Cinema and Modernism

Cinema and Modernism

DAVID TROTTER

Blackwell
Publishing

BLACKWELL PUBLISHING
350 Main Street, Malden, MA 02148-5020, USA
9600 Garsington Road, Oxford, OX4 2DQ, UK
550 Swanston Street, Carlton, Victoria 3053, Australia

The right of David Trotter to be identified as the Author of this Work has been asserted in accordance with the UK Copyright, Designs, and Patents Act 1988.

First published 2007 by Blackwell Publishing Ltd

2   2007

Library of Congress Cataloging-in-Publication Data

Trotter, David, 1951-
  Cinema and modernism / David Trotter.
    p. cm. – (Critical quarterly book series)
  Includes bibliographical references and index.
  ISBN-13: 978-1-4051-5982-1 (pbk. : alk. paper)
  ISBN-10: 1-4051-5982-0 (pbk. : alk. paper) 1. Motion pictures and literature. 2. English literature – 20th century – History and criticism. 3. Modernism (Literature) I. Title.

  PN1995.3.T76 2006
  791.4309′041–dc22
                    2006034249

A catalogue record for this title is available from the British Library.

Set in 10 on 12 pt Palatino
by Macmillan India

For further information on
Blackwell Publishing, visit our website:
http://www.blackwellpublishing.com

For Kasia

Contents

Foreword by Colin MacCabe   ix

Acknowledgements   viii

1   Introduction   1
2   The Literature of Cinema   17
3   D. W. Griffith   49
4   James Joyce and the Automatism of the   87
     Photographic Image
5   T. S. Eliot   125
6   Virginia Woolf   159
7   Charlie Chaplin   181

Index   203

Acknowledgements

A part of chapter 2 was published in an earlier form in *Critical Quarterly* 46:4 (December 2004), and is reprinted with the permission of Blackwell. A part of chapter 5 was published in an earlier form in *Modernism/Modernity* 13:2 (April 2006), and is reprinted with the permission of the Johns Hopkins University Press. A part of chapter 6 was published in an earlier form in *Film Studies* 6 (Summer 2005), and is reprinted with the permission of Oxford University Press.

Foreword

The academic study of film and literature has not flourished in our time. Much of the initial impetus for the setting up of schools of English after the First World War found its energy in an opposition to the horrors of mass culture of which film was often portrayed as the most horrific. This disdain of literary academics for the masterpieces of the cinema was not confined to the Anglophone world. Of course, there was always an early recognition of the possibilities of what the French called the Seventh Art, but the efforts of pioneers in film criticism in France, England or America took place outside the groves of academe. When André Bazin founded his magazine *Cahiers du cinéma* in 1952, his audience gathered in cine-clubs, not in lecture theatres, and indeed Bazin had earlier taken the decision to renounce his academic career in order to devote himself to the study of film.

All this changed in the seventies when the political demand to study contemporary culture and the considerable body of film criticism already established (most notably the work of Bazin and *Cahiers*) enabled the study of film to find a growing place within the university. Bazin himself, however, might have been astonished by the way in which the new academic discipline of film studies was often constituted as autonomous, functioning in an aesthetic void where any reference to literature was at best jejune and at worst disqualifying.

The reasons for this are not complicated. Film started life as a genuinely new artistic medium whose beginnings were in the fairgrounds and music halls far removed from any connection either with literature in particular or with traditional high culture in general. Even when film began to borrow from the other arts, and most importantly from literature, there was a continuous critical effort to stress film's unique qualities, particularly the universality of the silent image, a stark contrast to language-limited literature. If the advent of the talkies destroyed this claim to universality, important critical discourses continued to appeal to notions of pure cinema, of film, which had to be appreciated in its difference from other arts.

These intellectual tendencies were offered institutional reinforcement as film studies began to develop within the universities. It was perhaps inevitable that young critics and scholars keen to develop their brave new subject sought institutional independence from the largely literary departments in which they had developed their interests, perhaps also inevitable that older critics and scholars were pleased to see the back of an unwelcome distraction. What is more surprising is that even in those departments where local histories determined that film and literature were housed under the one roof, a very strict demarcation separated the professional worlds of literary and film scholarship.

These academic developments, however, look more than bizarre if one moves outside the university to look at the worlds of film and literature. The twentieth century – and the twenty-first is so far no different – saw an ever greater interpenetration of these two worlds. From Graham Greene's film criticism to Salman Rushdie's claim that *The Wizard of Oz* was his greatest literary influence, writers have thought and written about the cinema in ever greater numbers. At the same time cinema has from its second decade sought much of its source material in literature and there is almost no major novelist or dramatist in the last century who has not earned part of his or her living either from the direct sale of their work or by the writing of screenplays.

The magazine *Critical Quarterly* has from the mid-eighties sought to sponsor and promote work which focused on the complicated interrelations between the worlds of film and literature. It is no exaggeration to say that David Trotter's *Cinema and Modernism* is the most important book on this topic yet written and it is therefore an ideal title to launch a new series of *Critical Quarterly* books whose aim is to bring the most original academic work to the widest possible audience.

Trotter's work takes off from, and offers an overview of, one of the few areas of academic scholarship that has begun to investigate this complicated interrelation. Curiously enough this does not originate in film scholarship but from a long overdue literary critical reconsideration of the relations between cinema and modernism. It could be said unkindly that it has taken literary students of modernism more than half a century to notice the elephant in the sitting room. However, literary criticism in its modern form was largely designed by Eliot and Richards in the late 1920s as a device to render the elephant invisible. The close reading of difficult modern literary texts was the explicit psychic therapy to cure the facile forms of attention encouraged by modern popular culture, above all by the cinema. Cinema and literary modernism were antithetical and could not be put into any kind of common theoretical framework.

The first step out of this carefully constructed intellectual box has come only in the last two decades with a host of scholarship demonstrating the intensity of modernist interest in cinema. The two most obvious instances of this interest are Joyce's establishment of the first cinema in Dublin and the late-twenties magazine *Close-Up*, but the examples multiply. Indeed, Trotter's own book makes a substantial contribution to this scholarship with its focus on early letters of Eliot, which show how thoroughly Eliot had mastered the grammar of early narrative cinema.

Much of this recent scholarship, however, has wanted to stress the relations between cinema and literature as one of technique and above all the technique of montage as it was understood in the light of the great

Russian film-makers of the 1920s. Trotter wants to object to this on two grounds. First, this comparison is often woefully ahistorical. Both *Ulysses* and *The Waste Land* (favoured candidates for this comparison) are published long before this Russian cinema has been shown in the West. More significantly, this ahistorical emphasis on technique obscures something much more important, which is a shared concern of modernist writing and early mainstream cinema with the implications of a world in which representation without an intervening consciousness is possible.

It was, of course, Bazin, in his essay 'The Ontology of the Photographic Image', who stressed this feature of the camera, and Trotter's book is the product of a deep engagement with the French thinker. Indeed, Trotter's main thesis elaborates an aside of Bazin, which characterised the relations between twentieth-century literature and cinema not as direct influence or borrowing but as a 'certain aesthetic convergence'.[1] It is this convergence that Trotter is concerned to delineate, and he locates it firmly in the cinema's double impersonality – its automatic reproduction of a reality that it cannot intervene to change and its indifference to the audience before which it is projected.

This indifferent automatism had become an aesthetic concern before the Lumière brothers developed the 'last machine'; one can find it in writings as different as symbolist poetry or the Naturalist novel. Trotter's genius is to trace from a series of brilliant local readings and histories – a letter of Eliot, an essay of Woolf's, accounts of the first cinema projections in Dublin – a general account of Joyce's Dublin, Eliot's waste land and Woolf's Mrs Ramsay which demonstrates beyond question the convergence that links modernist masterpiece to mainstream cinema.

Trotter, however, is concerned with a much more comprehensive recasting of the cultural history of modernism than a simple demonstration of the centrality of the cinema to three great modernist classics. His ambition is to demonstrate that the convergence is exactly that; a matter not simply of literature deepening its investigation of impersonality through a meditation on the camera and the screen but also of the cinema itself addressing these fundamentally modernist questions.

If Trotter's book constitutes a magisterial correction of the last two decades of literary scholarship on modernism, it also acts as a kind of critical culmination of the past two decades of early cinema history, the great scholarly achievement of modern film studies. This book is unthinkable without the work of Tom Gunning and Charles Musser, Ben Brewster and Lea Jacobs, but it uses that work, which has given us so much better an understanding of the specific history of the cinema, to place Griffith and Chaplin at the centre of the most general debates about modernism.

Trotter's book is nowhere more salutary than in its insistence that modernism has always been concerned with the real, that modernism's interruption of conventional forms of representation is at the service of more urgent realities. Auerbach at the end of his discussion of Woolf's *To the Lighthouse* puts it best: 'What takes place here in Virginia Woolf's novel is precisely what was attempted everywhere in works of this kind (although not everywhere with the same insight and mastery) – that is to put the emphasis on the random occurrence, to exploit it not in the service of a planned continuity of action but in itself. And in the process something new and elemental appeared: nothing less than the wealth of reality and depth of life in every moment to which we surrender ourselves without prejudice'.[2]

What Trotter does is to show us, at the centre of the two greatest exponents of American silent cinema, Griffith and Chaplin, this very same reality and depth of life, this surrendering without prejudice. Modernism is not here to be opposed to mass culture but is to be found at its centre. It has been fashionable in recent years to dismiss modernism as 'elitist'. Trotter's book makes clear the ignorance on which such facile populism rests. The modernist emphasis on the random occurrence is – and this is as clear in Griffith and Chaplin as it is in Woolf, Eliot and Joyce – part of a fundamental democratisation of life, the bringing into focus of what Auerbach called 'the elementary things which men in general have in common'.

The delights of this book are many. It provides an expert guide through the bibliographies of both recent literary criticism of modernism and recent historical work on silent American cinema. It offers a re-engagement with the classic texts of film theory, most notably Bazin and Heath. It offers delightfully close readings of both film and literature, text and context. Above all it makes clear why modernism, which provided the founding literary texts for the establishment of English as a university discipline, cannot be understood without reference to the early cinema and, furthermore, why that cinema cannot be fully appreciated without reference to literary modernism.

COLIN MacCABE
September 2006

Notes

1   André Bazin, *What Is Cinema?*, vol. 1 (Berkeley and Los Angeles: University of California Press, 1967), 63.
2   Erich Auerbach, *Mimesis: The Representation of Reality in Western Literature* (Princeton: Princeton University Press, 2003), 552.

Introduction

'The short story', Elizabeth Bowen declared in 1944, 'is a young art: as we now know it, it is the child of this century.' Since 1900, the young art had been taken up assiduously, and often to superb effect, by most if not all of the British and American writers whom we would now characterise as modernist. It had, in Bowen's view, a visual counterpart, or rival. 'The cinema,' she went on,

> itself busy with a technique, is of the same generation: in the last thirty years the two arts have been accelerating together. They have affinities – neither is *GS* sponsored by a tradition; both are, accordingly, free; both, still, are self-conscious, show a self-imposed discipline and regard for form; both have, to work on, immense matter – the disorientated romanticism of the age.[1]

The short story as a literary form will only feature intermittently in this book. But the argument I aim to advance is based on the premise Bowen floats: that there were significant affinities between early cinema and literary modernism. Bowen's categories of affinity are perhaps too lightly sketched to sustain extensive analysis of the relation between literature and cinema during the modernist period. Even so, they point us in the right direction. During those years, literature and cinema were indeed, in her adroit phrase, busy with a technique; and they did self-consciously seek out new forms, at once fragmentary and encyclopaedic, to fit the immense matter of modern life. Bowen herself will reappear in the argument as the author of one of the finest short stories ever written about movie-going.

Modernist writing in English constitutes a capacious and by no means stable historical and theoretical category encompassing a wide variety of engagements with the idea of the new in texts published (for the most part) during the first half of the twentieth century.[2] Cinema has been proposed with increasing frequency as an illustrative or explanatory context for some or all of those engagements.[3] The great majority of the enquiries into literary modernism's relation to cinema undertaken during the past thirty years have been committed implicitly or explicitly to argument by analogy. The literary text, this argument goes, is *structured like a film*, in whole or in part: it has its 'close-ups', its 'tracks' and 'pans', its 'cuts' from one 'shot' to another. Writers and film-makers were engaged, it would seem, in some kind of exchange of transferable narrative techniques. The transferable narrative technique which has featured most consistently in debates about modernist writing in English is montage. Michael Wood, indeed, proposes that the 'principle of montage', together with the 'construction of imaginary space through the direction of the gaze', was 'quintessentially modernist'.[4] It is a principle active, according to an already voluminous scholarship, throughout the work of James Joyce. *The Waste Land* has recently been described as the 'modern montage poem par excellence'.[5]

There has always been an advantage in thinking of the modernist literary text as though it were a film structured by the principle of montage, if montage is understood in its basic sense as the juxtaposition of two or more images. Moments in that text do seem to invite, indeed almost to require, analysis in terms of the 'construction of imaginary space' either through montage or through camera-movement (pan, track, tilt).[6] These are affinities I intend fully to acknowledge. However, I do also believe that recent criticism has been at once too loose, in its attribution to the modernist literary text of just about any cinematic technique going (including some which were not going at all when the work in question was written); and too tight, in its insistence on one particular kind of montage as that text's primary method. There are historical and theoretical reasons for scepticism on both counts.[7]

Louis MacNeice remembered encountering the poems of T. S. Eliot for the first time in 1926, when he was in his final year in school: 'we had seen reviews proclaiming him a modern of the moderns and we too wanted to be "modern".' To someone his age, MacNeice recalled, *The Waste Land*'s literary allusions and 'anthropological symbolism' meant nothing. What did help was a ticket to see the movies. 'The cinema technique of quick cutting, of surprise juxtapositions, of spotting the everyday detail and making it significant, this would naturally intrigue the novelty-mad adolescent and should, like even the most experimental films, soon become easy to grasp.'[8] That might have been, and yet be, entirely true; and still not tell us anything at all about how the poem came to be written as it was written. For experimental cinema did not arrive in Britain until the founding of the London Film Society in 1925 (a development whose consequences I explore at length in chapter 6). The view the novelty-mad adolescent reading *The Waste Land* in 1926 would have taken of its 'cinematic techniques' already differed significantly from the view the author took (if he took a view) in devising them. In chapter 5, I show that Eliot was familiar with montage practice as developed in mainstream cinema during the period immediately before and during the First World War. But that is in itself no reason to read *The Waste Land* as though it were an experimental film (indeed, it's a reason not to).

There is a history, in short, to literature's affinities with cinema. I shall argue throughout this book that such affinities should only be established – and put to use in literary criticism – on the basis of what a writer might conceivably have known about cinema as it was at the time of writing. Historically, the term 'montage' acquired in a short period of time a range of not always entirely compatible meanings.[9] For the most part, it came to be understood as referring either to the combination of two shots in such a way as to generate an effect or meaning not discernible in either shot alone, or to the sort of conceptual or rhythmical cutting associated in particular with Sergei Eisenstein. P. Adams Sitney identifies reverse angle cutting as the 'montage formula' which by the end of the First World War had become the basis of narrative continuity in cinema. Modernist montage arose out of the reinvigoration of this formula through 'playful hyperbole' and other means in films made from the mid-1920s onwards.[10] Michael North's meticulous survey of small magazines has made it clear that the intellectual prestige of the movies, and thus of montage as transferable narrative technique, peaked during the late 1920s, when Eugene Jolas's *transition* found room for various experiments in 'logocinema'.[11] Whatever its virtues, no account of modernist montage along these lines can tell us how and why works of literature conceived during the previous decade, works such as *Ulysses* and *The Waste Land*, came to be written as they were written.

Where literature and film are concerned, argument by analogy fails not only on historical but also on theoretical grounds. Literature is a representational medium, film a recording medium. The freedom modernist literature sought was freedom from the ways in which the world had hitherto been represented in literature. The freedom film sought (initially, at any rate, if not for very long) was freedom from representation: the freedom merely to record. For the recording arts constituted, as James Monaco has put it, 'an entirely new mode of discourse, parallel to those already in existence'. The new mode of discourse eventually made it possible to record, on film, tape, or disc, any event whatsoever that could be seen or heard. From the beginning, Monaco adds, film and photography were neutral; the media existed before the arts. The art of film thus developed by a process of replication. 'The neutral template of film was laid over the complex systems of the novel, painting, drama, and music to reveal new truths about certain elements of those arts.'[12] Film as medium before film as art: that fact, or the awareness of that fact, made all the difference, from literature; and continues to make all the difficulty, for arguments by analogy. 'For the first time,' André Bazin was to observe of the photographic image, 'between the originating object and its reproduction there intervenes only the instrumentality of a nonliving agent.'[13] The relation between cinema and literature can best be understood as a shared preoccupation with the capacities and incapacities of that which distinguishes one from the other: the instrumentality of a nonliving agent.

I propose here to substitute for the model of an exchange of transferable techniques the model of parallelism. In my view, the literature of the period and the cinema of the period can best be understood as constituting and constituted by parallel histories.[14] Some early film-makers shared with some writers of the period a conviction both that the instrumentality of the new recording media had made it possible for the first time to represent (as well as to record) *existence as such*; and that the superabundant generative power of this intrumentality (the ever-imminent autonomy of the forms and techniques it gave rise to) put in doubt the very idea of existence as such. The conviction's ground was technological fact: film as medium before film as art. When modernist writers thought of cinema, they thought of an image of the world made automatically: an image which, due to the original and durable excess in it of record over representation, contains either more or less of the world than would the image which would occur under comparable circumstances to a human observer. Film, Marianne Moore pointed out in 1933, 'like the lie detector of the criminal court, reveals agitation which the eye fails to see'.[15] In his essay on 'The Work of Art in the Age of Mechanical Reproduction' (1936), Walter Benjamin drew an influential distinction between the 'pictures' obtained by painter and cameraman: the painter's is 'total', whereas the cameraman's consists of 'fragments' assembled under a new 'law'. For Benjamin, the camera was a surgeon's scalpel which laid bare the 'optical unconscious'.[16] By obstinately seeing as the human eye does not see, film became a meta-technology: a medium whose constant subject matter was the limits of the human.

'Any effective account of modern culture', Jonathan Crary has maintained, 'must confront the ways in which modernism, rather than being a reaction against or transcendence of the processes of scientific and economic rationalization, is inseparable from them'.[17] Modernism has generally been understood, in recent scholarship, as a peculiar openness to modernity at its most enabling (sometimes a fearsome prospect).[18] Hugh Kenner argues that the affinity Eliot and many of his contemporaries felt with technological change had profound consequences for their writing. 'If Eliot is much else,' Kenner notes, 'he is undeniably his time's chief poet of the alarm clock, the furnished flat, the ubiquitous telephone, commuting crowds, the electric underground railway'. There is even a hint at cinema. For the 'hooded hordes' which swarm over endless plains, in the final section of *The Waste Land*, stumbling in the cracked earth, 'may', Kenner adds, 'have been literal impressions of World War I newsreels.'[19]

Garrett Stewart has recently offered an admirably challenging description of modernist literature's affinity with cinema which promises to move the whole debate decisively beyond argument by analogy, in the direction of the idea of parallel histories. During the course of a wide-ranging enquiry into the 'material transformations' of photography into cinema, Stewart brings a reading of literary experiment to bear on a reading of film in order to clarify the 'special kind of newness' accruing to photographic imprint when it enters into the 'motorized disappearance', frame after frame, which constitutes cinematic process. His emphasis is on the 'shared modernist strain, in every sense, of literary and filmic textuality': on the 'photogrammatic track' as the 'underlying stuff of the apparition'; and on writing as *écriture*, as text in production. The 'filmic', Stewart proposes, stands to the 'cinematic' as *écriture* to 'classic narrative'; one is modernist, the other merely modern.[20] Stewart's insistence on textuality has in effect reanimated the poststructuralist readings of Eliot, Pound, Joyce and others prevalent in the 1970s and 1980s. To think in terms of photographic imprint or 'photogrammatic' track is to think once again in terms of what Maud Ellmann has called a 'poetics of impersonality'.[21]

We might say, then, that modernism's axiom or formula was literature as (recording) medium *before* literature as (representational) art: an axiom or formula sprung, at that particular 'moment' in history, by the sudden pre-eminence of a medium which was from the outset, and remained at least for the ten years or so after its invention in 1895, a medium rather than an art. Film did not easily relinquish its neutrality. To begin with, the uses to which the medium was put ranged from scientific enquiry through education and reportage to light entertainment. The Lumière camera-projector was in itself all of these things: a prototype, an exhibit, and a stunt. Only from 1903, at the very earliest, did film become primarily a narrative art. The production of fictional films outstripped the production of factual films for the first time in 1907.[22] I shall argue that what fascinated modernist writers about cinema was the original, and perhaps in some measure reproducible, neutrality of film as a medium. Texts by Eliot, Joyce, Wyndham Lewis, and Virginia Woolf look back, in their affinity with cinema, to that original neutrality of film as a medium, rather than forward to montage as the apotheosis of cinematic narrative art. Dorothy Richardson, in an essay published in January 1929 in *Close Up*, the first British journal of film theory, spoke of the 'innocence' of the first movies.

> They were not concerned, or at any rate not very deeply concerned, either with idea or with characterisation. Like the snap-shot, they recorded. And when plot, intensive, came to be combined with characterisation, with just so much characterisation as might by good chance be supplied by minor characters supporting the tailor's and modiste's dummies filling the chief roles, still the records were there, the snap-shot records that are always and everywhere food for a discriminating and an undiscriminating humanity alike.[23]

Richardson's evocation of the 'snap-shot record' – of the image not yet bound up with and into narrative – eloquently expresses the motive for modernism's investment in cinema. Even in 1933, long after the transition to sound, and thus to enhanced narrative plausibility, Marianne Moore still held, as we have seen, to the medium's potential as a mode of scientific enquiry. To what extent, then, did these writers succeed in disintegrating their own literary art back into (the fantasised trace of) text's original neutrality as a medium? And how?

In defining modernist textuality, Stewart draws productively on Fredric Jameson's analysis of a passage in E. M. Forster's *Howards End* (1910). The novel's opening chapter consists of three letters from Helen Schlegel to her sister Margaret, describing her visit to the Wilcox family at Howards End, and the sudden strong attraction she feels towards the younger son, Paul. Chapter 2 ends with the arrival of a telegram from Helen announcing the end of the affair. The telegram, however, has arrived too late. For their aunt, the formidable Mrs Munt, is already in a train on the way down to Howards End. Chapter 3 finds Mrs Munt installed at one and the same time in a comfortable seat (facing the engine, but not too near it) and, Jameson explains, a 'cinematographic kind of space'. Gazing out of the window, she gazes into a framed scene; or frames the scene by her gaze. What is significant about this moment, Jameson adds,

> is not some possible influence of nascent cinema on Forster or on the modernist novel in general, but rather the confluence of the two distinct formal developments, of movie technology on the one hand, and of a certain type of modernist or protomodernist language on the other, both of which seem to offer some space, some third term between the subject and the object.[24]

For Jameson, Stewart observes, that third term is in effect the (literary/ photographic) apparatus, the 'disembodiment of perception by technique'. 'Modernist writing is neither predominantly impressionist nor expressive (since both imply the intervening subjectivity of an author) but in some new way strictly technical, a prosthesis of observation in the mode of inscription.' What Stewart discerns in *Howards End*, and then in an enhanced form in *Heart of Darkness* and *Finnegans Wake*, is 'an *automatism* of language beneath the intentionalities of inscription'. There was, he claims, a 'cultural commonality' between 'automated image projection' and 'the depersonalized verbal techniques of a modernist stylistic "apparatus"'.[25]

Stewart's broad 'textualist theory' of the 'adjacent inscriptive media of film and literature' strikes me as consistently illuminating. Since the argument turns on 'confluence' alone, rather than a conjuncture more often asserted than proven, he is able, as the proponents of montage as transferable narrative technique are not, to read each medium closely, and often to brilliant effect, in terms appropriate to its specific 'textuality'. The very broadness of the theory, however, can create problems.

In the first place, Stewart's programmatic lack of interest in the author (or Author, or author-function) damagingly flattens out his analysis of the literature of the period. In Forster and Joseph Conrad, Stewart argues, as in Joyce, the 'mechanisms of linguistic articulation' have been 'brought forward' as the 'suppressed material basis (phonemic even when not phonic or oral) of all lexical processing'.[26] But brought forward *how*, and to what effect? By whom? And why, at this moment in history? Forster, in particular, seems an odd choice as the vehicle or screen for a display of the 'mechanisms of linguistic articulation'. He surely owes his inclusion less to anything he might himself actually have said or done than to Jameson's need to fill the proto-modernist slot in an abstract scheme of the evolution of literary practice during the first years of the century.

'The train sped northward,' Forster wrote of Mrs Munt's journey, 'under innumerable tunnels.'[27] Stewart discerns in this sentence a 'writing beneath the written' which offers 'the near equivalent in prose for the filmic beneath the cinematic'. Trains, he notes, ordinarily pass through rather than under tunnels. Forster, perhaps, was aiming at assonance; that is, at literary *style*. He could, however, have squeezed out a little more assonance still if he had substituted 'numberless' for 'innumerable'. Stewart's conclusion is that he was not, in fact, after style. He had put the 1890s behind him. What happens instead, in this sentence, is something altogether more modern. The unexpected 'under' ruffles narrative transparency just enough for writing to emerge for an instant from beneath the written. What 'innumerable' does, in conjunction with 'tunnels', as 'numberless' would not have done, is to bring forward into view the modernist apparatus of depersonalised technique. For each word incorporates a 'pictogram' – '*nn* and then again *nn*' – of side-by-side tunnels.[28] Forget the *fin-de-siècle*. This could be a line in a poem by Ezra Pound. There, at the centre of Jameson's 'cinematographic kind of space', exactly where it ought to be, Stewart has spotted an irruption of textuality.

Forster, of course, did not conceive of himself as an Imagist *manqué*. *Howards End* was a (mildly) polemical fiction designed, as its nineteenth-century precursors had been before it, to alert a middle-class readership to the extent of the damage done to the body politic by the increasingly bitter antagonism between two separate 'nations': 'England', founded on 'local life' and 'personal intercourse'; and 'Suburbia', glossy product of the 'superficial comfort exacted by businessmen'.[29] Arnold Bennett thought that the book had been a success because it had got itself 'talked about' by the 'right people'.[30] The function of the paragraph describing Mrs Munt's journey was to give the right people something to talk about. Mrs Munt herself could not be considered up to the task. Engrossed in her mission, she has, we are told, neither the will nor the ability to grasp the social and political significance of the world she gazes out at through the carriage window. 'To history, to tragedy, to the past, to the future, Mrs Munt remained equally indifferent.'[31] Forster, however, has already demonstrated his superiority to her by discovering in the terrain through (or 'under') which she is conveyed a figure for her state of mind. The assonance created by the unexpected 'under' throws enough emphasis on to those 'tunnels' for them to remain in our minds until the paragraph's unfolding enables us to convert descriptive detail into metaphor. Mrs Munt, engrossed in her task, suffers, of course, from tunnel-vision. In this novel, the author alone, and then with great deliberation, rises above engrossment, above partiality. He does so again, once Mrs Munt has arrived at her destination, by distinguishing in an absolute manner between England and Suburbia. The paragraph, in short, constitutes a traditional exercise in the use of literary style (assonance) for rhetorical purposes (to establish the authority of the narrative voice). Any irruption of the modernist apparatus within it is insignificant.

v   A comparable doubt must attend Jameson's discovery in Forster's description of Mrs Munt's train journey of a 'cinematographic kind of space'. We surely cannot establish what it might have meant to propose such a 'space', in a novel published in 1910, without some reference, however tentative, to the spaces proposed in films its author could actually have seen. Such enquiries have been hindered by gaps in the historical record: lack of information about the nature and extent of a writer's interest in cinema. They have also been hindered in theory, or by theory. There has been a systematic failure, in discussions of early cinema and literary modernism, to take proper account either of films made before the First World War, or of films made after it for a mass audience.[32] The second objection to Stewart's theory is that it applies only to films based on the deliberate (self-conscious) 'multiplication of shots through editing': French and Russian experimental cinema of the 1920s, and the 'modernist valedictions' of the 1960s and 1970s.[33] The theory is, in this respect, representative. I know of no study of early cinema and literary modernism which does not restrict itself to the avant-garde.

Stewart does acknowledge the historical significance, as something 1920s modernism sought to 'retrieve' from its own rapid 'normalisation', of what Tom Gunning has termed a 'cinema of attractions'. Gunning proposes that the films made during the cinema's first ten years or so, whether in the documentary mode associated with Lumière, or in the narrative mode associated with Georges Méliès, should be understood as presentations compatible with – and indeed to some extent derived from – popular entertainments such as variety theatre and the magic-lantern show.[34] What counts, in them, is not that absorption of the spectator into diegesis undertaken by classical Hollywood cinema: cinema as voyeurism, or unacknowledged scopophilia, in Christian Metz's terms.[35] What counts, instead, is exhibitionism: the display of views or accomplishments to an audience authorised, in turn, to exhibit itself.

These very early films require consideration in their own right – rather than as something lost, and then retrieved – for two reasons. The first is that, as I have already indicated, the writers who should interest us most gave them plenty of consideration, and not just for nostalgia's sake. The second is that film's neutrality as a medium was not erased by, or in, its constitution as a narrative art. To the contrary, the narrative films which became the industry's staple product from 1907 onwards artfully reintroduce or re-enact the medium's founding neutrality as and when they can. The writers who will most concern me here were a great deal more interested in cinema, as Stewart defines it, than they were in film. We need to take full account of the gradual and uneven development of a cinema of attractions into a cinema designed above all to tell stories. I shall accordingly devote separate chapters to particular phases in the careers of two film-makers who made very substantial contributions to that development, D. W. Griffith and Charlie Chaplin. In chapter 4, I examine narrative films by George Loane Tucker, Griffith, Abel Gance, King Vidor, and Carl-Theodor Dreyer which, although varying widely in scope and tone, all exploit the lateral tracking shot as an artful departure from 'natural' lines of sight which brings back into view the medium's neutrality as a medium.

My hypothesis is that some modernist writers found in film's neutrality as a medium a stimulus to the reintroduction or re-enactment of the neutrality of literature, or in some cases of writing itself, as a medium. It was not cinema which made literary modernism, but cinema's example. If that was indeed the case, as I hope to show, we need to ask why. What was so wonderful about neutrality, about the automatism of the camera's-eye view? To answer those questions, we must first set aside the current understanding of technology's appearance on the scene as always and everywhere a matter of 'crisis' or 'threat'. Sara Danius, for example, has argued that the modernist aesthetic informing the work of Thomas Mann, Marcel Proust, and James Joyce was 'inseparable from a historically specific crisis of the senses, a sensory crisis sparked by, among other things, late-nineteenth- and early-twentieth-century technological innovations, particularly technologies of perception'.[36] According to James Lastra, cinema has 'come to stand for "modernity" itself, seeming to emblematize in the most compelling and even visceral way the frequently violent shifts in social and cultural life, especially the newly possible (if not inevitable) forms of spatial, temporal, and sensual restructuring'. The 'threat' posed by the emergence of new media during the early years of the twentieth century, Lastra concludes, was that of the 'spectre' of the inhuman within human experience.[37] I have no doubt that cinema's exposure of the inhuman within human experience was often conceived as threat or crisis. But there is as far as I am aware no reason to assume, as so many commentators have done, that it could not be conceived otherwise.

According to R. L. Rutsky, technology comes to life, or is willed into life, in modernism. Modernist machines are often the product of an occult or supernatural knowledge, a black magic (a white magic, even), rather than of engineering and of the dystopian representations which surrounded engineering in Romantic aesthetic theory. If modernism saw the 're-emergence of the technological in the aesthetic sphere', Rutsky notes, this was a 'realm still haunted by a transcendent, living "spirit", by the desire for the eternal and the immutable'. Thus, the doctor-magician figures in German Expressionist cinema not only reduce human beings to automata, but bring objects to life. In either case, the result is a combination of the scientific-technological and the spiritual-magical figured as a living machine.[38] The spectres inhabiting German Expressionism are cause for concern, to be sure, but not necessarily for panic.

The attitude Eliot, Joyce, Woolf, and Lewis took to visual technologies and their exposure of the inhuman within human experience was by no means utopian, of course. They were above all, I think, *curious*: apprehensive, perhaps, and often scornful, but also convinced that the camera's-eye view - the re-enactment, artfully or not, of film's neutrality as a medium – would prove a fruitful addition to the repertoire of ways in which the world might be known. Their literary modernism was an acknowledgement that existence as such (the only topic left for literature, they felt) would never appear otherwise than out of proportion: at once personal and impersonal; at once impossibly close (too much presence), and marked indelibly by remoteness, by what has been left out of the picture, by what has gone missing (too much absence). Cinema's defining drama of inclusion and exclusion showed them the way to existence as such, which was now all there was, or could be, virtually. The point was not – or not only – to match the fidelity of the photographic (or phonographic) record. It was, rather, to change the angle (a camera-thought, this, already) on the human as thus far constituted in the archive of representations.

Cinema's example provoked in some modernist writers a will-to-automatism. These writers *chose*, in certain texts, the 'disembodiment of perception by technique'. For literary modernism should not be regarded as the product of a machine age.[39] It was, rather, a wilful enquiry into the age's wilful absorption in the kinds of automatic behaviour exemplified by machinery in general, and by the new technologies of perception in particular. 'But, of course,' as Eliot famously observed in 'Tradition and the Individual Talent' (1919), 'only those who have personality and emotions know what it means to want to escape from these things'.[40]

The will-to-automatism, it hardly needs saying, is still with us. How could it not be, in the era of the World Wide Web, text messaging, virtual reality technologies, and windowed desktop multimedia applications? Jay David Bolter and Richard Grusin have discerned in the process of remediation by which new digital media define themselves in relation either to older analogue media, or to each other, a 'double logic' of immediacy and hypermediacy. Remediation takes a variety of forms. The new medium can act as a vehicle for the old; or refashion it by incorporating it in part; or absorb it entirely. In each case, though, a double logic operates. 'Our culture wants both to multiply its media and to erase all traces of mediation: ideally, it wants to erase its media in the very act of multiplying them.' Each new medium must be at once transparent as never before, a window on a homogeneous world; and opaque as never before, its own object, a windowed array of heterogeneous representations.[41] There is no shortage of will-to-automatism in remediation's double logic.

It is not my purpose to argue that literary modernism remediated cinema: that it took on montage in order to render itself at once newly transparent and newly opaque. Modernist writers did something far more interesting than that. Cinema's example enabled them to discern in the process of mediation itself, in the original and recoverable neutrality of the new medium's approach to existence as such, the double logic Bolter and Grusin discern in the process of remediation. They understood that this double logic is driven by contrary but mutually dependent desires: to be utterly transparent, to be utterly opaque. The will-to-automatism was the instrument with which writers and film-makers explored the double desire at once for presence to the world and for absence from it. Modernism, then, should not be regarded as the 'pre-history of cyberspace'.[42] But it gives us as good an idea as we are likely to get of what it is that we look for when we enter cyberspace: to be at once a window, and windowed.

My subject is the scavenging for presence- and absence-effects which so decisively informed the work of early-twentieth-century writers and film-makers. The chapters which follow offer a general though far from comprehensive account of that activity. Future research into the topic may well prove more particular. It may well find in historical instances of the representation of class, race, and gender a focus for enquiry in the circumstances under which mediation's double desire made itself felt.[43] What I have attempted here is an introduction to the topic, by way of case-studies, rather than a fully grounded history.

Chapter 2 describes what some writers (Henry James, Frank Norris, D. H. Lawrence, Elizabeth Bowen) saw in the new medium of cinema. What they saw made them think about the lack of proportion necessary to any attempt to view the world as it actually is: too much presence, too much absence. I also suggest that stereoscopy, a visual medium remediated both in literature (Joyce, Proust) and in film, put to spectacular use the conflict between immediacy and hypermediacy constitutive of mediation itself. The 'world' viewed through the stereoscope is at once abstract – a receding arrangement of separate planes – and very nearly tangible. Chapter 3 discovers both abstraction and tangibility in some of the films D. W. Griffith made for the Biograph Company between 1908 and 1913. Griffith's Biograph films are usually seen as a laboratory for the development of the narrative techniques which transformed film from a medium into an art. I value them for the *sense* they make of the world, by a deliberate reversion to film's neutrality as a medium, as well as for the *meaning* they make on its behalf, by the elaboration through montage of a mediated (or even hypermediated) cinematic discourse.

Tangibility, however, was not what most film-makers had in mind, or what would have been visible in their films, during the long transition, after 1907, to a cinema of narrative integration. Chapter 4, accordingly, shifts the emphasis from the desire to be transparent to the desire to be opaque. Its topic is the remediation of the first Dublin documentaries in the 'Wandering Rocks' episode of *Ulysses*. The ceremonies of recognition and acknowledgement which begin and end the episode burlesque into opacity the very similar ceremonies which structured the films Dubliners were most likely to see, in Dublin in 1904. I compare the absence-effects generated by its hypermediacy to those generated by the lateral tracking shots which found favour with some film-makers from 1913 onwards. The lateral tracking shot is the least anthropomorphic, and therefore most opaque, of all camera-movements.

Eliot and Woolf, I argue in chapters 5 and 6, were keen students of cinema's equal accommodation as a medium to experiences of near-tangibility, on one hand, and of otherwise unimaginable remoteness, on the other. Tiresias, in *The Waste Land*, a mere observer, and yet the poem's chief protagonist, throbs between the desire for presence and the desire for absence. In that respect, he resembles Prufrock, the observer-protagonist of his own 'love song'. But he is, for all his antiquity, the more modern of the two. Prufrock's visual technology of choice had been the magic lantern, staple of Victorian home entertainment; Tiresias's, I shall suggest, is the mutoscope. What came between them was Eliot's rapidly developing interest in cinematic technique. Woolf found in cinema a way to conceive death, rather than desire. The key passage in her brilliant essay on 'The Cinema' (1926), written at the same time as the 'Time Passes' section of *To the Lighthouse* (1927), concerns documentary cinema's definitive capacity to show us people as they are when we are not there in person to witness their behaviour. 'We see life as it is when we have no part in it.'[44] Prompted by her reflections on that capacity, I think, Woolf was able to imagine constitutive absence in *To the Lighthouse*, as she had not been able to in *Mrs Dalloway* (1925). Between them, Eliot and Woolf can be said to have taken full measure of the potent implications of cinema's 'disembodiment of perception by technique'.

Bolter and Grusin unequivocally align modernism with an opaque hypermediacy.[45] This seems to me an opinion worth revising. I have tried hard throughout this book not to associate Joyce, Eliot, and Woolf with some kind of 'deconstruction' of the mimetic techniques which, from Albertian perspective to photorealism, have underwritten immediacy in art. These writers took as much (if not more) pleasure in presence-effects as they did in absence-effects, for reasons which I have begun to sketch. The operation of a double logic of immediacy and hypermediacy produced in literature and film a descriptive method which, rather than deconstructing mimesis, as modernism is routinely said to, actually enhances it; an enhancement I shall define, in chapter 7, with reference to Lewis's *The Childermass* (1928), and to films by Charlie Chaplin, as hypermimesis, or imitation for imitation's sake.

These are all rather abstract formulations. I want now to add some historical detail. The enquiry will range widely, in the chapters which follow, through and around the parallel histories of early cinema and modernist literature. But its focus will remain on the kinds of curiosity registered in F. T. Marinetti's 'Technical Manifesto of Futurist Literature', of 11 May 1912:

Nothing more interesting for the Futurist poet than the movement of a keyboard on a mechanical piano. The cinematograph gives us the dance of a thing that divides and reassembles without human intervention. It gives us the backward plunge of a diver whose feet rise out of the sea and spring violently back onto the diving board. It gives us a man running at 200 kilometers an hour. So many movements of matter beyond the laws of intelligence . . .[46]

Notes

1   'The Short Story', in Elizabeth Bowen (ed.), *The Faber Book of Modern Stories* (London: Faber and Faber, 1944), 7–19, p. 7.

2   For a succinct and authoritative account of what the category as currently defined might or might not be thought to include, see Tim Armstrong, *Modernism* (Cambridge: Polity, 2002), ch. 2.

3   See, for example, Susan McCabe, *Cinematic Modernism: Modernist Poetry and Film* (Cambridge: Cambridge University Press, 2005). McCabe explores the 'impact' of 'new cinematic modes of representation' on the poetry of Gertrude Stein, William Carlos Williams, H.D., and Marianne Moore.

4   'Modernism and Film', in Michael Levenson (ed.), *The Cambridge Companion to Modernism* (Cambridge: Cambridge University Press, 1999), 217–32, pp. 222–3.

5   Thomas L. Burkdall, *Joycean Frames: Film and the Fiction of James Joyce* (London: Routledge, 2001), 8–17; McCabe, *Cinematic Modernism*, 40.

6   For an illuminating example of this approach, see Keith Williams, 'Short Cuts of the Hibernian Metropolis: Cinematic Strategies in *Dubliners*', in Oona Frawley (ed.), *A New & Complex Sensation: Essays on Joyce's 'Dubliners'* (Dublin: Lilliput Press, 2004), 154–67.

7   Maria DiBattista makes the theoretical case for not 'conflating' the literary with the cinematic persuasively in 'This Is Not a Movie: *Ulysses* and Cinema', *Modernism/Modernity*, 13:2 (2006), 219–35. But her own use of cinematic terminology in relation to *Ulysses* is itself, strictly speaking, anachronistic.

8   'Eliot and the Adolescent', in Tambimuttu and Richard March (eds), *T. S. Eliot: A Symposium* (London: Frank Cass, 1948), 146–51, pp. 146, 150.

9   For a start, the term meant different things in different languages. In German, as James Pettifer pointed out thirty years ago, it can refer to simultaneous as well as successive assemblage: James Pettifer, 'Against the Stream: *Kuhle Wampe*', *Screen*, 15 (Summer 1974), 49–64, p. 64.

10   *Modernist Montage: The Obscurity of Vision in Cinema and Literature* (New York: Columbia University Press, 1990), 17–19, 38.

11   *Camera Works: Photography and the Twentieth-Century Word* (Oxford: Oxford University Press, 2005), ch. 2.

12   *How to Read a Film: Movies, Media, Multimedia*, 3rd edn (New York: Oxford University Press, 2000), 38–9.

13   'The Ontology of the Photographic Image', in *What Is Cinema?*, trans. Hugh Gray, 2 vols (Berkeley: University of California Press, 1967–71), vol. 1, 9–16, p. 13.

14   For a comparable approach to the relation between cinema and psychoanalysis, see the essays collected in Janet Bergstrom (ed.), *Endless Night: Cinema and Psychoanalysis, Parallel Histories* (Berkeley: University of California Press, 1999).

15 'Fiction or Nature?', in *Complete Prose*, ed. Patricia C. Willis (London: Faber and Faber, 1987), 303–8, p. 308.

16 'The Work of Art in the Age of Mechanical Reproduction', in *Illuminations*, trans. Harry Zohn (New York: Schocken, 1969), 217–52, pp. 233 4.

17 *Techniques of the Observer: On Vision and Modernity in the Nineteenth Century* (Cambridge, MA: MIT Press, 1993), 85.

18 Tim Armstrong, *Modernism, Technology, and the Body: A Cultural Study* (Cambridge: Cambridge University Press, 1998).

19 *The Mechanic Muse* (Oxford: Oxford University Press, 1987), 25, 34.

20 *Between Film and Screen: Modernism's Photo Synthesis* (Chicago: University of Chicago Press, 1999), 266. For an alternative account of relations between the emergence of new communication technologies and modernism's 'unbinding of textuality', see Donald F. Theall, *Beyond the Word: Reconstructing Sense in the Joyce Era of Technology, Culture, and Communication* (Toronto: University of Toronto Press, 1995); and *James Joyce's Techno-Poetics* (Toronto: University of Toronto Press, 1997).

21 *The Poetics of Impersonality: T. S. Eliot and Ezra Pound* (Cambridge, MA: Harvard University Press, 1987). Ellmann's argument, like Stewart's, derives in part from Jacques Derrida's reflections on Plato and Stéphane Mallarmé: 'The Double Session', in *Dissemination*, trans. Barbara Johnson (Chicago: University of Chicago Press, 1981), 189–316. See *Poetics of Impersonality*, 83–4; *Between Film and Screen*, 273. Derrida's essay is also an important point of departure for Christophe Wall-Romana's argument that Mallarmé, a keen observer of technological development, either wrote or made plans for various 'cinematic sublations of the page and the book': 'Mallarmé's Cinepoetics: The Poem Uncoiled by the Cinématographe, 1893–98', *PMLA*, 120 (2005), 128–47, pp. 141–2. Wall-Romana's use of the term 'montage' is not supported by analysis in detail either of his primary text, *Un coup de dés*, or of films Mallarmé might conceivably have seen.

22 The most complete data available relate to the American film industry. For a concise account, see Charles Musser, 'Moving towards Fictional Narratives: Story Films Become the Dominant Product, 1903–1904', in Lee Grieveson and Peter Krämer (eds), *The Silent Film Reader* (London: Routledge, 2004), 87–102.

23 'Pictures and Films', in James Donald, Anne Friedberg, and Laura Marcus (eds), *Close Up 1927–1933: Cinema and Modernism* (London: Cassell, 1998), 186–9, p. 188.

24 'Modernism and Imperialism', in Terry Eagleton (ed.), *Nationalism, Colonialism, and Literature* (Minneapolis: University of Minnesota Press, 1990), 43–66, p. 53. Cinema's kinship with the railroad has been the subject of a good deal of scholarship. See Lynne Kirby, *Parallel Tracks: The Railroad and Silent Cinema* (Exeter: University of Exeter Press, 1997).

25 *From Film to Screen*, 281, 283, 285.

26 Ibid., 286.

27 *Howards End* (Harmondsworth: Penguin Books, 1941), 15.

28 *From Film to Screen*, 283.

29 *Howards End*, 16.

30 *Books and Persons* (London: Chatto and Windus, 1917), 291–2.

31 *Howards End*, 15.

32   In the latter respect, Miriam Hansen's emphasis on classical Hollywood cinema as a vernacular modernism could yet prove salutary: 'The Mass Production of the Senses: Classical Cinema as Vernacular Modernism', *Modernism/Modernity*, 6 (1999), 59–77. Her description of the shaping of that vernacular will have to be modified to take into account the consequences of an insistent return to the 'pre-classical'.

33   *From Film to Screen*, 311, 282, 293.

34   Gunning developed the idea of the cinema of attractions in a series of highly influential essays first published during the 1980s. See, for example, 'An Unseen Energy Swallows Space: The Space in Early Film and its Relation to American Avant-Garde Film', in John Fell (ed.), *Film Before Griffith* (Berkeley: University of California Press, 1983), 355–66; and 'The Cinema of Attractions: Early Film, Its Spectator, and the Avant-Garde', reprinted in Thomas Elsaesser (ed.), *Early Cinema: Space, Frame, Narrative* (London: BFI Publishing, 1990), 56–67.

35   *Psychoanalysis and the Cinema: The Imaginary Signifier*, trans. Celia Britton et al. (Basingstoke: Macmillan, 1982), 58–80, 91–7, p. 63.

36   *The Senses of Modernism: Technology, Perception, and Aesthetics* (Ithaca: Cornell University Press, 2002), 3. Danius's reference, it is worth noting, is consistently to film theory of the 1920s and after: Leger, Vertov, Eisenstein, Moholy-Nagy, Benjamin.

37   *Sound Technology and the American Cinema: Perception, Representation, Modernity* (New York: Columbia University Press, 2000), 4, 7.

38   *High Techne: Art and Technology from the Machine Aesthetic to the Posthuman* (Minneapolis: University of Minnesota Press, 1999), 24, 36.

39   Danius mounts an effective critique of the various highly influential commentaries, by Marshall Berman, Stephen Kern, Friedrich Kittler, and others, which characterise literary modernism as no more than a reaction to technological modernisation: *Senses of Modernism*, 43–6. For a comparable debate concerning early cinema's opennness to modernity, see Ben Singer, *Melodrama and Modernity: Early Sensational Cinema and Its Contexts* (New York: Columbia University Press, 2001), ch. 4; and Charlie Keil, '"To Here from Modernity": Style, Historiography, and Transitional Cinema', in Keil and Shelley Stamp (eds), *American Cinema's Transitional Era* (Berkeley: University of California Press, 2004), 51–65.

40   'Tradition and the Individual Talent', in *Selected Prose*, ed. Frank Kermode (London: Faber and Faber, 1975), 37–44, p. 43.

41   *Remediation: Understanding New Media* (Cambridge, MA: MIT Press, 1999), 45–9, 5–6.

42   Theall, *Beyond the Word*, 21.

43   Karen Beckman, for example, has usefully proposed the 'vanishing woman' who appeared (and disappeared) in so many turn-of-the-century vaudeville acts, and subsequently became a staple of the cinema of attractions, as just such a focus: *Vanishing Women: Magic, Film, and Feminism* (Durham: Duke University Press, 2003). 'Hovering in the space between absence and presence,' Beckman observes, 'she challenges us to think not only about the "presence" of particular women, but also about the very possibility of presence per se' (p. 68). I propose the films D. W. Griffith made with Blanche Sweet as a comparable focus: 'The Space Beside: Lateral Exposition, Gender, and Urban Narrative Space in D. W.

Griffith's Biograph Films', forthcoming in Andrew Webber and Emma Wilson (eds), *Cities in Transition* (London: Wallflower Press, 2007).

44 'The Cinema', in *The Crowded Dance of Modern Life*, ed. Rachel Bowlby (Harmondsworth: Penguin Books, 1993), 54–8, p. 55. It is characteristic of the retrospective cast of literary reflections on cinema that her examples should be taken from newsreels made in 1926, and in 1910.

45 *Remediation*, 38–9.

46 *Selected Poems and Related Prose*, trans. Elizabeth R. Napier and Barbara R. Studholme (New Haven: Yale University Press, 2002), 77–80, p. 79.

2

The Literature of Cinema

Characters in novels began to go to the movies almost as soon as there were movies to go to. By 1899, Frank Norris's McTeague, a San Francisco dentist, was already trying to impress his girlfriend Trina Sieppe and her family with tickets to a variety show. The programme includes a musical farce and a display of skirt-dancing, as well as acrobats, ventriloquists, and – the main feature – an exhibition of films. That is what cinema largely was, in 1899: a selection of brief scenes of everyday life shown as a ten- or twenty-minute 'turn' in a variety programme. Trina's mother, Mrs Sieppe, is moved to tears by some yodellers in Tyrolese costume who sing songs about mountain tops. 'Instantly she remembered her childhood and her native Swiss village.' McTeague himself proves more susceptible to the main feature.

> McTeague was awe-struck.
> 'Look at that horse move his head,' he cried excitedly, quite carried away. 'Look at that cablecar coming – and the man going across the street. See, here comes a truck. Well, I never in all my life! What would Marcus say to this?'
> 'It's all a drick!' Exclaimed Mrs Sieppe, with sudden conviction. 'I ain't no fool; dot's nothun but a drick.'
> 'Well, of course, mamma,' exclaimed Trina, 'it's – '
> But Mrs Sieppe put her head in the air.
> 'I'm too old to be fooled,' she persisted. 'It's a drick.'
> Nothing more could be got out of her than this.[1]

The contrast Norris draws here, between the effect of live performance and the effect of the mechanically reproduced image, soon became, and was to remain, a feature of responses to cinema. Live performance, in which artist and audience share a time and place, has the effect of restoring Mrs Sieppe immediately to herself, to what she is and always has been. By contrast, the documentary films which so impress McTeague, while they inspect afresh a world he already knows inside out, can scarcely be said to restore him through that inspection to himself, to what he is and always has been. For there is no disguising the fact that the images of which they consist have been captured at some other time in some other place from where he now is. McTeague has been shown a world which fits him like a second skin, a world which (it might seem) requires his presence in order fully to exist – at the very moment when he is decisively absent from it, when it can be seen once again to exist without him. At once so close to the scene viewed that the very grain of familiar motion (a tramcar, a man crossing the street) becomes apparent, and remote from it, not at all viewing it as a human observer would view it, the films reek of the uncanny. McTeague will not know what to make of them until he has consulted Trina's modish cousin Marcus Schouler. Mrs Sieppe, however, has her own term for such hypermediation: 'dot's nothun but a drick.'

On 28 December 1895, in Paris, the Lumière brothers, Louis and Auguste, gave the first commercial showing of the films they had made with their new invention, the Cinématographe, a combined camera and projector. Their stock-in-trade was the nonfiction 'actuality'. Taken in long shot, almost invariably from a fixed camera, and lasting about fifty seconds, actualities comprised all of whatever it was that took place in front of the camera, staged or unstaged, essential or inessential, during the fifty seconds. Workers pour out through a factory-gate; a train arrives in a crowded station, and passengers alight; some courageous (or handsomely paid) pedestrians try to cross the Champs-Elysées in the rush-hour; fire-engines clamour down a city street; a small boat heads out to sea.

It is said that the the first viewers of *Arrival of a Train at La Ciotat Station* (1895) took drastic evasive action as the locomotive, looming larger and larger as it draws gradually to a halt, appeared to burst out of the screen at them. 'In the distance,' reported an observer present at the film's first showing in London, in February 1896,

> there is some smoke, then the engine of the express is seen, and in a few seconds the train rushes in so quickly that, in common with most of the people in the front rows of the stalls, I shift uneasily in my seat and think of railway accidents.[2]

Thinking of railway accidents rapidly became a habit among audiences as the Lumière films fanned out, in the early months of 1896, across Europe and the United States. Cinema's unique claim to realism lay, as Tom Gunning observes, in 'its ability to convince spectators that the moving image was, in fact, palpable and dangerous, bearing towards them with physical menace'.[3] Before long, however, audiences were being invited to laugh at any impulse they might yet harbour to dive out of the way. The British pioneer R. W. Paul used the Lumière effect of frontal assault to construct a 'primitive' spectator: a spectator for whom the cinema was still new, still replete with physical menace. The rustic protagonist of *The Countryman and the Cinematograph* (1901) responds in different ways to different kinds of stimulus: a woman dancing, a train entering a station, and a rural courtship. He ogles the dancer, flees in panic from the locomotive, and tries to intrude on the courtship. For him, it's all magic, and it's all real. By 1901, then, cinema had already remediated itself. The Edison Company duly paid Paul the tribute of shameless imitation, in *Uncle Josh at the Moving*

Show (1902). Like McTeague, Uncle Josh is a rube, a simpleton let loose in a technological wonderland, fit only to be awe-struck.

McTeague belongs to what one might call the literature of early cinema: a literature in which people go to the movies, or in which metaphoric use is made of reference to film effects. Nobody goes to the movies in Norris's *The Octopus* (1901), but the hero, relaxing into the 'strange hypnotic condition' which precedes sleep, finds that the day's doings have passed before his imagination 'like the roll of a kinetoscope'.[4] The kinetoscope, Thomas Edison's peepshow machine, in which films ran on a loop or 'roll', gave a number of writers some welcome assistance in imagining mental process. It enabled Jack London, for example, to grasp the essential duality of human consciousness, forever split, or so he thought, between modern reason and ancient instinct. The narrator of *Before Adam* (1907) describes how he, a 'modern man', entered into dreams in which he saw through the eyes of his 'prehistoric ancestor' or 'other-self', 'and in the consequent strange dual personality was both actor and spectator'.[5] By the time he published *Martin Eden*, two years later, London had found a new term for that strange dual personality. Martin watches with ironic detachment as his brutal 'other-self' ferociously beats another man into pulp. 'It was to him, with his splendid power of vision, like gazing into a kinetoscope. He was both onlooker and participant.'[6] Already the cinema had begun to figure for the novelist the double logic of immediacy and hypermediacy relentlessly at work in modern experience.

No novelist relied more consistently or to greater advantage on metaphor than Henry James, and it is therefore no surprise that cinema should appear as a figure of speech in a compelling late story, 'Crapy Cornelia' (1909). James had picked out for figurative use the rather startling effect in the first actualities of movement into and through the foreground of the shot. The standard lens of the silent era yielded about 28 degrees of horizontal coverage, in stark contrast to the 200-degree field available to a person with two eyes.[7] As long as the action it framed took place at a set distance from the camera, or in recession from it, this discrepancy did not cause any problems. But movement towards and past the camera could easily result in an effect of looming or frontal assault. In 1896, a commentator in the *British Journal of Photography* observed that 'a grotesque and unnatural effect is produced when, in taking a street scene, for instance, vehicles and pedestrians approach to within a few feet of the camera, and jerk themselves out of the picture, so to say'.[8] Carriages, explained Maxim Gorky, who first saw the Lumière films at a variety show in Nizhni Novgorod in 1896, move 'straight at you, into the darkness in which you sit', while people loom larger and larger as they come close: the train entering the station seems actually to enter the auditorium.[9] The distortion produced by movement towards and past the camera is troubling, ultimately, because it discloses our externality to the scene. We seem to be right there, in front of it, so palpable are the movements on display, so dangerous. And yet we cannot be, because if we had been, we would have 'taken it all in' quite like this, with a machine's inflexible stare. The immediacy cinema gives, it also takes away.

In March 1900, James took his niece Peggy and three of her friends to 'a first-class variety entertainment (with "biograph" war-pictures &c,)' at the Alhambra. An Alhambra Theatre programme for 5 March 1900 includes, at no. 13 on the bill, 'Actual War Pictures by the Chronoscope', which is presumably what the party saw. The Boer War then at its height had proved a godsend to documentary cinematographers everywhere.[10] 'The affair was most successful,' James reported happily: 'Peggy is a highly-developed Pro-Boer (& seemed surprised that *I* am not).'[11] For both uncle and niece, the interest lay primarily in the military event and its politics, rather than in the quality of the mechanically reproduced image. There was not much of the McTeague about them. When James alluded to cinema, however, in 'Crapy Cornelia', he had something other than topicality in mind. His allusion was to the effects of the sort of film made not in 1909, the year of the story's publication, or even in 1900, when Peggy had so ebulliently taken him to task, but in, say, 1895. For the literature of cinema continued to dwell on its original effect (on the effect of its originality).

The story's fictional premise is straightforward: White-Mason, a middle-aged bachelor and one of the few surviving representatives of 'old' New York, is about to pay a visit to the ultra-chic and unashamedly rich Mrs Worthingham, with a view to a proposal. White-Mason is something of a virtuoso of the missed encounter. He has already proposed marriage to three different women; and now feels, with Mrs Worthingham in prospect, that he was right, in each case, 'to have put himself forward always, by the happiest instinct, only in impossible conditions'.[12] Arriving at her house, he discovers that she has polished her 'lustre' up for the occasion (to his eyes, the modern is always dazzling); and that there is someone else present, 'a small black insignificant but none the less oppressive stranger' (p. 226), whom he proceeds to ignore.

Emboldened by the welcome he receives from Mrs Worthingham, White-Mason pictures to himself the marriage he will contract with her as the view from 'a great square sunny window that hung in assured fashion over the immensity of life' (p. 227). He frames, as a number of James's protagonists do, though not always with marriage in mind, an enabling prospect. For Tony Tanner, it is *The Ambassadors*, above all, which makes of the view from above both a reassurance and a guarantee of meaning in life. Lambert Strether's 'progress in Europe', Tanner says, should be regarded as an 'ascent to a balcony'.[13] In 'Crapy Cornelia', however, the prospect or picture is rudely interrupted. An 'incongruous object' looms, suddenly, usurping the 'privilege of the frame'.

> The incongruous object was a woman's head, crowned with a little sparsely feathered black hat, an ornament quite unlike those the women mostly noticed

by White-Mason were now 'wearing', and that grew and grew, that came nearer and nearer, while it met his eyes, after the manner of images in the cinematograph. (p. 228)

In the first films, movement towards the camera had laid the framing of the scene bare as a machine's-eye view. It had defined that scene as one at which, for all its immediacy, the viewer could not have been present. Here, the looming demonstrates White-Mason's necessary absence from the scene of proposal: from the prospect or picture of marriage so gloriously established in his own mind. The hat belongs to the third person present, Cornelia Rasch, an old friend, a survivor of 'old' New York, now returned from Europe, and renewing acquaintances. Even after Cornelia has left, White-Mason cannot bring himself to propose to Mrs Worthingham. For he was never really *there*, he now understands, for all the immediacy of the lustre so assiduously polished up, to see her as she is. Mrs Worthingham represents a balcony he was never likely to ascend to. Crapy Cornelia becomes instead the focus of his thoughts, thus ensuring that he will remain until his death the virtuoso of the missed encounter.

McTeague and 'Crapy Cornelia' belong to the literature of early cinema: one makes dramatic, the other figurative, use of cinema's new eminence, soon to become pre-eminence, as a medium. Cinema had to be reckoned with, as institution and as method. It passed into modernist knowledge, and modernist knowingness.[14] There can be no clearer evidence of this than the curious experimental poem (or verse drama) Ford Madox Ford published in 1923: *Mister Bosphorus and the Muses or a Short History of Poetry in Britain*.

Mister Bosphorus was Ford's *Dunciad*: an assault equally on British philistinism and on the British climate. A lengthy subtitle describes it as a 'variety entertainment' in four acts, 'With Harlequinade, Transformation Scene, Cinematograph Effects, and Many Other Novelties, as well as Old and Tried Favourites'. Act 2, scene 1 is set in a workhouse in Clerkenwell. Mr Bosphorus and Mr Bulfin, pauperised poet and pauperised critic, converse on a 'fore-stage', while moving pictures of scenes from East End life appear on a screen behind them. The cinematograph effects which seem most to have impressed Ford were the use of explanatory intertitles, and, especially, rapid changes of shot-scale.

(*On screen*: A London street in an obviously poor quarter. Old, small houses. Shops beneath. Two shops shown, preternaturally large. One is a pawn-broker's, the three golden balls protruding; the other an undertaker's, coffin-lids standing outside. The film shifts; pawnbroking establishment vanishing, the undertaker's seems to jump, rather unsteadily, at the spectator.)

The director of this 'film' has evidently cut from an establishing long shot of the two adjacent shops to a medium shot of one of them, which thus appears to jump unsteadily out at the spectator. Ford was having enough fun with the effect to try it again. '*The screen* performs another Close-up or whatever is the technical term. Pawnbroker's shop jumps at audience.' In the 1910s, the term 'close-up' could well have applied to the kind of relatively distant view Ford has in mind here, perhaps with one or more actors occupying the foreground. By 1923, however, it had come to mean what it means today: a cut-in shot of a face, or some other detail. Ford uses it in this sense during the development of the scene in the pawnbroker's shop. '*Close-up* shows waves of emotion on widow's face.'[15]

Mister Bosphorus entertainingly remediates film by its representation of 'cinematograph effects'. Indeed, it provides valuable evidence concerning the ways in which films were actually 'seen' in the years immediately after the First World War. Ford was by no means alone, for example, in his conception of changes in shot-scale as bringing segments of the world viewed, or indeed of the screen itself, abruptly forward towards the viewer. It is not quite right, however, to say, as Max Saunders does, that the poem amounts to a 'cinematic presentation of a series of "dissolving views"'.[16] Dissolve is one thing the views do not do; and they are in any case pretty much restricted to the single scene set in the Clerkenwell workhouse. Literature, rather than film, was Ford's model. *Mister Bosphorus* incorporates a parody of the opening section of *The Waste Land*; and probably owes something as well, as Saunders points out, to the 'Circe' episode in *Ulysses*. Ford felt he had to know about, and was entertained by, cinematograph effects. But he did not lay claim to a theory of cinema. He had not thought through the implications of the camera's-eye view for literature.

My primary focus, here, will be on texts which, whether or not anyone in them goes to the movies (as in *McTeague*), or has his or her behaviour explained by reference to or representation of film effects (as in 'Crapy Cornelia' and *Mister Bosphorus*), do yield such an understanding or theory of cinema, whose 'disembodiment of perception by technique' they have to some extent made their own. The literature of cinema will on occasion provide a context for the understanding of cinema literary texts propose. In chapter 5, I discuss *The Waste Land* in relation to Katherine Mansfield's 'Pictures' and John Rodker's *Adolphe 1920*; in chapter 6, I discuss *Mrs Dalloway* and *To the Lighthouse* in relation to Rudyard Kipling's 'Mrs Bathurst', Mary Butts's 'In Bloomsbury', and Elizabeth Bowen's 'Dead Mabelle'. In general, however, the literature of cinema, whether modernist or non-modernist, was not a new literature. Dramatic or figurative use of cinema and its effects made little or no difference, in itself, to the shape taken by most of the literary texts in which it was incorporated. We can get a preliminary sense of the difference an understanding of cinema might actually make to literature from a brief consideration of D. H. Lawrence's *The Lost Girl* (1920).

The Lost Girl and the rise of the Latin Lover

D. H. Lawrence left England, in November 1919, in a state of near-destitution. *The Rainbow* was still out of print, *Women in Love* had not yet been published, and there was generally little or no demand for his work. He needed to make some money quickly. He began to revise and expand a story he had set aside in 1913, about the Eastwood family of George Henry Cullen, a tradesman famous for his flights of entrepreneurial fancy. The story became *The Lost Girl*, written rapidly between 9 March and 5 May 1920, with a view to commercial publication. One of those flights of fancy was a cinema known as Cullen's Picture Palace.

Alvina Houghton, like Florence Cullen, has trained as a nurse, but at 28 finds herself back at home 'withering towards old-maiddom', as we learn at the start of a chapter entitled 'Houghton's Last Endeavour'.[17] 'Now so far,' the narrator adds, 'the story of Alvina is commonplace enough. It is more or less the story of thousands of girls' (p. 83). Alvina, however, is no ordinary person. 'If help came, it would have to come from the extraordinary. Hence the extreme peril of her case' (p. 84). The help which does eventually come for the 'lost girl' comes also, and unexpectedly, given its author's antipathy to cinema, for *The Lost Girl*. Both heroine and novel find redemption from ordinariness through the agency of James Houghton's final endeavour, a Pleasure Palace.

Woodhouse (Eastwood) already boasts a cinema, the Empire. An itinerant impresario and conman called Mr May persuades Houghton to establish a variety theatre in the slum district of Lumley (Langley Mill). Like the variety theatre to which McTeague takes the Sieppes, the Pleasure Palace in Lumley will combine live acts with a programme of films assembled by Mr May: *The Human Bird*, a 'purely descriptive' Norwegian ski-ing film; *The Pancake*, a comedy; and a serial, *The Silent Grip*. The turns include Miss Poppy Traherne, a lady in innumerable petticoats, and the acrobatic Baxter Brothers. Alvina provides the piano accompaniment (p. 107). The novel is set in the years immediately before the First World War, when purpose-built cinemas showing films only had begun to construct a mass-audience, without as yet displacing the older variety-format, which still survived in working-class districts.[18] The variety-format enables Lawrence, as it had enabled Norris, to compare the effect of live performance with that of the mechanically reproduced image. The comparison alters the course of the novel.

For Lawrence stages a debate about cinema. The debate brackets the arrival in Lumley of the most spectacular of the live acts, the Natcha-Kee-Tawara, a troupe consisting of Madame Rochard and four young men whose great turn is a 'Red Indian scene' (p. 120). Of the young men, one is French, another French Swiss, the third German Swiss and a famous yodeller, and the fourth Italian. The chapter introducing the Natcha-Kee-Tawara opens with the first phase of the debate. The 'interest' upon which Mr May's promotions are based remains 'the human interest in living performers and their living feats'. He cannot believe that the colliers and factory girls crowding the Woodhouse Empire want 'everything in the flat' (p. 116): that is, cinema. Alvina explains this preference with a little help from film theory. She argues that the 'common people' feel jealous of anyone who does anything they themselves are not capable of doing. They find themselves 'up against' the performer's singularity, or otherness, right there on the stage in front of them, and cannot abide it. 'They hate anything that isn't themselves. And that's why they like pictures. It's all themselves to them, all the time.' They can 'spread themselves' over a film, 'and they *can't* over a living performer'. Extraordinary feats 'done on the film' pose little threat because they do not involve 'flesh-and-blood people'. The 'life' movies possess is a function of the people who watch them, who therefore find in them nothing to be jealous of (p. 116).

aud, –
ence

Well, it's a theory. At issue is the fact often noted by commentators from Walter Benjamin onwards that in the cinema, unlike the theatre, actors and audience never coincide: for one party to be present, the other must be absent.[19] Christian Metz, for example, remarks that in the theatre the world viewed (the 'given') is 'physically present, in the same space as the spectator'; whereas the cinema only ever offers the given 'in effigy, inaccessible from the outset, in a primordial *elsewhere*'. That primordial elsewhere is the other 'scene' of absence itself, 'which nonetheless represents the absent in detail, thus making it very present, but by a different itinerary'.[20] To Mr May, to Alvina, to Lawrence himself, such an elsewhere or other scene looks very much like no place at all, a mere flatness. The feats performed there cannot have any life to them.

Life, it would seem, is what the entertainers have in abundance, for Alvina, if not for the common people. 'Queer cuts these! – but just a little beyond her.' Alvina watches them from a distance she would like to cross, particularly when it comes to the Japanese strongman, whose richly tattooed body and 'toad-like lewdness' fascinate her. 'Odd, extraneous creatures, often a little depressed, feeling life slip away from them. The cinema was killing them' (p. 119). Most fascinating of all are the Natcha-Kee-Tawara, who advertise their arrival by parading up and down the main street of Woodhouse in full Red Indian kit, the Italian, Ciccio, on a bay horse, 'flickering hither and thither in the rear, his feathers swaying, his horse sweating, his face ghastlily smiling in its war-paint' (p. 141). Cinema, it might seem, has already got into Ciccio, as he 'flickers' hither and thither in the rear.

The parade occasions the second phase of the debate about cinema. To Miss Pinnegar, the supervisor of Houghton's work-girls, the Natcha-Kee-Tawara parade is transparently a performance, and therefore uninstructive. 'It's not like the cinema, where you see it and take it all in at once; you *know* everything at a glance' (p. 142). Cinema delivers a certain knowledge, and delivers it at once, immediately. It makes absence present in a way no mere presence ever could be. Miss Pinnegar's thesis concerning cinema brings Alvina 'back to consciousness' after the 'delicious excitement' of the parade (of live performance). It is now the performers who seem 'unreal' to her, 'the actual unrealities: while the ragged dithering pictures of the film were actual, real as the day' (p. 143). Alvina bitterly resents this awakening. She has lost for ever the reassurance of Mr May's conviction that film is merely flat.

There is a problem, here, for Alvina, and for Lawrence, because Ciccio, who will redeem her from ordinary old-maiddom, and the novel from traditional narrative method, is the consummate live performer: rather, he is the live performer understood as the embodiment of masculinity, of dark (that is, blind, pre-verbal, purely sensuous) unknowing. Both need to persuade themselves that Mr May is right about the actuality of live performance, and Miss Pinnegar wrong. Alvina gives it her best shot. After her father's death, she enlists in the Natcha-Kee-Tawara, seduces (or is seduced by) Ciccio, and follows him to Italy. Lawrence, for his part, has to find a way to represent Ciccio's actuality: an actuality powerful enough to redeem a young woman from ordinary existence (from the kind of existence an ordinary novelist, Arnold Bennett, say, would have enjoyed describing). *The Lost Girl*, he explained to Compton Mackenzie on 11 June 1920, was different from his other work: 'not immediate, not intimate – except the last bit: all set across a distance'.[21] That last bit, which describes events after James Houghton's death, has as its subject Alvina's redemption by and through Ciccio's actuality (his live performance, one might say). It purports to bridge the distance established by traditional narrative method between the narrator's point of view and the protagonist's, to cross over; as Alvina, rescued by Ciccio, will cross over with him into some other, less ordinary life. Live performance *is* the bridge, then, for heroine and author alike.

And yet the only way in which the novel can grasp Ciccio, during this last bit, is as the object of Alvina's gaze. 'It was the clean modelling of his dark, other-world face that decided her – for it sent the deep spasm across her' (p. 179). Alvina knows him, that is, not as Mr May knows the liveness of a live performance – by the appreciation of presence, of flesh-and-blood singularity – but as Miss Pinnegar knows the film-image, as actual unreality: by the way in which the modelling of his face works on her from afar.

In that respect, Ciccio resembles Gerald Crich, in *Women in Love*. As Linda Ruth Williams has shown, Gudrun Brangwen, Gerald's lover, is represented as needing to make him into a representation, 'and at a proper cinematic distance', in order to know him fully. *Women in Love*, throughout, and *The Lost Girl*, in its last bit, do not so much achieve a new immediacy, in their representation of masculinity, as substitute one kind of distance for another: that of cinema for that of traditional narrative method. Gerald, as Williams puts it, with Metz's formulation of the difference between cinema and theatre in mind, has been made into spectacle: 'a framed image *over there*, not a present actor'.[22] The same could be said of Ciccio, whose 'other-world face', like Gerald's, is highly visible in its clean modelling, and yet somehow unseen, or spectral, because always 'over there'. Alvina's seduction by Ciccio is staged as a movement into the dark, into sensuous unknowing; but his power depends on her continuing absorption in the *sight* of his 'lustrous dark beauty'. She succumbs to him because she desires above all to preserve him as a spectacle: because she 'could not see him ugly', as he really is (as anyone really is) in ordinary life (p 202). Ciccio, the 'dark Southerner', seems like a proto-Valentino: the creation of a single fan, as Valentino and the other Hollywood Latin Lovers were to be of many.[23] For Alvina, the choice is not between seeing Ciccio and not seeing him; it is between seeing him beautiful and seeing him ugly. To see him beautiful is to be redeemed: by the Latin Lover's flickering hither and thither, by spectacle, by cinema. Miss Pinnegar has won the argument.

Lawrence, I think, knew that she had. *Women in Love*, his most uncompromisingly experimental work, is often uneasily close, in its representation of sexual mesmerism, to the stereotypes of popular fiction, themselves rapidly taken up by Hollywood.[24] In *The Lost Girl*, Alvina Houghton joins the Natcha-Kee-Tawara voluntarily, but her incorporation into the 'tribe' thereafter follows the pattern of the captivity narratives informing American frontier-myth in general, and James Fenimore Cooper's *The Last of the Mohicans* in particular. Alvina goes native. The chapter describing her seduction by Ciccio is entitled 'Alvina Becomes Allaye'. Indeed, the names Lawrence chose for his Red Indian troupe may owe something to Cooper's novels, which he had reread for *Studies in Classic American Literature*, written in 1917, and revised in 1920, and then again in 1923. Equally revealing, perhaps, is Mr May's description of the whole episode as 'almost *White Slave Traffic*, on Madame's part' (p. 228). White slavery – the entrapment of white women into prostitution by (for the most part) 'alien' criminal gangs – was the up-to-date version of the Indian captivity narrative. The panic white slavery engendered made it a hot topic for a narrative cinema intent on combining sensationalism with a moral reform agenda (no surprise that *The Inside of the White Slave Traffic* should appear from the Moral Feature Film Company in 1913). The kidnapping scene in *The White Slave Girl*, a Danish film of 1911, evidently stirred Franz Kafka's imagination.[25] Mr May could have had in mind not so much a phenomenon as a specific film, or kind of film. Such films certainly existed, and would not have been out of place at Houghton's Pleasure Palace in Lumley.

It seems to me fair to conclude that the need to take account in his novel of George Henry Cullen's commitment to the idea of a Picture Palace provoked Lawrence into an understanding of cinema, which in turn had profound consequences for the way in which the novel came to be written. Or, rather, for the way in which it came partly to be written. *A Lost Girl* remains, in many respects, not all that far from the kind of novel Arnold Bennett might have considered writing about a woman like Alvina Houghton. It is full of implication, nonetheless, for the analysis of modernist literature's relation to narrative cinema. Before pursuing that implication further, I want first to examine what it might have meant to say, as Miss Pinnegar does, that in cinema you '*know* everything at a glance'. In the final section of this chapter, I will describe the specific life-likeness (the array of presence-effects) generated by the stereoscope, a visual technology which caught the attention of writers and film-makers alike. The world viewed through a stereoscope is, I shall suggest, at once immediate and hypermediated.

Stereoscopy: modernism and the 'haptic'

In the 'Proteus' episode of *Ulysses*, Stephen Dedalus, crossing Sandymount Strand, considers at some length Bishop Berkeley's proposition that reality is made in the mind. 'The good bishop of Cloyne took the veil of the temple out of his shovel hat: veil of space with coloured emblems hatched on its field.'[26] According to Stephen's redaction of Berkeley, the visible world is a 'veil of space' or flat screen onto which emblems differentiated by colour have been (divinely) projected. How come, then, that we experience it in three dimensions?

> Coloured on a flat: yes, that's right. Flat I see, then think distance, near, far, flat I see, east, back. Ah, see now: Falls back suddenly, frozen in stereoscope. Click does the trick. (p. 48)

Flatness is what we see, Stephen reckons, depth (or distance) what we think we see. The third dimension has been produced mechanically, by a conjuring trick, a scene-change in the theatre of the mind. 'Signatures of all things I am here to read,' he had previously told himself, with a nod at Jakob Boehme's *De Signatura Rerum*; and criticism, taking that particular hint, now routinely casts him as an exegete or semiotician of the visible.[27] However, his subsequent reflections on the veil of space do not encourage further resort to the Renaissance sage. His own rapid experiment has demonstrated that the perception of depth *reconfigures* the world, and that it doesn't really help to imagine the process as a reading of signatures. What enables him to come to a conclusion about the nature of the visible is not recondite visual theory, but the visual practice constituted by a mechanism at once mundane and utterly entrancing: the stereoscope.

The basic principle of stereoscopy is simple. Paired images made with a twin-lens camera produce, when seen through a binocular stereoscope, a startling illusion of three-dimensionality. The mind converts the flatness of the images set side by side on a piece of cardboard into depth. Click (adjustment to the appropriate focal length) does the trick. By 1904, it was a trick easily performed. The stereoscope had received its first major exposure at the Great Exhibition of 1851; production of the device, and of images for use in it, was soon on an industrial footing. By 1858, the London Stereoscopic Company had a trade list of more than 100,000 titles. The invention of a cheap hand-held model established the stereoscope as a staple of home entertainment. By the end of the nineteenth century there were millions of images in circulation: views, for the most part, of location, of architecture and landscape; but also of events, some actual, some staged.[28] Scientific applications were proposed, from time to time, in surgery, or aerial reconnaissance.[29] But stereoscopy was, above all, a medium of mass-entertainment. It survived as such until the 1930s; indeed, it still survives, here and there, on the stalls outside heritage sites, as a marketable gadget. The basic effect it produces, of hyper-reality, cannot fail to enthrall; the flimsier the apparatus, the duller the image viewed, the more profound the enthralment. On the whole, however, we have forgotten what it means to view or to think stereoscopically.

It is, of course, the purpose of phenomenological theories of film to get to grips with enthralment by the moving image: with what David Clarke has described as cinema's 'sensorial immediacy'.[30] Clarke poses in relation to cinema a question originally posed by Maurice Blanchot in relation to imagery in general. 'What happens when what you see, even though from a distance, seems to touch you with a grasping contact, when the manner of seeing is a sort of touch, when seeing is a *contact* at a distance?'[31] In film theory, the question has been pursued most productively with the aid of the distinction made by the art historian Aloïs Riegl (1858–1905) between two kinds of visual experience: the optical, which delivers a survey, an account of (and accounting for) distinguishable objects in deep space; and the haptic, which feels its way along or around a world conceived as an infinitely variable surface, alert to texture rather than outline. In haptic experience, the manner of seeing is, as Blanchot puts it, a 'sort of touch'. Riegl himself spoke of a 'haptic' (*haptein* = to fasten) rather than a 'tactile' look, because he did not want it to be understood as a literal touching.[32] The optical manner of seeing stands back from the world, withholds itself in and for survey, or surveillance (it will become the bad gaze of twentieth-century cultural theory); the haptic, so fast (in both senses) in its fastening, is a form of attachment.

Two recent books have demonstrated the concept's enduring explanatory force. In *The Skin of the Film*, Laura Marks examines the ways in which audiovisual media evoke, 'within their own constraints', the senses of smell, taste, and touch. She argues that such evocations have been used to inform and make sense of the experience of moving from one culture to another. Intercultural cinema 'appeals to contact – to embodied knowledge, and to the sense of touch in particular – in order to recreate memories'. It does so by drawing attention to the texture both of the world and of the medium itself. In a move full of implication for cinema of all kinds, Marks opposes 'haptic visuality' to the meaning generated by narrative.[33] In *Atlas of Emotion*, Juliana Bruno explores the relation between visual fastening and kinesthesis (our ability to sense our own movement in space). For her, the haptic is an 'agent in the formation of space'. It plays 'a tangible, *tactical* role in our communicative "sense" of spatiality and motility, thus shaping the texture of habitable space and, ultimately, mapping our ways of being in touch with the environment'. Bruno argues that cinema is the latest (or next to latest) in a series of configurations of a 'topographical "sense"' which cannot be understood entirely in terms of perspectivism, or of a theory of the gaze. Cinema, she concludes, has established 'its own sentient way of picturing space'.[34]

Marks situates the work of contemporary intercultural film-makers within a 'history of tactile looking' in cinema in general. The appeal of the first films, she observes, was to bodily rather than narrative identification.[35] For Bruno, cinematic kinesthesis descends 'genealogically' from an eighteenth-century 'spatial curiosity', or hunger for vistas and views. The 'haptic consciousness' once fed by panoramas and travel literature was to find further and even more lavish sustenance in the travelling shots of the first Edison actualities.[36] Antonia Lant has pointed out that the emergence of cinema in the 1890s coincided with the development of haptic theory in art criticism. The haptic qualities Riegl and others had seen in ancient Egyptian art found an analogue, Lant argues, in cinema's 'novel spatiality': a teeming flatness often made vivid, during the early years, by the incorporation of ancient Egyptian motifs.[37] In my view, an understanding of stereoscopy can help us to define that phase in the 'education of the eye' which also includes early cinema.[38]

The stereoscope provided a point of reference for those theorists who sought to demonstrate that visual media had evolved, within their own constraints, a sentient way to picture space. In *The Problem of Form in Painting and Sculpture* (1893), a work decisive for Riegl, the sculptor Adolf Hildebrand argued that the eye perceives space in two modes, optical and kinesthetic, the one appropriate to distance from the object of vision, the other to a close-up view. The term Hildebrand found for kinesthesis was 'stereoscopic vision'. A painting, he said, might belie its own flatness by an appeal to kinesthetic perception. It might produce a 'stereoscopic impression'.[39] The psychologist Hugo Münsterberg, writing in 1916, believed that the same was true of cinema.

> The stereoscope thus illustrates clearly that the knowledge of the flat character of pictures by no means excludes the actual perception of depth, and the question arises whether the moving pictures of the photoplay, in spite of our knowledge concerning the flatness of the screen, do not give us after all the impression of actual depth.[40]

The stereoscope is the historically specific visual technology which haptic theory requires to make its case in relation to that phase of the education of the eye which includes early cinema.

It is, however, crucial to understand, and has not sufficiently been understood, that the reality effect produced by the stereoscope is *variable*: objects in the middle or far distance appear to be arranged along planes separated from each other by a void; while objects in the foreground, solid enough to touch, assume an astonishing palpability. In the most incisive account yet offered of the stereoscope's role in the constitution of a 'modern observer', Jonathan Crary observes that its distinctive feature is the organisation of the image as a sequence of receding planes. 'We perceive individual elements as flat, cutout forms arrayed either nearer to or further from us. But the experience of space between these objects (planes) is not one of gradual and predictable recession; rather, there is a vertiginous uncertainty about the distance separating forms.' There are some similarities, Crary adds, between the stereoscopic image and classical stage design, which synthesises flats and real extensive space into an illusory scene. The stereoscope could in this respect be said to have remediated theatre. Like Stephen Dedalus, Crary grasps the theatricality of the process by which the mind makes an image out of retinal difference. Nothing, however, he goes on, 'could be more removed from Berkeley's theory of how distance is perceived than the science of the stereoscope'. This 'quintessentially nineteenth-century device', which constructs relief through an organisation of optical cues, undid Berkeley, who had always regarded depth perception as a function of movement and touch, rather than of sight. For Crary, the stereoscope was the product and vivid embodiment of a new (modern) emphasis on the 'autonomy and abstraction' of vision.[41]

It is important, however, not to overestimate the extent to which the stereoscope delivers autonomy and abstraction. In the composition of many stereoscopic images, theatricality gives way to something else altogether. Crary himself points out that the purpose of such images, in the eyes of those who produced them, 'was not simply likeness, but immediate, apparent *tangibility*'.[42] The overwhelming illusion of tangibility is a product of the assertiveness with which objects in the foreground occupy space: the feeling that one could reach out and touch them, or be touched by them. Two visual systems, optical and haptic, inform stereoscopy. It may have been their coexistence – rather than, as Crary suggests, the replacement of one by the other – which gave the stereoscope a role in the constitution of a modern viewing subject. Of the two effects it generated, of tableau and of tangibility, the less memorable, the less disturbing, in 1850, or in 1900, or in 1910, because it could be understood as hypermediacy, as a representation of theatre, must surely have been the former.

It was tangibility on which Oliver Wendell Holmes, inventor of the handheld stereoscope, laid the emphasis, in an essay published in 1859. 'By means of these two different views of an object,' Holmes argued,

> the mind, as it were, *feels round it*, and gets an idea of its solidity. We clasp an object with our eyes, as with our arms, or with our hands, or with our thumb and finger, and then we know it to be something more than a surface.[43]

When the image seizes on it, Blanchot says, 'the gaze is drawn, absorbed into an immobile movement and a depth without depth'. To be absorbed by an image is thus not simply to be sucked into it (*sorbere*), but to be sucked into it away from (*ab*) where one once stood. By this account, absorption pre-empts meaning (the meaning that might be delivered by perspective, by an 'optical' look). 'What fascinates us, takes away our power to give it a meaning, abandons its "perceptible" nature, abandons the world, withdraws to the near side of the world and attracts us there.'[44] Viewed stereoscopically, objects in the foreground abandon their perceptible nature; a loss, or a gain, easily measured against that other view on offer, the view of objects in the middle and far distance, as in a theatre.

To look through a stereoscope is to feel the need for a theory of the haptic. But the incorporation of historical instance into a theory sometimes alters the theory. Haptic theory seems committed to Benjamin's thesis that film is an art of shocks in rapid succession: in cinema, as in the street, every touch at a distance is an assault, a lightning strike. The Dadaist work, Benjamin wrote, was 'an instrument of ballistics'.

> It hit the spectator like a bullet, it happened to him, thus acquiring a tactile quality. It promoted a demand for the film, the distracting element of which is also primarily tactile, being based on changes of place and focus which periodically assail the spectator.

What the stereoscope offers, by contrast, even at its least comfortable, is not shock, but absorption; and the whole point about absorption is that it is in itself utterly unshockable. It has already drawn us away from that place where we might suffer shock. In Benjamin's view, spectatorship is a necessary and productive act of defence. 'Man's need to expose himself to shock effects is his adjustment to the dangers threatening him.'[45] Absorption, by contrast, is neither offensive nor defensive.[46]

In February 1911, Franz Kafka, looking for a way to pass the time while on a business trip to the northern Bohemian cities of Friedland and Reichenberg, stumbled upon an apparatus known as the Kaiserpanorama, with which he had been familiar in his youth.[47] The Kaiserpanorama was a device invented by the scientist and optical entrepreneur August Fuhrmann for the public and profitable display of his collection of glass stereoscopic photographs. First installed in Breslau in 1880, and then in Berlin in 1883, it was soon in operation at some 250 venues in cities in Germany, Austria, and elsewhere. The first Kaiserpanorama was about fifteen feet in diameter and could accommodate twenty-five spectators, who would simultaneously view different images illuminated by small lamps. The images rotated from one viewer to the next at roughly two-minute intervals, a bell ringing as they were about to change. In a later model, separate coin slots were installed at each viewing station.[48] The mechanism, in short, allowed for individual absorption into the reality effect generated by each image.

What Kafka saw in the Kaiserpanorama was scenes set in Italian cities.

> Brescia, Cremona, Verona. People inside like wax figures, their soles fixed to
> the ground on the sidewalk. Funerary monuments: a lady with a train trailing
> over a short flight of steps pushes a door slightly ajar and looks back as she
> does so ... The scenes more alive than in the cinematograph, because they
> allow the eye the stillness of reality. The cinematograph lends the observed
> objects the agitation of their movement, the stillness of the gaze seems more
> important. Smooth floor of the cathedrals in front of our tongue. Why is there
> no combination of cinema and stereoscope in this way?[49]

Kafka was quite explicit about the two kinds of looking the stereoscope
invited. On the one hand, there are figures in the middle and far distance
poised like wax figures, the soles of their shoes fixed to the ground; on the
other, there is a foreground immediately in front of the tongue, almost
tangible in its solidity. The first effect could be compared to a theatrical
tableau or museum display; the second, an immobile movement, or depth
without depth, is unique to the medium. Kafka, at the Kaiserpanorama, was
looking to be absorbed. One of the stereoviews he saw was entitled
'Funerary Monument to a Widow'.[50] His written account omits any
reference to the widow, the monument's *raison d'être*. It does not make
anything out of, or indeed even envisage, the tableau of a woman entering
her own tomb. Instead, Kakfa laps up whatever is solid in the image: a
garment trailing over some steps, pressure on a door, a backward glance.
Or, he laps up the solidity of an image which has abandoned its perceptible
nature. Existence (that which has been felt round) precedes essence (the
monument as monument).

A brief survey of some commonplace, though by no means representative, stereoviews should help to establish their hapticity. Look at *Fountain in
Hyde Park* (fig. 1) through a stereoscope and the figures of the two men in
the rowing-boat recede; they clearly belong, despite the stare one of them
gives the camera, to a world set back beyond (and below) the fountain, a
world steadied by the contour of the far bank, which rises gently up to a
path, and some elegant, sun-dappled woodland. The mind can certainly
feel its way into those depths, take a virtual stroll. More remarkable,
however, and perhaps more unsettling, is what occupies the foreground:
water which does not so much fall from the fountain's basin, as festoon it
stringily, or curdle at its foot. In *Modern Painters*, John Ruskin had described
how a storm beats the sea 'not into mere creaming foam, but into masses of
accumulated yeast, which hang in ropes and wreaths from wave to wave'.
Even Turner, he said, would have struggled to paint the yeastiness of these
'writhing, hanging, coiling masses', these 'clotted concretions'.[51] The very
insistence of Ruskin's language is an absorption, an attempt to feel round
and so come to terms with that which has abandoned its perceptible nature.
The fountain in Hyde Park scarcely provokes such intensity of awe verging
on nausea. But stereoscopy has endowed it, too, with clotted concretions.

Figure 1   *Fountain in Hyde Park.* Stereoview. J. F. Jarvis. Author's collection.

An image withdraws to the near side of the world, and attracts us there, holds us fast.

Quicker Way to Spread the News (fig. 2) is an excellent example of the staged scenes which became increasingly popular towards the end of the nineteenth century. It puts on display a new means of communication, and the woman using it, whose handsomeness has been rounded off stereoscopically for our benefit, set solidly in knowable space. Again, though, an image has withdrawn to the near side of the merely perceptible world. The view's most remarkable feature is the solidity of the metal rail whose corner protrudes into the room, somewhere in front of our tongue, as Kafka might have put it; indeed, the triangular shape it forms *is*, in some ways, a kind of prosthetic tongue. This tongue touches the elaborately prepared scene on the raw. Its tip rests up against an object which would seem to have no place in it, no meaning: a handkerchief laid casually on the chair. The news which is spreading has passed the handkerchief by (though it may yet activate the fan the woman holds). What stereoscopy's haptic consciousness touches, here, is (the illusion of) contingency itself.

Some stereoviews deliberately 'foreground' the haptic-contingent. In *Foreign Offices, London* (fig. 3), stereoscopy attributes to the building itself a volume entirely appropriate to the dignity of its function. But the eye is drawn magnetically away from the building to the clump of rushes on the near side of the vista. In this case, the haptic-contingent could even be said to obtrude on the vista, to spoil it. Oliver Wendell Holmes had long since noted the violence inherent in the stereoscopic foreground. 'The scraggy branches of a tree in the foreground run out at us as if they would scratch our eyes out. The elbow of a figure stands forth so as to make us almost uncomfortable.'[52] The lower the angle of the shot, the livelier the potential discomfort. In *Houses of Parliament* (fig. 4), the building itself recedes magnificently, but without interest, while the barges in the foreground compel by the sheer weight and intricacy of clotted concretion. I like to imagine the photographer waiting for a particularly ripe selection of detritus to swim into view before taking the shot. But draw back a little further, and absorption dwindles, that sense of being between sight and touch. *Houses of Parliament and Towers of Westminster Abbey* (fig. 5) frames its object altogether too comfortably. The balance established by the higher angle of the shot between foreground and background (between authority, commerce, and leisure) returns the image to its perceptible nature, to mere pictorialism.

Stereoscopy, then, involves the visualisation of tangibility. That which we might want to touch takes shape in front of our eyes. The shape it takes is that of its own tangibility. There is a choice, here, of a low angle; and potentially a politics, an education of the eye in the pleasures of the haptic-contingent. The stereoscope, although for the most part put to genteel use, was in itself democratic, as Holmes had been the first to recognise. 'A painter shows us masses; the stereoscopic figure spares us nothing, – all

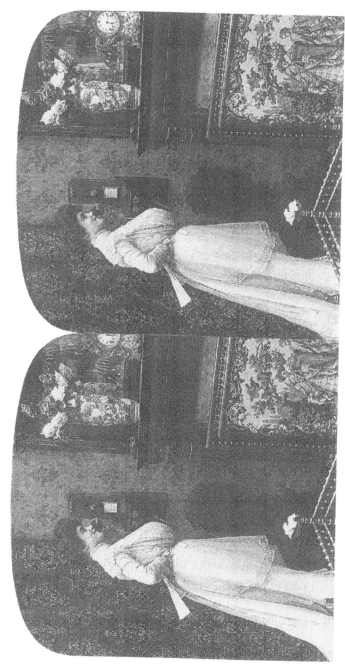

Figure 2 *Quicker Way to Spread the News.* Stereoview. H. C. White Co. Author's collection.

Figure 3 *Foreign Offices, London.* Stereoview. No publisher's name. Author's collection.

Figure 4   *Houses of Parliament, London, England.* Stereoview. J. F. Jarvis. Author's collection.

Figure 5   *Houses of Parliament and Towers of Westminster Abbey.* Stereoview. Keystone View Company. Author's collection.

must be there, every stick, straw, scratch, as faithfully as the dome of St Peter's, or the summit of Mont Blanc, or the ever-moving stillness of Niagara. The sun is no respecter of persons or of things.' Examining stereoviews of Ann Hathaway's cottage, Holmes noted the marks and stains left by passage through the doorway. Whenever it gives us a group of houses, he added, the stereoview 'insists on finding' a clothes-line.[53]

The choice of a low angle might, of course, indicate lowness in general. 'The stereoscope as a means of representation was inherently *obscene*,' Jonathan Crary remarks, drawing upon the term's folk etymology, 'in the most literal sense. It shattered the *scenic* relationship between viewer and object that was intrinsic to the fundamentally theatrical setup of the camera obscura.'[54] And it was indeed used, from the very early days, for purposes of obscenity. 'It was not long', Baudelaire complained in 1859, 'before thousands of pairs of greedy eyes were glued to the peepholes of the stereoscope, as though they were the skylights of the infinite.'[55] Substantial collections of pornographic stereoviews survive.[56] Here, the mind does, as Holmes had put it, *feel round* the object represented. Linda Williams has written illuminatingly about the 'new porno-erotics of corporealized observation' of which these images were a part.[57]

Baudelaire's homily had been provoked by a society woman's request to see some pornographic stereoviews ('Let me see; nothing shocks me').[58] The decision to become absorbed was not restricted by gender. Representations of stereoscopes in use, and of the Kaiserpanorama, show a full complement of female viewers.[59] Restriction by class is harder to assess, but presumably eased as the instrument itself became more widely available. Pornographic stereoviews were usually in colour, and therefore relatively expensive. Generally speaking, though, the stereoscope's grasp on the haptic-contingent – this sight of something which is not exactly visible, which is more or less than visible – can be understood in relation to the 'new mode' of reflexivity, at once modernist and vernacular, that Miriam Hansen has described in Hollywood movies.[60]

A hankering after three-dimensionality is as old as cinema itself. In 1903, the Lumière brothers produced a stereoscopic version (in two-colour format) of one of their earliest actualities, *Arrivée d'un train à La Ciotat*.[61] To British film-makers of this period, the phenomenon of motion parallax – the stereoscopic effect created when the camera moves in a curve around a scene in which more than one plane is visible – offered the enticing prospect of a 3-D cinema which did not require the use of special projectors or viewing arrangements.[62] Cecil Hepworth, perhaps the most inventive of them all, continued to experiment with stereoscopic effects. *Up the River with Molly: A Stereoscopic Gem* (1921) puts the camera on a punt on the Thames and moves it across, or rather into and around, a series of conspicuously layered scenes (Molly was Hepworth's dog). Giovanni Pastrone said that in *Cabiria* (1914) he had moved his camera along curved tracks in order to create a stereoscopic effect, an 'impression of relief'.[63] On 28 June 1920, Abel Gance told Charles Pathé that he had discovered a proper stereoscopic process; one reel of *Napoléon* was in fact shot in 3-D, but left out of the final print on the grounds that it was more likely to fascinate the eye than the heart.[64] In one of the last essays he wrote, Eisenstein maintained that cinema's stereoscopic effect was at its most 'devastating' when the image, 'palpably three-dimensional, "pours" out of the screen into the auditorium'. A cobweb bearing a gigantic spider hangs 'somewhere between the screen and the spectator'; the branches of a tree 'overhang' the auditorium.

> Different calculations during the filming force the image either into Space, endlessly extended to the sides and in depth, or into three-dimensional Volume, moving in materially towards the spectator and positively palpable.[65]

Hepworth, Pastrone, Gance, and Eisenstein are all of central importance to my argument. It is because the images these film-makers created are so palpable, because they move in with such intensity on a spectator not present at their creation, that they speak of absence, of what has gone missing from them.

On the whole, though, film-makers seem to have aimed at no more than an approximation to stereoscopic effects. The most productive of those approximations, in use from the very beginning in films such as G. A. Smith's *Grandma's Reading Glass* (1900), was the close-up, understood as a cut-in enlargement of detail. Increasingly, the close-up served the purposes of narrative, dramatic, or allegorical clarification. However, there is evidence to suggest that the use of close-ups continued to cause a certain unease. Company executives at Biograph notoriously objected to the close-ups D. W. Griffith had begun to introduce into his films. 'The actors look as if they were swimming – you can't have them float on, without legs or bodies!'[66] The cut-in shot made it hard to understand the relation of part to whole; it severed foreground from background. Eisenstein was to criticise Griffith's close-ups for their independence of the contexts in which they occur. In his view, such shots should not show or present, but designate, or give meaning, as a unit of montage; whereas Griffith's merely show or present. Quite, Siegfried Kracauer responded, with the close-up of Mae Marsh's hands in the trial scene in *Intolerance* in mind: 'the face appears before the desires and emotions to which it refers have been completely defined, thus tempting us to get lost in its puzzling indeterminacy.' Big close-ups, Kracauer went on, 'metamorphose their objects by magnifying them'.[67] Such metamorphoses seem to me to involve something more than indeterminacy. They involve that visualisation of tangibility also proposed by the stereoscope's grasp of the haptic-contingent. What is at issue, in cinema as in stereoscopy, is a rapid alternation of prospects: a movement to and fro between framed theatrical tableau and a foreground full, as Vachel Lindsay put it, of 'dumb giants', of bodies in 'high sculptural relief'.[68]

One purpose served by such high sculptural relief had to do with what Noël Burch calls the close-up's 'erotic vocation'.[69] In this respect, there was a considerable overlap, both of subject matter and of technique, between early cinema and the stereoscope. For example, in *Don't Get Above Your Business* (fig. 6), the high sculptural relief into which the woman's stockinged foot and the man's measuring hands have been thrown makes it quite clear why the transaction might prove a cause for concern. It enables us, like the man seated in the background, to visualise tangibility. Other versions of the view provide the woman with a wary chaperone. Edison's *The Gay Shoe Clerk* (1903) transposes the scene from small-town cobbler's shop to metropolitan emporium. It consists of three shots. In the first shot, a young woman and her chaperone, both dressed with utmost respectability, enter the emporium. The young woman takes a chair, while the clerk offers her a selection of shoes. She chooses one, and he crouches on a stool, slips it onto her foot, and starts to lace it up. Cut in on the axis to a close-up of the foot. The young woman slowly raises her skirt, almost to the knee, revealing in the process a fair amount of undergarment. The close-up does not merely enlarge; it enacts, as Kracauer might have said, a metamorphosis. Foreground has been severed from background. Although not seen in relief, the section of leg on display has been transformed from an object of vision to the object of something like touch. Cut back to the initial long shot. The clerk, as though still inhabiting the idyll of desire created in close-up, cannot stop himself getting above his business. He rises up and leans forward to kiss his inviting customer. The chaperone suddenly realises what is going on, and sets about him brutally with her umbrella. Desire has shown itself, and been punished. The two women leave.

The scene returns us to *Ulysses*: if not to Stephen Dedalus on the beach, in 'Proteus', then to Leopold Bloom on the beach, in 'Nausicaa', an episode which has many connections with 'Proteus'. Realising that she has Bloom's full attention, Gerty MacDowell 'just lifted her skirt a little but just enough' (p. 340). She sees the 'meaning' in his look.

> He was looking up so intently, so still and he saw her kick the ball and perhaps he could see the bright steel buckles of her shoes if she swung them like that thoughtfully with the toes down. She was glad that something had told her to put on the transparent stockings thinking Reggie Wylie might be out but that was far away. Here was that of which she had so often dreamed. (p. 342)

Katherine Mullin has shown convincingly that the medium in which Joyce conceived the erotic encounter between Gerty and Leopold Bloom was that of a specific modern visual technology: the mutoscope.[70] The mutoscope was a motion picture device consisting of photographs mounted sequentially on a cylinder driven by a hand-crank. After masturbating, Bloom reimagines the experience as a visit to a mutoscope parlour.

> A dream of wellfilled hose. Where was that? Ah, yes. Mutoscope pictures in Capel street: for men only. Peeping Tom. Willy's hat and what the girls did

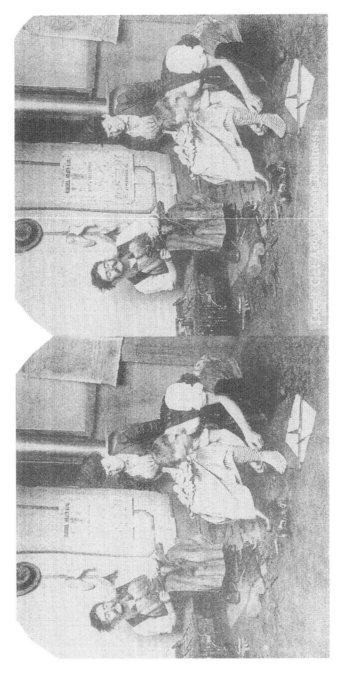

Figure 6 *Don't Get Above Your Business*. Stereoview. Universal Stereoscopic View Co. Author's collection.

with it. Do they snapshot those girls or is it all a fake. *Lingerie* does it. Felt for the curves inside her *deshabille*. (pp. 351–2)

As Mullin points out, Gerty's 'returned look' at Bloom imitates the collusive glance to camera of the heroine of mutoscope scenarios such as *Willie's Hat and What the Girls Did with It*, who reveals her reciprocal longing at the same time as her body.[71] What the mutoscope did not do, of course, was foreground the haptic-contingent. The intensity of the encounter between Bloom and Gerty, in which each touches and is touched by the other's look, seems to demand a further context: that of the close-up's erotic vocation. Bloom's thoughts about the mutoscope are preceded by the memory of an incident earlier that morning, described in 'Lotus Eaters', when a tram passing had cut off a glimpse of a woman's ankle, as she mounted her carriage outside the Grosvenor Hotel. Then, his pique had found a cinematic metaphor. 'Flicker, flicker: the laceflare of her hat in the sun: flicker, flick' (p. 71).[72] The analogy in that case might be with G. A. Smith's *As Seen through a Telescope* (1900), in which a close-up renders a woman's ankle in high sculptural relief. Bloom does not own a stereoscope. Perhaps he doesn't need one. He is already a connoisseur and advocate of the haptic-contingent.

For Stephen Dedalus, as we have seen, the stereoscope is proof of the autonomy and abstraction of the visible. Its tableau-effect appeals to him rather more strongly than its tangibility-effect. In this respect, he could be compared to the narrator of *A la recherche du temps perdu*, evidently a connoisseur of hypermediacy, who imagines that watching a play in performance must be like looking into a stereoscope.[73] To be sure, Stephen has the occasional Ruskinian moment on the beach. He closely observes a dog halted at the ocean's 'lacefringe', barking at the waves. 'They serpented towards his feet, curling, unfurling many crests, every ninth, breaking, plashing, from afar, from farther out, waves and waves' (p. 46). But the observation exists for the sake of the rhythm it has generated. 'Lacefringe' is brilliantly apt, but stops short of absorption into the world, because it has not removed Stephen from his habitual literariness; it has not drawn him over to where the image stands. Tangibility eludes the epithet, as it also eludes a merely rhythmic prose. Stephen is a Ruskin without Ruskin's taste for the haptic-contingent, without Ruskin's nausea. How much of the world does he want to see? How much of the world might he have seen, if he hadn't, as we eventually learn, broken his glasses the day before?

Notes

1 *McTeague: A Story of San Francisco*, ed. Jerome Loving (Oxford: Oxford University Press, 1995), 78, 84.

2 *The Sketch*, 18 March 1896, 323; quoted by Yuri Tsivian, *Early Cinema in Russia and Its Cultural Reception*, trans. Alan Bodger (Chicago: University of Chicago Press, 1994), 135.

3 'An Aesthetic of Astonishment: Early Films and the (In)credulous Spectator', *Art & Text*, 34 (1989), 31–45, p. 32.

4 *The Octopus* (London: Thomas Nelson, n.d.), 184.

5 *Before Adam* (London: T. Werner Laurie, 1929), 108–9.

6 *Martin Eden* (Harmondsworth: Penguin Books, 1967), 118. I am grateful to Kasia Boddy for drawing my attention to these two passages in London's work.

7 David Bordwell, *On the History of Film Style* (Cambridge, MA: Harvard University Press, 1997), 182.

8 Quoted by Stephen Bottomore, 'Shots in the Dark: The Real Origins of Film Editing', in Thomas Elsaesser (ed.), *Early Cinema: Space, Frame, Narrative* (London: BFI Publishing, 1990), 104–13, p. 111.

9 'The Lumière Cinematograph', in *The Film Factory: Russian and Soviet Cinema, 1896–1939*, trans. Richard Taylor, ed. Taylor and Ian Christie (London: Routledge & Kegan Paul, 1988), 25–6, p. 26.

10 On the filming of the war, see Simon Popple, ' "But the Khaki-Covered Camera Is the *Latest* Thing": The Boer War Cinema and Visual Culture in Britain', in Andrew Higson (ed.), *Young and Innocent? The Cinema in Britain 1896–1930* (Exeter: Exeter University Press, 2002), 13–27; and Elizabeth Grottle Strebel, 'Imperialist Iconography of Anglo-Boer War Film Footage', in John L. Fell (ed.), *Film Before Griffith* (Berkeley: University of California Press, 1983), 264–71.

11 *Correspondence of William James*, vol. 3, *William and Henry 1897–1910*, ed. Ignas K. Sknepskelis and Elizabeth M. Berkeley (Charlottesville: University of Virginia Press, 1994), 111. It was not Henry's first visit to the movies. In 1898, he told a correspondent that he had just been to the 'cinematograph – or whatever they call it' to see a film of the Corbett-Fitzsimmons fight, which took place at Culver City, Nevada, on 17 March 1897: Leon Edel, *Life of Henry James*, 2 vols (Harmondsworth: Penguin Books, 1977), vol. 2, 230.

12 'Crapy Cornelia', first published in *Harper's Magazine*, in October 1909, then in *The Finer Grain* (1910), reprinted in *The Jolly Corner and Other Tales*, ed. Roger Gard (Harmondsworth: Penguin Books, 1990), 221–48, p. 223. References will henceforth be included in the text.

13 'The Watcher from the Balcony: *The Ambassadors*', in Harold Bloom (ed.), *Modern Critical Views: Henry James* (New York: Chelsea House, 1987), 105–23, p. 110.

14 And, of course, into the knowledge of writers whom we would not normally describe as modernist, such as Bernard Shaw and H. G. Wells. Shaw's opinions have been gathered in *Bernard Shaw on Cinema*, ed. Bernard F. Dukore (Carbondale: Southern Illinois University Press, 1997). On Wells, see Keith Williams, *Realist of the Fantastic: H. G. Wells, Modernity, and the Movies* (Liverpool: Liverpool University Press, 2007).

15 *Mister Bosphorus or a Short History of Poetry in Britain* (London: Duckworth, 1923), 42, 44, 49.

16 *Ford Madox Ford: A Dual Life*, 2 vols (Oxford: Oxford University Press, 1996), vol. 2, 124.

17 *The Lost Girl*, ed. John Worthen (Cambridge: Cambridge University Press, 1981), 81. References will henceforth be included in the text.

18 In Britain, the earliest purpose-built cinemas date from 1907. Before then, films had been screened more or less anywhere, 'in village halls, in church halls, as part of the variety programme in music-halls, in schools, in empty shops with the front windows knocked out and replaced by porticos, in tents, and by

travelling showmen in magnificent portable theatres': Audrey Field, *Picture Palace: A Social History of the Cinema* (London: Gentry Books, 1974), 16. Nicholas Hiley has correlated the boom in cinema-building in Britain, from 1907 to 1914, with dramatic increases in the production of fiction films, and films over twenty-five minutes in length: ' "At the Picture Palace": The British Cinema Audience, 1895–1920', in John Fullerton (ed.), *Celebrating 1895: The Centenary of Cinema* (London: John Libbey, 1998), 96–103, p. 98.

19   This fact is central to the argument developed in Benjamin's celebrated essay on 'The Work of Art in the Age of Mechanical Reproduction', in *Illuminations*, ed. Hannah Arendt, trans. Harry Zone (London: Fontana, 1970), 219–53.

20   *Psychoanalysis and the Cinema: The Imaginary Signifier*, trans. Celia Britton, Annwyl Williams, Ben Brewster, and Alfred Guzzetti (Basingstoke: Macmillan, 1982), 61.

21   *Letters*, vol. 3, ed. James T. Boulton and Andrew Robertson (Cambridge: Cambridge University Press, 1984), 549.

22   *Sex in the Head: Visions of Femininity and Film in D. H. Lawrence* (Hemel Hempstead: Harvester Wheatsheaf, 1993), 86–7.

23   See the exemplary account by Miriam Hansen, *Babel and Babylon: Spectatorship in American Silent Film* (Cambridge, MA: Harvard University Press, 1991), ch. 11.

24   On the oblique but nonetheless intriguing relation between *Women in Love* and E. M. Hull's bestselling desert romance, see Billie Melman, *Women and the Popular Imagination in the Twenties: Flappers and Nymphs* (Basingstoke: Macmillan, 1988), 100; David Trotter, *The English Novel in History 1895–1920* (London: Routledge, 1993), 184–93; Williams, *Sex in the Head*, 82–3.

25   Hanns Zischler, *Kafka Goes to the Movies* (Chicago: University of Chicago Press, 2003), 33–43.

26   *Ulysses*, ed. Jeri Johnson (Oxford: Oxford University Press, 1993), 48. References will henceforth be included in the text.

27   'The world exists before him (there must be a text to be read)', Johnson explains, 'but comes alive *to him* in the act of "reading" it' (*Ulysses*, 784). There has also been a tendency to make out of Stephen Dedalus's ruminations on Sandymount Strand a universally applicable epistemology. 'The modality of the visible', Nicholas Miller concludes, 'is ineluctably textual: to see is to read': *Modernism, Ireland and the Erotics of Memory* (Cambridge: Cambridge University Press, 2002), 23.

28   The account given by William C. Darrah in *The World of Stereographs* (Gettysburg, PA: W. C. Darrah, 1977) remains the most comprehensive. According to Darrah, the stereoscope, 'though but one type of photograph, was the first visual mass medium' (p. 2).

29   P. Camecasse and R. Lehman, *La Chirurgie enseignée par la stéréoscopie* (Paris: J. B. Baillière, 1906); L.-P. Clerc, *Applications de la photographie aérienne* (Paris: O. Doine et fils, 1920).

30   'Introduction: Previewing the Cinematic City', in David Clarke (ed.), *The Cinematic City* (London: Routledge, 1997), 1–18, p. 8. Crucial points of reference for this approach are Gilles Deleuze's two books on cinema, *Cinema 1: The Movement-Image*, trans. Hugh Tomlinson and Barbara Habberjam (London: Athlone, 1986), and *Cinema 2: The Time-Image*, trans. Hugh Tomlinson and Robert Galeta (London: Routledge, 1989); and Vivian Sobchack, in *The Address of*

the Eye: A Phenomenology of Film Experience (Princeton: Princeton University Press, 1992).

31　'The Essential Solitude', in *The Gaze of Orpheus*, trans. Lydia Davis (New York: Station Hill, 1981), 63–77, p. 75.

32　Riegl developed his theory of haptic looking in *Problems of Style: Foundations for a History of Ornament*, first published in 1893, trans. Evelyn Kain (Princeton. Princeton University Press, 1993); and *Late Roman Art Industry*, first published in 1901, trans. Rolf Winkes (Rome: Giorgio Bretschneider Editore, 1985). The explanation of his choice of terminology occurs in an essay of 1902, 'Late Roman or Oriental?', trans. Peter Wortsman, in Gert Schiff (ed.), *German Essays on Art History* (New York: Continuum, 1988), 173–90, p. 190. See Michael Podro, *The Critical Art Historians* (New Haven: Yale University Press, 1982), ch. 5; and Margaret Iversen, *Aloïs Riegl: Art History and Theory* (Cambridge, MA: MIT Press, 1993).

33　*The Skin of the Film: Intercultural Cinema, Embodiment, and the Senses* (Durham: Duke University Press, 2000), ch. 3, esp. pp. 129, 137. The methodology of 'connective materialism' Marks describes in the Introduction to *Touch: Sensuous Theory and Multisensory Media* (Minneapolis: University of Minnesota Press, 2002) is very much to my purpose here.

34　*Atlas of Emotion: Journeys in Art, Architecture, and Film* (London: Verso, 2002), 6, 8.

35　*Skin*, 170–71.

36　*Atlas*, 171–2.

37　'Haptical Cinema', *October*, 74 (1995), 45–73. See also her 'The Curse of the Pharoah, or How Cinema Contracted Egyptomania', *October*, 59 (1992), 87–112.

38　The phrase is Peter de Bolla's: *The Education of the Eye: Painting, Landscape, and Architecture in Eighteenth-Century Britain* (Stanford: Stanford University Press, 2003).

39　*The Problem of Form in Painting and Sculpture*, trans. Max Meyer and Robert Morris Ogden (New York: G. E. Stechert, 1907), 21–2, 24–6.

40　*The Photoplay: A Psychological Study* (New York: Dover, 1970), 20.

41　*Techniques of the Observer*, 116–32, 59, 62, 14. For Crary, the stereoscope, rather than photography, is in epistemological terms cinema's true precursor, because the image it offers is at once subjective and lodged in (or at) the observer's body.

42　*Techniques of the Observer*, 123–4.

43　'The Stereoscope and the Stereograph', in Alan Trachtenberg (ed.), *Classic Essays on Photography* (New Haven, CT: Leete's Island Books, 1980), 72–82, p. 75.

44　'Essential Solitude', 75.

45　'Work of Art', 240, 252. For the incorporation of Benjamin's hypotheses into haptic theory, see Lant, 'Haptical Cinema', 68–9; Marks, *Skin*, 171; Bruno, *Atlas*, 247, 250. Miriam Hansen's argument that Hollywood 'produced and globalized a new sensorium' also draws heavily on Benjamin (and on Siegfried Kracauer): 'The Mass Production of the Senses: Classical Cinema as Vernacular Modernism', *Modernism/Modernity*, 6 (1999), 59–77. Steven Shaviro's account of the violent tactility of the film image defines spectatorship as an act not so much of defence as of masochism: *The Cinematic Body* (Minneapolis: University of Minnesota Press, 1993).

46　In trying to define the kinds of visuality rendered by the stereoscope, I have drawn inspiration from De Bolla's account of the emergence in Britain in the 1760s of a 'sentimental look'. 'Neither gaze nor glance, the sentimental look operates via a fully somatic insertion into the visual field. It makes the body present to sight, and in so doing it stimulates the cognitive process of affective response.' De Bolla argues that certain paintings by Joseph Wright of Derby educated the eye by captivating it: *Education of the Eye*, 11, 66.

47 Zischler, *Kafka Goes to the Movies*, 25.
48 Stephen Oettermann, *The Panorama: History of a Mass Medium* (New York: Zone Books, 1997), 229–33; Bernard Comment, *The Panorama* (London: Reaktion Books, 1999), 70–71.
49 Quoted in translation in Zischler, *Kafka*, 25–6.
50 It is reproduced by Zischler: *Kafka*, 29.
51 *Works*, ed. E. T. Cook and Alexander Wedderburn, 39 vols (London: Longmans, Green, 1907), vol. 3, 569–70.
52 'Stereoscope', 77.
53 Ibid., 77, 80.
54 *Techniques of the Observer*, 127.
55 'The Modern Public and Photography', in *Classic Essays on Photography*, 83–9, p. 87.
56 *The Stereoscopic Nude 1850–1930*, ed. Serge Nazarieff (Cologne: Benedikt Taschen, 1993).
57 'Corporealized Observers: Visual Pornographies and the "Carnal Density of Vision"', in Patrice Petro (ed.), *Fugitive Images: From Photography to Video* (Bloomington: Indiana University Press, 1995), 3–41.
58 'Modern Public', 87.
59 Crary, *Techniques of the Observer*, 123; Oettermann, *Panorama*, 231; Comment, *Panorama*, 70.
60 'Mass Production of the Senses', 69–70.
61 R. M. Hayes, *3-D Movies: A History and Filmography of Stereoscopic Cinema* (Jefferson: McFarland, 1989), 3. For some extremely suggestive remarks about the influence of stereoscopy on the 'particular way of looking' developed in the early Lumière films, see Thomas Elsaesser, 'Louis Lumière – the Cinema's First Virtualist?', in Elsaesser and Kay Hoffmann (eds), *Cinema Futures: Cain, Abel or Cable?* (Amsterdam: Amersterdam University Press, 1998), 45–61, pp. 59–61.
62 Stephen Herbert, *Theodore Brown's Magic Pictures: The Art and Inventions of a Multi-Media Pioneer* (London: The Projection Box, 1997), ch. 6.
63 Interview given in 1949, cited in Noël Burch, *Life to Those Shadows*, trans. Ben Brewster (London: BFI Publishing, 1990), 181.
64 Norman King, *Abel Gance: A Politics of Spectacle* (London: BFI Publishing, 1984), 185. For Gance's comments on the 3-D scenes, see Kevin Brownlow, *Napoléon: Abel Gance's Classic Film*, rev. edn (London: Photoplay Productions, 2004), 131.
65 'About Stereoscopic Cinema', *Penguin Film Review*, 8 (1949), 35–45, pp. 38–9.
66 'What I Demand of Movie Stars', in Harry M. Geduld (ed.), *Focus on D. W. Griffith* (Englewood Cliffs: Prentice Hall, 1971), 50–54, p. 52.
67 *Theory of Film: The Redemption of Physical Reality* (Princeton: Princeton University Press, 1997), 47–8.
68 *The Art of the Moving Picture* (New York: Modern Library, 2000), 68. First published in 1915.
69 *Life to Those Shadows*, 29.
70 *James Joyce, Sexuality and Social Purity* (Cambridge: Cambridge University Press, 2003), ch. 5.

71   Ibid., 164.

72   In her eagerness to conceive this incident as a 'proto-cinematic spectacle', Sara Danius mistakenly assumes that Bloom has himself boarded a tram, and that the flickering laceflare of the lady's hat has been produced by sunlight's refraction by the windows of another tram which moves past the one he is in: *The Senses of Modernism: Technology, Perception, and Aesthetics* (Ithaca: Cornell University Press, 2002), 166. The desire to find cinema in the novel seems in this case to have led to the creation, on Joyce's behalf, of a wholly new scene.

73   *The Way by Swann's*, trans. Lydia Davis (Harmondsworth: Penguin Books, 2003), 75.

3

D. W. Griffith

There is an odd moment in Eisenstein's essay on 'Dickens, Griffith, and the Film Today' (1944) when the discussion turns to the passer-by in the modern story in *Intolerance* who interrupts a conversation in the street between the 'suffering boy and girl'. 'I can remember next to nothing of the couple,' Eisenstein remarks, 'but this passer-by, who is visible in the shot only for a flashing glimpse, stands alive before me now – and I haven't seen the film for twenty years!'[1] The suffering boy and girl are in the first timid throes of courtship when the passer-by pushes aggressively between them. The story of their subsequent embattled existence, told melodramatically in the terms Griffith had perfected during his years at Biograph, anchors his millennial theme in contemporary experience. It becomes the very condition of the film's intelligibility. And yet what 'stands alive' before Eisenstein, with a force no merely narrative or melodramatic clarification could deliver, is a passer-by who comes abruptly into view, and then is gone for ever.

Of course, the passer-by *is* intelligible, as an omen of the obstacles life (or at least the divisive meddling of moral reformers) will throw in the couple's way. But that intelligibility does not excite Eisenstein. What excites him is a presence as palpable as anything produced by cinema's stereoscopic effects: an image which moves in materially on the spectator, which pours out of the screen, which overhangs the auditorium. The effect of the passer-by's presence, like that of some of the stereoscopic images I discussed in the previous chapter, turns on its sheer contingency, its (appearance of) just happening to happen. It is a revelation of chance, by chance. That which is strikingly palpable is that which *appears* (in both senses) without design. The palpable is the hidden 'other side' of our relentless determination to attribute meaning and value to events in the lived world. Or so Eisenstein seems to have thought. For he goes on to contemplate other 'unforgettable figures' in Griffith's films, figures who seem to have strayed in 'directly from the street' for their one and only appearance on film.[2]

It is an arresting thought: Griffith as a third Lumière brother, an exponent of the actuality principle, a proto-neo-realist. The purpose of this chapter is to pursue that thought to some kind of conclusion. For it is not one Eisenstein entertained for very long. Passing the passer-by swiftly by, the essay proceeds to develop the brilliant account of Dickens and Griffith as exponents of montage which is its enduring legacy to film theory, and in which it has been followed by most of those who have written about Griffith's films.

Narrative, or rather narrative's intelligibility, was the major preoccupation of the trade journals at the time when Griffith began to direct for Biograph.[3] Griffith, of course, not only felt that pressure, but turned it to his own advantage. Intelligibility – the attachment of effect to cause, action to motive – became his medium, and his trademark. 'The basis of the American classical cinema's narrative aesthetic was compositional unity rather than realism,' Kristin Thompson observes. 'Reality might be full of random events and coincidences, but the film-makers sought to motivate as much as possible causally.'[4] 'Indeterminism is banished from the studio,' Vladimir Nabokov was to remark, with studio-era Hollywood in mind.[5] But it had not yet been banished, I shall argue, from the various studios in which Griffith made his films for Biograph. These films recapitulate an accident-prone (accident-friendly) 'cinema of attractions' even as they clear the way for a 'cinema of narrative integration' shaped at the level both of content and of form by the logic of cause and effect.[6]

Intelligibility worked as Griffith worked it, strenuously, even to excess, became an end in itself; and thus a puzzle, or a topic, something the films were *about*, rather than a demonstration of expertise, an art concealing art. Such strenuousness, a response to pressures from within and from beyond the industry, was a feature of a 'transitional' style in American cinema, in the years before the First World War, a style which shaped its emergence as mass-medium.[7] With Griffith, however, it became something more than a response to pressures. Grasped in its extreme form, in his Biograph films, it provides a point of view from which to explore a little further what Kristin Thompson terms the 'predominance of narrative structure over the systems of time and space' in classical Hollywood style.[8] Indeed, it might enable us to re-examine the concept of 'narrativisation' first put forward by film theory in the 1970s, and more recently brought to bear, with the psychoanalysis stripped out, on the transitional style in American cinema.[9]

According to Stephen Heath, narrativisation entails a 'constant conversion to narrative, catching up the spectator as subject in the image of the narrative and in the film as its narration'. The 'narrative film', Heath observes, 'can only seek to maintain a tight balance between the photographic image as a reproduction of reality and the narrative as the sense, the intelligibility, of that reality'.[10] But are sense and intelligibility, as this formulation proposes, the same thing? Should sense and intelligibility both be ranged unequivocally on the side of narrative? Might there not be a sense generated by or in the photographic image which yet falls short of intelligibility? My argument here is that the consequence of the work Griffith did for Biograph between 1908 and 1913 was to establish such a distinction. The Biograph films consistently make sense of the world, in ways I shall describe, as well as – through narrative's intelligibility, which was also intelligibility's narrative, its assumption of predominance over an emergent mass-medium – a meaning and value for it. The sense is in the images which pour out of the screen.

The Biograph years were Griffith's most literary, as his wife Linda Arvidson later recalled.[11] Adaptation from literature enhanced the status of cinema, and the well-made story, or novel, or play had a great deal to teach film-makers about narrative structure.[12] But Griffith did not go to literature for structuring devices alone. He went to it, too, for its understanding of the 'systems of time and space' which constitute the lived world. 'The task I'm trying to achieve', he told an interviewer in 1913, 'is above all to make you see.'[13] The words this declaration echoes are those of a novelist. 'My task which I am trying to achieve', Joseph Conrad explained in the preface to *The Nigger of the 'Narcissus'* (1897), 'is, by the power of the written word to make you hear, to make you feel – it is, before all, to make you *see.*'[14]

In the first section of this chapter, my topic is the excess in Griffith's attempt to systematise narrative in and for film. That surplus intensity gave rise, I argue, to an anti-system by which we are made to see, not meaning and value, but their opposite, or limit. In the second section, I propose a theoretical framework for the definition of anti-system, or counter-narrative: another story, about what is most lived in the lived world, which may not be what is most lively, or most life-like, and which chance reveals, or certain kinds of hardship. Sections three and four develop readings of the anti-system or counter-narrative at work in two types of Biograph film: the stories derived from poems by Tennyson and Kingsley, of men at sea, and the women who wait for them on land; and the essays in social criticism which adapt some of the methods of Naturalist fiction. An example of each type was among the films singled out in December 1910 by a distributor who wrote to the New York *Dramatic Mirror* to contrast Griffith's achievements at Biograph with the Pathé *films d'art*:

> While the French pictures were very fine they did not compare in originality and beauty to those unnamed films d'art produced by the American Biograph, the films d'art players contenting themselves with turning out beautiful imitations of plays, photographed, while the Biograph originated an entirely new art in such pictures as *The Unchanging Sea*, *The Way of the World* and a picture the name of which I forget but which we call the 'wheat' picture – a new art in which poetry, the stage and painting were all called upon to make one exquisite form of expression.[15]

The Unchanging Sea (1910) and its more ambitious successor, the two-reel *Enoch Arden* (1911), will feature prominently here; as will *A Corner in Wheat* (1909), the most celebrated of the essays in social criticism, and *its* successor, *The Usurer* (1910). There is, indeed, in these films, a new and compelling art.

Narrative cinema

A great deal of attention has been paid to the Biograph films, over the past twenty years, in ground-breaking books by Joyce Jesionowski, Tom Gunning, and Scott Simmon, and more recently in the informative commentaries supplied by contributors to the relevant volumes of Paolo Cherchi Usai's *Griffith Project*.[16] The major emphasis in this work is on Griffith's achievement in developing his own idiosyncratic but widely influential version of a cinema of narrative integration. Revisionist historians have agreed with Eisenstein in associating Griffith with montage in general, and parallel editing in particular. They have proven even less willing than Eisenstein to be distracted by speculation about the role of passers-by and the like.

Iris Barry, who in the 1930s acquired many of the Biograph titles for MOMA, thought that Griffith's most substantial achievement had been the 'disjunctive method of narration' evident in *The Lonely Villa* (1909) and *The Lonedale Operator* (1911). She drew attention to the cuts-on-action which enhance parallel editing in the latter: 'there is no waste footage – no deliberation in getting on with the story.'[17] Tom Gunning has redescribed this disjunctive method as a 'narrator system' whose omnipresent and supreme device was parallel editing. The narrator system was an 'extreme expression' of the norms of a cinema of narrative integration. 'With Griffith,' Gunning concludes, 'the emphasis on the tasks of storytelling is brought to a particular intensity.'[18] What interests me is the system in the narrator system: the extremity of that attitude to storytelling.

In Gunning's account, the narrator system produced both a new articulation of time and space, in the cross-cut race to the rescue, and a new articulation of character: the disclosure of feeling through cinematic discourse (above all, through montage). Griffith first mastered the latter effect in *After Many Years* (1908), a version of Tennyson's *Enoch Arden* which tells of a shipwrecked man and the woman who waits for his return; a version shot, not insignificantly, in New Jersey (that is, for the most part in the studio), rather than in California. According to Linda Arvidson, in an anecdote Eisenstein seized on eagerly, Griffith's proposal to cut between the husband on a desert island and the wife at home caused consternation among Biograph executives. 'How can you tell a story jumping about like that?' Griffith replied to the effect that what was good enough for Charles Dickens, whose stories jump about all over the place, was good enough for him.[19] In his hands, the jumping about acquired a transcendental function, as Gunning ably demonstrates. Shot 8 shows John Davis, on the desert island, gazing at a locket, and kissing the image it contains. Shot 9 shows not the image in the locket, but the woman herself on the porch of the family home, arm outstretched. These gestures express the 'emotional motivation' for the cut: the couple's longing for each other, a longing which 'overcomes' geography. The cut has created a 'space of the imagination', Gunning notes; and it has done so by interrupting the gesture of the kiss, by 'terminating' it at a point of maximum intensity. The placement of the cut bears witness to the 'force' of parallel editing as a 'manufacturer of meaning'. In Gunning's view, *After Many Years* reveals the 'essence' of 'psychological editing'.[20]

Parallel editing soon acquired a further function, over and above suspense, as in *The Lonely Villa* and *The Lonedale Operator*, and psychological intensity, as in *After Many Years*: a function most apparent in the various Biograph essays in social criticism, which use it to contrast the fortunes of the rich and the poor, in order to condemn the former. 'The contrast edit', as Gunning puts it, 'primarily compares the content of shots ideologically, expressing a paradigmatic relation, a comparison of types.' Thus, in *The Song of the Shirt* (1908), the first shot shows a seamstress leaning over her sister's sickbed in a slum apartment, the second the owner of the company she works for surrounded by his obsequious minions. The two have not yet met: the contrast edit expresses the 'abstract relation' between them, the economic dependence of one on the other.[21] Geography has been overcome, in this case, by an economic analysis conducted on behalf of the narrator system itself, rather than by mutual longing. Transcendence through disjunctive method – the manufacture of meaning – has produced moral judgement.

In Gunning's account, the extremity of a narrator system based on disjunctive method lies in its abstraction: its capacity to abs-tract, to draw meaning out of and separate it from material embodiment or practice. So powerful is his emphasis on abstraction through editing that it colours significantly the equally informative analysis of devices other than editing: devices such as the organisation of pro-filmic elements, and the framing of the image (for example, the remarkable pans which open and close *The Country Doctor*).

Gunning regards such devices as part of the narrative strategy Griffith began to develop in 1908 or 1909. Combined with parallel editing, he argues, they would yield a 'style of extraordinary abstraction'.[22] I find Gunning's account of the narrator system entirely persuasive. But the Biograph films do not seem to me to be abstract through and through.

The photographic image, Gunning observes, shows more forcefully than it can tell. There is always in it an excess of mimesis over meaning. Mimesis itself, of course, already has, from the outset, from the moment it comes into play, the potential to be meaningful. It carries an invitation to interpret. But one might say that there customarily remains, in the photographic image, an excess of indeterminate over determinate meaning; or, in my terms, of sense over intelligibility. 'Automatically present', Gunning adds, 'are details of posture, costuming, and gesture whose verbal description would overwhelm a written text.' An 'excess of photographic reality' is as characteristic of the films shot by the Edison Company in its Black Maria as it is of the Lumière actualities. 'Film *shows* automatically, recording a world of contingent events and unimportant details.' There is sense in such scenes before, and perhaps after, there is intelligibility. The narrator system does not make sense; it makes intelligibility out of sense. Griffith's filmic discourse 'bends' its own 'excessive realism' into story, Gunning says; it 'carves' story out of photographed reality.[23]

Gunning's terms hint at the violence involved in this overcoming. Parallel editing destroys the specificity of space and time. Each narrative space becomes a zone. In cross-cut races to the rescue such as *The Lonely Villa* and *The Lonedale Operator*, assailant and liberator only ever *pass through*, on their way to somewhere else, to where the victim is – or, rather, to where the victim awaits their arrival, since she too occupies a zone rather than a space (a time of expectation). The only furnishing of any note in the room where the victim awaits rescue is that which connects one zone to another (the telephone in *The Lonely Villa*), or time present to time future: the clock in *The Fatal Hour* (1908) whose hands will trigger the gun aimed at the female detective when they reach twelve. In the race to the rescue, time, like space, is relative: a zone rather than a duration. Meanwhile, the cut-on-action, which interrupts the rhythm by which a person might establish her or his being in the world, uniformly converts sense into intelligibility. The husband in *The Lonely Villa* does not engage in any activity unrelated to his family and its plight. His job is to go away and then come back again, just in time. He is all meaning.

Much the same could be said of the consequences of Griffith's equally forceful use of parallel editing and the cut-on-action for psychological or moral purposes. Who knows or cares what the marooned John Davis might have got up to on his desert island? His job, too, is to go away and then – after many years, and much gazing at the image in the locket, but just in time – come back again. Mrs Davis meanwhile exists for us solely in and through what the *Biograph Bulletin* terms a 'prophetic hope': that is, in relation to another place, where her husband might be, and another time, when he might return to her.[24] As Jesionowski notes, Shot 9's cut-in on the axis, which shows Mrs Davis on the porch of the family home reaching out to him (to the thought of him), 'tightens the familiar image around her'.[25] This tightening excludes the lived world: everything in the immediate environment which does not contribute to prophetic hope. She, too, is all meaning (an intelligibility drawn out of and separated from material embodiment).

The terms used by historians to describe the narrator system reflect their understanding of the pressures Griffith and other film-makers were under, to produce complete and coherent narratives for a rapidly expanding and diversifying audience. The narrator system was an industrial necessity. It worked supremely well, for Griffith, as a strategy. But we need also to consider its extremism: that in it which sought to eclipse, rather than merely to subordinate, the systems of space and time; that in it which sought to put intelligibility in the place of sense, meaning in the place of material embodiment.[26] What the narrator system had to overcome was both the residual formlessness of photographed reality and the constitutive automatism of the photographic image. The medium's resistance provoked in Griffith a determination, over and above the strict requirements of strategy, to be utterly abstract. It provoked him, one could say, to hypermediacy.

That resolve is not a function of parallel editing and the cut-on-action, though these devices express it most fully. It also inheres in diegesis. By definition, the race to the rescue occurs as the climax and conclusion of a narrative film. But the specific conversion it accomplishes, of sense into intelligibility, of material embodiment into meaning, has more often than not been prepared for diegetically. Thus, the opening shot of *The Lonely Villa* shows the burglars in conference in the foreground, behind a bush; a sidewalk leads in the direction of the establishment they have designs on. The next shot takes us inside that establishment. It shows us the parlour, where the family has assembled, and where much of the subsequent action will take place. The servants ask for the night off. Shots three and four show them on their way out of the house, in the corridor leading to the front door, and then on the verandah. Shot 5 revisits the burglars in their hiding-place outside. This bracketing of the views of the interior (shots two, three, and four) has in effect abolished the very idea of an ordinary or unremarkable event. Understood from outside, from the point of view of the ruffians lurking in the undergrowth, the scene with the servants indicates that a time will come, soon, after Mr Cullison's departure, when the women of the house are on their own, and thus vulnerable. Like Mrs Davis's gesture, this mundane negotiation about a night off is *solely* prophetic. It has a meaning, in relation to the future, but no sense. The gestures which constitute it are already impalpable. The bracketing converts the corridor and the verandah from an inhabited environment into zones through which the ruffians must pass in order to get at the women.[27] In the climactic race to the rescue, editorial technique completes the work of abstraction begun by the (literal and metaphoric) foregrounding of the burglars in shots one and five. Thus indeterminism is banished from the studio.

The narrative convention which establishes the presence of the burglars in shots one and five as a hermeneutic threshold – the point at which interpretation commences, the point beyond which the demand must be above all for intelligibility – is itself no mere narrative convention, but already propaganda. It gives voice to a widespread and persistent anxiety about the dangers confronting the family, the bourgeois home. Such dangers are the very stuff of Griffith's Biograph films.[28] Moral panic about ruffians lurking in suburban undergrowth has primed the narrative for abstraction. Griffith's determination to be abstract occupies that anxiety, at once bound by it and able to put it to strategic use.

No wonder, then, that another and even more virulent moral panic, the international White Slavery obsession of the pre-war years, should have proved a godsend to a film industry intent on combining sensationalism with the politics of reform.[29] *The Fatal Hour*, whose climax represents one of the earliest examples of the cross-cut race to the rescue, took as its subject a 'stirring incident' of the 'Chinese white slave traffic'. 'Much has been printed recently by the daily press on this subject,' the *Bulletin* was to claim, 'but never has it been more vividly depicted than in this Biograph production.' A viewer stirred by the press coverage would find herself or himself, on entering the auditorium, already beyond the hermeneutic threshold, and therefore suspicious from the outset of what the *Bulletin* terms the villain's 'glib, affable manner'. Further coaching in suspicion is at once provided diegetically by the woman detective, whose 'shrewd powers of deduction' enable her to penetrate that manner, and by so doing put her in danger.[30] A viewer coached always to interpret for the worst – to understand that the relentless forward movement of the clock-hand, seen in close-up, means that help may not arrive in time – is exactly what parallel editing requires.

Such coaching begins to look like a disciplinary programme.[31] However, the instruction on offer can scarcely be considered an instruction in business skills or good citizenship. It is, rather, an instruction in a kind of madness. Consider the figure of the detective, permanently on hand, in the popular genre fiction of the period, and increasingly in films, to lead us across the hermeneutic threshold. There is no such thing as matter, animate or inanimate, in detective fiction, 'the epistemological genre *par excellence*'.[32] The protagonist's arrival on the scene (any scene, however mundane) converts every material trace in the vicinity into a clue. Even the corpse, should one arise, is a text edited by assassination. What the detective does is to abstract it yet further, into pure meaning: a meaning which at once takes the place of material embodiment, and is thus, at the moment when it finally yields the assassin's identity, in every sense a 'solution'. The female detective in *The Fatal Hour* is in her own way as much a creature of prophetic hope as the heroine of *After Many Years*, both while exercising her shrewd powers of deduction on the affable villain, and while helplessly bound and gagged as the fatal hour approaches.

It is tempting to say that detection (in books and films, at any rate) involves the deployment of a benign paranoia which, although the suspicions upon which it is founded turn out to be accurate, within the diegesis, nonetheless isolates the detective, as the disease itself isolates the sufferer, by enabling her or him to find significance in events and phenomena nobody else regards as in the least bit remarkable. Richard von Krafft-Ebing, whose *Textbook of Insanity* exemplifies the late-nineteenth-century understanding of paranoia, described it as a type of psychosis in which the patient develops an internally consistent delusional system of beliefs around the certainty that he or she is a person of great importance, and on that account subject to hostility and persecution. They hate me because I am special; I am special because they hate me. The paranoiac's delusions are 'systematised', Krafft-Ebing observed, and thus constitute a formal 'structure'. The power of that system or structure depends on its ability to eliminate randomness: to convert the material trace an event leaves in the world (its presence-effect, its sense) into a sign which only ever has one meaning. Unable to accept that the world really is as it seems, Krafft-Ebing thought, the paranoiac goes looking for secrets, for concealed motives and intentions. She or he notices 'behind' phenomena something which does not 'belong' to them.[33] In *The Psychopathology of Everyday Life*

(1901), Sigmund Freud was to remark that paranoiacs 'attach the greatest significance to the minor details of other people's behaviour which we ordinarily neglect, interpret them and make them the basis of far-reaching conclusions'.[34] It is just as well for the safety of civilisation as we know it that detectives do the same.

Paranoia is programmatically anti-mimetic: it puts the meaning and value produced by its own interpretative system *in place of* the world as it is, or as everyone except the paranoiac knows it. The kind of literature one would expect it to inform is that which, for whatever reason, does not set much stock by the accurate representation of the world as it is. In the first three decades of the twentieth century, a taste for paranoid fantasy distinguishes both avant-garde experiment and mass-market sensational fiction from respectable domestic realism.[35] Griffith's taste for paranoid fantasy stretched at least as far as spy fiction, a hugely popular genre in the years before the First World War (though more so in Europe than in America).

In *The Prussian Spy* (1909), set during the Franco-Prussian War of 1870, a French officer, coached in suspicion by sexual jealousy as well as by national emergency, surmises that the woman he loves has concealed his Prussian rival in a closet the door of which he thereupon proposes to use for target-practice. Mise-en-scène conveys all of this essential narrative information during a single lengthy shot. The second half of the film cross-cuts between the room containing the closet and a room above where the maid is attempting to pull the Prussian spy to safety through a trap-door. Stephen Higgins has remarked on the clumsiness of the long-drawn-out first shot, and on the 'palpable sense of anxiety' parallel editing and cuts-on-action create in those which follow.[36] There are *two* narrator systems at work, here. The first, operative through mise-en-scène, creates in the French officer a focus for our suspicions about the world as it is (or at least the world as it is in spy fiction). The second, operative through montage, transfers the responsibility for suspiciousness to the viewer, who must anxiously piece images together. Or we could say that the film incorporates two levels or phases of the abstraction of meaning from mimesis.

As Higgins's comment indicates, these two levels or phases sit rather uneasily together, in *The Prussian Spy*; as they do, perhaps, in other films of this period. Ben Brewster notes a similar division between expository preamble and 'dilated suspenseful climax' in *The Note in the Shoe* and *Confidence*, both released later in 1909.[37] That two techniques for the paranoid production of intelligibility should so reverberate against each other, in these films, is symptomatic of the extremism of Griffith's hypermediated narrative method.

It is no coincidence that Griffith should have made a theme, if not exactly of paranoia, then of the power of delusion to substitute an abstract order produced by its own interpretative system for the world. In *The Restoration* (1909) and *The House of Darkness* (1913), he devised memorable accounts of the damaging consequences of suspicion. The context Kristin Thompson and Eileen Bowser have proposed for these films is that of 'the newly emerging field of psychoanalysis'.[38] The context I would suggest is that of mainstream psychiatry, already well established by 1900, and very much the voice of authority in the definition and treatment of psychosis. The *Biograph Bulletin* explicitly advertised *The Restoration* as a case of 'misconstruction of intent'. 'Wrong impressions, converted ideas and hallucinations', it went on, in a quasi-psychiatric tone, 'have formed the greater part of the causes of calamity, and there is no stronger ideological force than jealousy.'[39]

According to Krafft-Ebing, the common causes of 'delusions of jealousy' in men are alcoholism and 'weak virility'.

> At first this arises by way of combination: accidental, but frequent visits of gentlemen in the house are thought to be for the wife. When she clears her throat it is a sign given to her lover hidden near by. Every noise at night is interpreted in the same sense. There is increasing avoidance of the wife, and brutal treatment of her may go to actual violence.[40]

The *Bulletin* describes Henry Morley, the protagonist of *The Restoration*, as suffering from an attack of 'hypochondriasis'. He is 'low spirited, irresolute of purpose, and in fact on the verge of nervous collapse'. Sexual jealousy deludes him into the firm conviction that he has seen his wife embracing a young man called Jack Dudley. It is in fact Mrs Morley's cousin Alice, shrouded in a shawl she has lent her (the scene itself is shrouded in darkness, with minimal illumination from a window at the right). Henry hits Jack over the head, and rushes from the house 'raving mad', certain that he has committed murder. Only when a doctor insists that the whole incident be re-enacted, with the scene fully lit, and Jack and Alice now transparently playing themselves, does he realise his error.

The House of Darkness is Griffith's most thorough investigation of mania. A review in *Moving Picture World* neatly summarises the plot, and reveals something the film itself does not reveal: the protagonist's profession.

> A noted judge is one of the most violent patients in the sanatorium until it is discovered that music has the power to quiet him. One day he escapes and going to the house of a former nurse, now the wife of a physician, he finds her alone. In his capacity as judge, he sentences her to die in five minutes. It is then by mere accident that the terror-stricken woman learns the power of music.[41]

The interest lies in the distortion of authority by madness, as it does in the case of the age's most famous paranoiac, Daniel Paul Schreber, also a 'noted judge', whose remarkable *Memoirs* (1903) became the subject of an essay by Freud.[42] Both judged to excess. The protagonist of *The House of Darkness* suffers from delusions of grandeur brought on, it may be, by delusions of persecution. He does not merely play judge; he plays god. 'You waster of time, you,' he scolds his terrified victim, via an intertitle: 'You die in five minutes.'

It is worth noting that Griffith went to considerable lengths to distinguish the specific delusion manifested by the protagonist from mania in general. The first two shots of the film, staged in eloquent depth, show two groups of inmates (one male, the other female) in the asylum grounds, in various poses of vacancy and distraction. 'Cases through poverty and overwork which we might prevent,' an intertitle announces. Then flashbacks describe the breakdowns suffered by two individual patients: a mother, previously seen in the right foreground of the group of women cradling a bundle of clothes, suffers the loss of her child; and a clerk, previously seen in the left foreground of the group of men, and identifiable by his visor, breaks down through overwork.[43] What connects these unfortunates, and distinguishes them sharply from the tendency to homicidal violence soon apparent in the behaviour of the judge, is their docility. *The House of Darkness* is not a film about mental disorder in general. It is, rather, like *The Restoration*, a film about the power of delusion.

The choice of suspiciousness as a theme seems to have inspired Griffith to new invention: an intricate racking of focus as Henry Morley stealthily pursues Jack Dudley through a garden, in *The Restoration*; or the judge's abrupt emergence out of a blurred background into crisp close-up, in *The House of Darkness*, as he approaches the house where his victim plays with a kitten.[44] We struggle to adjust to the enormity of the delusion taking violent shape (somewhere) in front of our eyes. The madman pulled suddenly into focus as he stalks his victim becomes a figure for his own particular madness: the tendency to identify something 'behind' phenomena which does not properly belong to them. Such experiments in the power of delusion were by no means restricted to films about psychopathology. In *The Drive for a Life* (1909), for example, a lengthy tracking-shot contrives to keep in view (more or less) both the motor-car in whose back seat a wealthy young man and his fiancée develop an oblivious intimacy and the horse-drawn buggy containing the young man's abandoned mistress. 'Jealousy,' the subsequent intertitle announces, a little superfluously. The theme evidently provoked Griffith into perfecting his narrator system, and not through montage alone. We 'receive' a film produced by that system, Gunning remarks, as though it 'has designs on us'.[45]

It is the mutual mirroring of paranoid form and paranoid content, in the Biograph films, which crystallises and lays bare their extremism. The effort at abstraction, relayed through mise-en-scène, cinematographic device, and montage, becomes apparent as just that, an effort at abstraction. I want now to argue, with reference to the Biograph coastal romances and essays in social criticism, that so much system could not but engender an anti-system. But we still need terms for that anti-system: for films which make sense as well as, or instead of, intelligibility. The next section therefore takes a turn into theory.

Back to ontology?

We have rather lost sight, in this concentration on system, of Eisenstein's passer-by. One commentator who never did lose sight of him was Siegfried Kracauer. For Kracauer, the ease with which Eisenstein recalled that moment in *Intolerance* was proof of cinema's enduring 'affinity' with 'haphazard contingencies'.[46] Griffith, in fact, looms surprisingly large – that is, larger than the current emphasis on the abstractness of his films would lead one to expect – in Kracauer's account of cinema as the 'redemption of physical reality'.

The primary function of the close-up of Annie in *After Many Years*, Kracauer proposed, was to 'suggest what is going on behind that face': to reveal character. Similarly, the close-up of Mae Marsh's clasped hands, in the trial scene in *Intolerance*, exposes the depth of her anguish. The function of such shots is to intensify our involvement in the 'total situation'. In support of this view, Kracauer cited Eisenstein's demonstration that the purpose of the close-up is 'not so much to *show* or to *present* as to *signify*, to *give meaning*, to *designate*'. For Eisenstein, the close-up should be understood as a 'montage unit'. Kracauer was not so sure.

> Consider again the combination of shots with the close-up of Annie's face: the place assigned to the latter in the sequence intimates that Griffith wanted us also to absorb the face for its own sake instead of just passing through and beyond it; the face appears before the desires and emotions to which it refers have been completely defined, thus tempting us to get lost in its puzzling indeterminacy.

The face, like Mae Marsh's hands, is 'an end in itself'. To Griffith, Kracauer continued, such 'huge' images of 'small material phenomena' were not only integral components of the narrative, but 'disclosures of new aspects of physical reality'. A film cannot adequately account for the 'emotional and intellectual events' which comprise it unless it 'leads us through the thicket of material life from which they emerge and in which they are embedded'.[47] The thicket of material life seems to have been an important metaphor for Kracauer, and it is one to which I shall return on several occasions in this book; though I am not sure that indeterminacy is the right term for the sense material life can be made to make on film (its failure to be fully intelligible).

André Bazin's classic essay on 'The Evolution of the Language of Cinema' affords Griffith what probably still seems to us his natural place as the first truly versatile exponent of montage. According to Bazin, montage involves the 'creation of a sense or meaning not objectively contained in the images themselves but derived exclusively from their juxtaposition'. One might note, here, as in Stephen Heath's comparable formula, the near-amalgamation of 'sense' with 'meaning' or 'intelligibility'. In montage, Bazin continues, the 'substance of the narrative' is an 'abstract result': maidens plus appletrees in bloom equal hope. His aim, of course, was to trace an alternative evolutionary descent through the work of those directors who had put their faith in reality rather than in the image: Robert Flaherty, Erich von Stroheim, and F. W. Murnau. 'In their films,' he maintained, 'montage plays no part, unless it be the negative one of inevitable elimination where reality superabounds. The camera cannot see everything at once but it makes sure not to lose any part of what it chooses to see.' Griffith, however, has rather surprisingly not been shown the door. 'These three directors do not exhaust the possibilities. We would undoubtedly find scattered among the works of others elements of nonexpressionistic cinema in which montage plays no part – even including Griffith.'[48]

You could say that my aim is to reconstruct a Bazinian Griffith by identifying the elements of a 'nonexpressionistic' method in some Biograph films. However, the terms Bazin developed for the sense cinema makes of the material life do not seem to me all that much of an improvement on those Kracauer was developing at the same time.[49] Montage, Bazin argued, 'by its very nature rules out ambiguity of expression'; whereas Wellesian depth of focus, by declining to lead the eye, reintroduces it.[50] Ambiguity incites (even if only to confound) an act of interpretation. It requires us to choose between two or more meanings; and then to recognise, productively, that we cannot. Much the same could be said of Kracauer's indeterminacy. But does cinema, when it is not being 'expressionistic', deal in *meanings* at all (Bazin has already collapsed sense into meaning)? Deborah Thomas remarks of a detail of decor in a scene in Capra's *It's a Wonderful Life* (1945) that although the detail does not 'mean' or 'symbolise' anything, it *resonates*.[51] One might expect that the accounts Kracauer and Bazin offer of cinema's redemption of physical reality would assist us to conceive and describe such resonance. And indeed they do. Both, however, are hampered, I think, by an addiction to meaning.[52] The effects I hope to describe in Griffith's Biograph films hesitate on, or have not yet arrived at, the hermeneutic threshold put into play by paranoia. Their *resonance* is what we need to understand: though that metaphor, in turn, may not prove entirely adequate.

One possible approach, long advocated by Peter Wollen, is to develop in relation to cinema the distinctions made by the American logician C. S. Peirce between different kinds of reference. Peirce distinguished between the *icon*, a sign which represents its object by similarity to it, by resemblance, or likeness; the *symbol*, which bears no resemblance to its object, and represents it by the force of law, or the force of convention; and the *index*, which becomes a sign by virtue of an existential bond between itself and its object (a weathercock signifies in so far as it is moved by the wind in a particular direction). One of Peirce's examples of an indexical sign is the photograph, created on the occasion when the light rays bouncing off an object first struck a chemical emulsion. The example enables Wollen to argue that cinema is a medium as reliant upon indexical as upon iconic signs. Indeed, he proposes a Peircean Bazin. 'It was the existential bond between fact and image, world and film, which counted for most in Bazin's aesthetic, rather than any quality of similitude or resemblance.'[53] More recently, Laura Marks has invoked that aesthetic in developing a 'sensuous theory' of the trace material objects leave on the surface of the film.[54] Film theory thrives on the concept of indexicality. The index, however, is only in exceptional circumstances a readily apparent feature of the photographic image itself. We should rather speak, as James Lastra does, of an 'indexical function' whose ground is 'the knowledge of how some kinds of signs are typically *produced*', and which therefore requires an inference on the beholder's part. Semiosis, in short, has its basis in historically specific social understanding.[55]

According to Mary Ann Doane, the proliferation of photographic images of one kind or another during the early decades of the twentieth century aroused a certain anxiety about the indexical function itself. The anxiety was that the embodiment of surplus representation in the shape of the photographic image had created a 'spatial continuum' without the gaps or lacks conducive to the production of significance. Sigmund Freud and Etienne-Jules Marey lost interest in the cinema, Doane argues, because it did not prove amenable to the abstraction required to illustrate the basic concepts of psychoanalysis and chronophotography. 'In its hyperindexicality it could not dissociate itself from the realm of the contingent or the material.'[56] What Freud openly admired in paranoia, by contrast, was its capacity to dissociate or abstract itself from the realm of the contingent and the material. His 1914 essay 'On Narcissism' examines in considerable detail the link between paranoia and the construction of speculative systems.[57] Doane concludes that the transition from actualities to narrative in early cinema was one way of 'ameliorating' fears about hyperindexicality.[58] Maybe someone should have taken Freud to see a Biograph when he visited America in 1909.

Doane's account very usefully historicises a preoccupation with, or fear of, the indexical function. It was a preoccupation fed, I think, with deliberate intent, by cinema's stereoscopic adventures, and by Griffith's own wilful plunge into the thicket of material life. If I speak of the consequences of that plunge as the production of an excess of presence-effect (of 'photographic reality', in Gunning's phrase), rather than as hyperindexicality, it is because the excess at issue should not necessarily be understood as an excess of one kind of sign only, or indeed as any excess of any kind of sign. Sometimes the thicket of life does not even provide the slightest opening to interpretation. Griffith's narrator system, far from abolishing the photograph's spatial continuum without gaps or lacks, in fact gave rise through its own impossible intensity to an anti-system. Sense, in the Biograph films, is intelligibility's anti-system, a counter-narrative which articulates contingency or the 'material life' as presence-effect. Montage, Bazin staunchly maintained, should be understood as one mode of storytelling among several, but *more abstract* than the others.[59] Griffith worked the less abstract modes as well. He worked immediacy.

The histories of literature and of aesthetic theory may help us further to define these less abstract modes. One of the specialisms developed by the European and American novel during the fifty years or so before the First World War was the articulation of contingency.[60] Acknowledgement of the historical significance of theatrical adaptation should not preclude enquiry into what Griffith might have learned (montage aside) by reading the novels and poems subsequently made into plays.[61] I shall try to show, through detailed analysis of particular Biograph films, that he did indeed read literature carefully.

What I am calling 'intelligibility' and 'sense', Martin Heidegger, in his major contribution to aesthetic theory, 'The Origin of the Work of Art', called World and Earth; and Fredric Jameson, in an essay on the work of Raymond Chandler which revises Heidegger from a late-Marxist perspective, calls History and Matter.[62] According to Jameson, World/History constitutes the 'ensemble of acts and efforts' whereby human beings have attempted to extract meaning from the 'limits and constraints' of their environment.[63] Hubert Dreyfus has described it as a 'cultural paradigm' whose function is to unify the 'scattered practices' of a group and hold them up to the members of that group as 'coherent possibilities for action'.[64] In Heidegger's view, the work of art serves that function: he has in mind the Greek temple. Dreyfus also adduces Clifford Geertz's Balinese cock-fight. Each represents a method or model in and through which an abstract or general knowledge can be organised.

'Earth, meanwhile,' Jameson continues, 'is everything meaningless in those surroundings and what betrays the resistance and inertia of sheer Matter as such.' Earth/Matter should be understood as a term for that which cannot be assimilated into paradigmatic meaning: death, contingency, finitude.[65] Jameson's formula seems to me a useful one, as revealing in relation to Griffith as it is in relation to Chandler. All I would add to it is that in Heidegger's account World involves an act of perpetual self-disclosure, whereas Earth forever withdraws itself, remains silent. 'A stone', he says, 'is worldless.'[66] Greek temples and Balinese cock-fights, on the other hand, serve no purpose at all unless the 'cultural paradigm' they bring into being remains fully intelligible to those frequenting them. Indeed, they do not so much produce intelligibility as perform it. I want to retain this emphasis, in order to separate what lies on one side of the hermeneutic threshold in Griffith's films – the point in a narrative or a scene at which suspicion becomes the rule – from what lies on the other.

What Jameson takes from Heidegger, and I take from him, is that these two dimensions of reality are 'radically incommensurable'; and that the task (of philosophy, of art, of politics) is not to heal this fundamental rift, but to exacerbate it and hold it open. Earth/Matter is not passive, but comes about precisely as that which cannot be generalised from, as anti-system to World/History's system. At the very moment when we have become convinced that the World is all World, art discloses the Earth within it, alien and inseparable. At the very moment when we become convinced that the Earth is all Earth, art discloses the World within it, alien and inseparable. For World, one might substitute History, or intelligibility, or hypermediation, or the sign (both iconic and indexical); for Earth, Matter, sense, immediacy, or the trace. Is it all a bit much to ask of Griffith? We shall see.

Sea-drift: Griffith on the coast

Griffith, Lillian Gish said, admired Walt Whitman's *Leaves of Grass* 'passionately'.[67] 'When we ran out of things to do with the Assyrian army,' Karl Brown was to recall of the filming of *Intolerance*,

> we went back to the studio and did some shots of Lillian Gish rocking a cradle, all to the tune of Walt Whitman's poetry, which Griffith recited with great feeling and surprisingly good delivery, considering how outstandingly lousy he was as an actor. It must have been one of his good days.[68]

The poetry and the poetry-reading belong, we might say, to the film's aspiration to the status of cultural paradigm; an aspiration to be impressed first on those making the film, and then on its audience. 'We must have Whitmanesque scenarios,' Vachel Lindsay had declared in *The Art of the Moving Picture*, which Griffith knew. The movies would complete what Whitman had begun. 'The possibility of showing the entire American population its own face in the Mirror Screen has at last come.'[69] As Miriam Hansen observes, the narrator system shaping *Intolerance* has assumed Whitman's 'grandiose compassion'; it, too, is the product of a 'poetic ego' which 'creates itself as it recreates history'.[70]

Griffith almost certainly read on, in the section of *Leaves of Grass* entitled 'Sea-Drift', past 'Out of the Cradle Endlessly Rocking'. The poem he would have come to next, 'As I Ebb'd with the Ocean of Life', tells a rather different story. Here, Whitman paces the shore of Long Island, his 'electric self' avid for 'types', for the emblem which would make a World of his poem. What he finds instead is Earth: the matter in the history constituted by the paradigmatic relation of land (father) to sea (mother), the flaw or blank spot in the Mirror Screen.

> Fascinated, my eyes reverting from the south, dropt, to follow those slender windrows,
> Chaff, straw, splinters of wood, weeds, and the sea-gluten,
> Scum, scales from shining rocks, leaves of salt-lettuce, left by the tide . . .

A fine mess. The stuff accumulated between land and sea – the product of both equally, but belonging to neither – recoils upon the poetic ego and its paradigms, so that Whitman no longer has any idea who or what he is, or how he might continue to make experience intelligible. The poetic ego does recover itself sufficiently to find, or to believe that it has found, a meaning in the encounter between land and sea. The poem, however, cannot be prised away from the 'friable shore', the 'trails of debris'.[71] Heidegger argued that the matter in art – the stuff of stone, colour, language, the medium's neutrality as medium – always resists meaning.[72] There is a kind of withdrawal, in 'As I Ebb'd', on the part of language: a failure, finally, to configure the land as father and the sea as mother. Description's sheer specificity (windrow, sea-gluten, salt-lettuce) compacts into an awkwardness which is the awkwardness of the contingent itself: of finitude, of death. Whitman has found Earth where he expected to find World.

Did Griffith, a sucker for cradles, also notice the sea-gluten? Rather more often, I think, than we might suppose. The evidence lies in the coastal romances which became a specialism after the winter trips to Southern California began in 1910: *After Many Years* (1908), *Lines of White on a Sullen Sea* (1909), *The Unchanging Sea* (1910), *Fisher Folks* (1911), *Enoch Arden* (1911). The basic plot is a simple one: Man goes to sea, and doesn't come back for a long time; meanwhile Woman waits for him on shore, scanning the horizon. The critical attention given to *After Many Years* has shown that the coastal romance allowed plenty of scope for parallel editing. It anchored the look 'over' the cut, from Woman at home to Man far away, in diegesis: in her look out for him over the waves breaking on the shore. That look is the instrument of the abstraction of meaning from mimesis. Material embodiment gives way to a gendered paradigm, a paradigm of gender: Man goes, Woman stays. No wonder, then, that Gunning should cite *Lines of White on a Sullen Sea* as his primary example of an 'imagistic' method in Griffith's work, which, combined with parallel editing, wrought a 'style of extraordinary abstraction'. In that film, Gunning says, the heroine's look out over the waves breaking for her faithless lover becomes an 'emblematic action' (enhanced in the crucial scene by a fade and by tinting). These devices lift the image out of a 'simple realistic diegesis'.[73]

A significant number of the coastal romances derive from poems, which might explain their propensity for emblematic action. Tennyson supplied the source for *After Many Years* and *Enoch Arden*; Charles Kingsley for *The Unchanging Sea*, and for *The Sands of Dee* (1912), which is coastal but not about fisher-folk; and William Carleton, supposedly, although I have not been able to track down the original text, for *Lines of White on a Sullen Sea*. The *Bulletin* does its level best to establish a diegetic motivation for the effect indicated by the title's mysterious formula. Day after day, we are told, Emily (the Woman left behind on the shore) 'scans the sullen sea which only brings back to the beach huge lines of white, which seem to taunt her as they break upon the sands'.[74] The *Bulletin* has to introduce the idea of immensity ('*huge* lines of white') in order to make the sea's sullenness something Emily cannot avoid noticing, something she might feel taunted by. The formula itself, however, seems rather to propose the idea of a material trace laid onto or over a sea of a particular colour (grey-green? pewter?). Sullenness, in any case, entails a certain passivity; it lacks the confidence to taunt. The heroine of coastal romance looks out *over* the breaking waves; her hope (endorsed, it may be, by a cut away to elsewhere) dissolves their substance. She does not see (the narrative does not see) the lines of white on a sullen sea. But the film's self-consciously poetic title insists that there is something in the view it offers of the world – a visual effect, an equivalent to sea-gluten and salt-lettuce – which will not be used up in meaning.

In 1912, in *The Moving Picture World*, the director Lois Weber defended the use of lines of poetry in intertitles as a way to develop rhythm and mood. Eileen Bowser has suggested that this is particularly true of *The Unchanging Sea*, based on Kingsley's 'The Three Fishers', in which a woman waits faithfully for her man; he endures shipwreck on a distant shore, and loss of memory, but eventually finds his way back to her.[75] The intertitles in *The Unchanging Sea* in fact alternate between atmosphere provided by Kingsley's poem and rather more prosaic supplements to narrative ('Will they ever return?'). The poem is about three fishermen, all of whom drown; the film allows one of them to survive, and to return. But a central sequence of shots does take the full measure of Kingsley's bleak articulation of finitude and death. It is introduced by an intertitle drawn from the poem:

> Three corpses lay out on the shining sands,
> In the morning gleam as the tide went down.
> And the women are weeping and wringing their hands,
> For those who will never come back to the town.

There is then a shot of a sea driving corpses and debris against a distant shore, and another intertitle drawn from the poem:

> For men must work and women must weep.
> And the sooner it's over the sooner to sleep;
> And good-bye to the bar and its moaning.[76]

The next shot shows the recovery of bodies from the sea; one man, clinging to a spar, is still alive. Thus the film carves its story of fidelity and restoration out of the poem's melancholia. Soon parallel editing puts the faithful man and the faithful woman back in touch through her look out over the breakers, across the cut; while the intertitles resume their matter-of-factness ('Restored to health but his memory a blank'). However, the bar and its moaning have not been obliterated; the shot of corpses and debris remains, as an anti-system, a visual counterpart to that element in poetic language which intelligibility cannot exhaust. The shot thus articulates contingency. This little sequence could be reckoned Griffith's 'As I Ebb'd with the Ocean of Life', his stab at sea-gluten and salt-lettuce.

In *The Unchanging Sea*, the foreshore emerges as a distinct territory, a space overwritten by traces, a space within which contingency can be articulated. The traces are those left not just by waves breaking, but by everyday human activities. Never before, as Jesionowski points out, had Griffith introduced so much 'stray material' into a suite of narrative images, without distracting from their force. We get to see quite a lot of life on the foreshore both in the village where the woman waits and in the village where the man slowly recovers. 'Both the husband and the wife are presented in dynamic situations that depict a process parallel to the immediacy of the separation the wife experiences.'[77] Those 'dynamic situations' depict a process parallel to the meaning abstracted from material embodiment by the narrator system.

In shot 18, the woman and her daughter walk on the beach. The young girl runs off down to the water to play, exiting frame left, while her mother gazes out over the breaking waves. A suitor approaches the woman, no doubt remarking as tactfully as possible that her husband is not going to come back. At this moment, the young girl reappears, down by the water; she has taken over the graphic margin (the lines of white, the foam produced by waves breaking on the sand) for animal spirits, for sheer ordinariness. Her mother now rejects the suitor, pointing emphatically at the horizon. As he shuffles off, she remains with her arm outstretched, while her daugher plays at the water's edge. Her refusal to be ordinary (to join her daughter, to remarry), exemplified by the look out over the breaking waves, will receive an immediate reward from the narrator system: a shot of her husband, alive. The processes thus beautifully rendered in this scene in parallel are those of the life as it is and life as it might be. The scene discovers Earth in World, and World in Earth.

Enoch Arden, Griffith's second version of Tennyson's poem, is more complex yet, because it explores to the full the moral consequences of an investment at one and the same time in life as it is and life as it should be. The first version, *After Many Years*, had been shot for the most part in the studio, Linda Arvidson recalled. 'Now we would do something g-r-a-n-d. "Enoch Arden" was such good movie stuff, and Mr Griffith was wondering how he could get it all into one thousand feet of film.'[78] He didn't, of course. *Enoch Arden* is a two-reeler;[79] and it certainly does do something grand with its Santa Monica location. It puts back, one might say, what the studio-bound *After Many Years* had left out, Tennyson's evocation of place:

> Long lines of cliff breaking have left a chasm;
> And in the chasm are foam and yellow sands;
> Beyond, red roofs about a narrow wharf
> In cluster . . .[80]

The good movie stuff in the poem is not just the story, I would suggest, but the 'stray material' of one kind or another.

Ben Brewster has emphasised the sheer extent of the cross-cutting, in *Enoch Arden*, between Annie down by the shore or in the family home and Enoch on the desert island or the ship which rescues him from it. In this respect, the film represents a 'highly refined variant' of a technique Griffith had been experimenting with since 1908.[81] But there is a difference, I think. The difference is that in *Enoch Arden* cross-cutting should be understood as one narrative mode among several, but *more abstract* than the others. The relation it constitutes between Annie at home and Enoch abroad becomes itself a topic of commentary, as other relations, constituted by other narrative modes, develop in parallel.

This dramatisation of and commentary on the look out over the waves (the look over the cut) begins with Enoch's departure on a ship to China, to regain his fortune. The scene of leave-taking on the beach, as the Man bids farewell, and then strides down to where the boat waits to take him out to the ship, while the Woman remains transfixed, is familiar from *Lines of White on a Sullen Sea*. In this case, however, there is someone else left behind: Philip Ray, Enoch's defeated rival, whose gaze comes if not between Annie and Enoch, then between us and Annie; Philip watches Annie watching Enoch. Griffith dramatises Annie's fixation, her eyes only for Enoch, by supplying her, as Tennyson had done, with a telescope.

24. (ext./mls) The ship. Raising sail. The boat approaches. Enoch tosses his bundle up on to the deck, and climbs after it. The ship moves slowly out of the frame, Enoch in the stern waving frantically.[82]

25. (ext./mls) Annie stands on the beach, her children on either side of her, watching the ship through a telescope. The line of foam where the sea breaks on the shore divides the frame horizontally.

26. (ext./ls) The ship recedes with agonizing slowness. Empty sea unfolds behind it. Cut only as it leaves the frame . . .

Intertitle: 'Ev'n to the last dip of the vanishing sail she watches it, and departed weeping for him.'

27. (ext./ms) Annie on the beach, with the children, telescope to her eye. The sea laps at her feet. She wipes the lens on her apron, takes a final look, and gives up. They leave. The waves break, for a second, on an empty shore.

Shots 26 and 27 deliberately refuse the cut-on-action, and thus establish a rhythm and mood in stark contrast to the parallel editing which will shortly unite Enoch and Annie in a phantom embrace. The emptiness they linger on is in fact not emptiness at all, but a different plenitude: the plenitude of matter, a sullen sea inscribed with white lines. Annie, telescope to her eye, looks out over that plenitude. The intertitle's slight revision of Tennyson insists on the difference between the telescopic or parallel-edited phantom embrace and an acknowledgement of finitude. Tennyson had written:

Even to the last dip of the vanishing sail
She watched it, and departed weeping for him . . .[83]

In Griffith's version, by contrast, Annie watches in an eternal present disjoined from the particular occasion of her departure weeping.

Her electric self, like Whitman's on Long Island, seeks only a type, an image of Enoch.

The foreshore, with the waves breaking on sand and rock, becomes a scene of disjunction. Like Emily in *The Unchanging Sea*, Annie refuses her persistent suitor, Philip, still faithful, as an intertitle puts it, to the hope of Enoch's return (shot 38). In a later scene, however, staging in depth at last folds Annie into itself, seizes her out of her abstraction. Philip again approaches Annie as she watches her children play down by the water. Griffith cuts to the desert island, and a despondent Enoch. Meanwhile, in the scene on the foreshore, the children have become increasingly absorbed in Philip's courting of Annie. The daughter's bonneted head in the background rhymes with Annie's in the foreground. Their heads are flanked by the rhyming tricorn hats of the son in the background and Philip in the foreground. This is already a family tableau, albeit on two separate planes. The planes coalesce as the children approach to surround the adults with their fervent solicitations. Annie accepts Philip, and they embrace. Mise-en-scène has become a commentary on the parallel editing which sustains the narrator system, as anti-system to its system. It now constitutes a moral argument as well as a technique: Annie should put her telescope away, should stop looking over the cut, should get on with her life.

The commentary of one technique on the other intensifies as the story reaches its climax with Annie's marriage to Philip, and Enoch's rescue. Griffith cuts between the process of rescue and the new home Philip has made for Annie and her children. Philip cautiously approaches Annie who, dozing in a chair by the open window, appears lost in a dream. She stretches her arms out in the direction of the window (off-screen left): that is, away from Philip, and by the direction-matching of previous cuts 'towards' Enoch, or wherever Enoch might be thought to be. However, the disjunction between husband and wife created by parallel editing's disjunctive method will soon heal over. A family tableau forms around her, with the child she has borne Philip at its centre. The disjunctive method, it would seem, no longer holds the power to abstract her from the new life she has made for herself.

Griffith, however, does not rely solely on the well-worn device of the family tableau to cure disjunction (to cure montage). He establishes the scene of Annie's dream by conducting us from the outside to the inside of the new home she has made for herself and her children with Philip.

> 60. (ext./ms) The rear of Philip's house. A window at the right. Spreading to its left, across the frame, is a spectacularly untidy climber rampant not only in its upward thrust, but in its bulge out into foreground space. When Philip and Annie enter from the left, they have more or less to force their way through this little stretch of jungle in order to approach the window. Clearly, the climber has become a topic of friendly debate. Annie handles it with an executioner's eye. Scope, perhaps, for home improvement?

The unruly climber is surely Kracauer's 'thicket of material life' incarnate. It plays an important part, I would argue, by its indexical function, in our dawning conviction that Annie has made the right choice.

Neither a symbol nor an element of 'simple realistic diegesis', the climber, like the tableau which succeeds it, asks to be understood as a plenitude. It, too, fills the screen. But it is, of course, a plenitude of a particular kind. It asks to be understood in its unruliness, and in its near-tangibility (its bristling or thrusting out at the viewer). The anti-system it constitutes cannot just be attributed to mise-en-scène. It relies, I believe, in its development as an anti-system, on an effect created by a specific visual technology: the stereoscope. The stereoscopic effect of interest here is the powerful illusion of tangibility which attaches to objects in the foreground of the image. As we have already seen, Oliver Wendell Holmes, inventor of the hand-held stereoscope, regarded this tangibility as a democratic exposure of the world as it is. I am not sure how stereoscopic Griffith really meant to be in depicting the 'thicket of material life' which so densely blankets the exterior of the house. What he most certainly did want to convey about it, however, was its tangibility and its unruliness.

On his return from the desert island, Enoch discovers that Annie and the children are no longer at the old home; he then learns from the landlady of the inn where he is staying that she has married Philip. Desperate for a sight of them, he approaches their new home. Immediately before his arrival, we see Philip and Annie once again inspecting the contentious climber, this time from inside the house. The plant's unruly bulk has in some sense set the agenda, by its articulation of contingency, for what follows. Annie tugs at one of the more obtrusive fronds. They retire, and close the window. Enoch and Annie's daughter brings the new baby into the room. A tableau forms. Meanwhile, Enoch, like Philip and Annie before him, but with greater caution, has pushed his way past or through the little stretch of jungle outside the window. He looks in. The tableau now includes Enoch and Annie's son. Griffith cuts between Enoch outside, aghast at what he sees, and the family inside. Enoch looks up to the sky, his head forced back into the climber, which trembles, then once more into the house (shot 81). He pulls away from the window, and topples or subsides backwards into the climber, which envelops him. A branch springs out at the viewer (shot 83). Enoch, having found the strength not to tell Annie of his return – or so an intertitle informs us – rushes away (shot 85).

What this wonderful scene enacts, partly through telling shifts between medium long shot and medium close-up, partly through near-stereoscopic tangibility, is Enoch's reabsorption, after his long absence, into the world as it is. Most notable of all, perhaps, in the latter respect, is shot 83, and the branch which springs out at the viewer. Oliver Wendell Holmes had noted the violence inherent in stereoscopy's unruliness. 'The scraggy branches of a tree in the foreground run out at us as if they would scratch our eyes out,' he wrote. 'The elbow of a figure stands forth so as to make us almost uncomfortable.'[84] Enoch's discomfort is our discomfort. The shot's near-stereoscopic effect articulates the contingency which the narrator system had always sought to abstract its stories from. Reversing the view taken by *After Many Years*, *Enoch Arden* insists that its hero and heroine should both live, however painful the consequences, in the here and now.

Biograph 'editorials'

A review of Griffith's *A Corner in Wheat* in the *New York Dramatic Mirror* of 25 December 1909 recognised its radically experimental nature. 'This picture is not a picture drama, although it is presented with dramatic force. It is an argument, an editorial, an essay on a subject of deep interest to all.'[85] Griffith had already produced one such 'editorial', *The Song of the Shirt* (1909), and he went on to produce several more: *The Usurer* (1910), *Gold Is Not All* (1910), *For His Son* (1911). 'All these films', Gunning observes, 'use parallel editing to contrast the fortunes of the upper and lower classes, morally condemning the heartlessness of greedy capitalists.' The analysis thus generated is social as well as moral. The first shot of *The Song of the Shirt* shows a seamstress leaning over her sick sister's bed, the second a factory-owner surrounded by obedient minions. The seamstress and the factory-owner have not yet met: the relation established by parallel editing is thus, as we've already seen, one of economic dependence alone. 'Editing pushes against the edge of abstraction,' Gunning concludes, 'a project which *A Corner in Wheat* would bring to a climax.'[86]

The Biograph 'editorials' have some claim to be regarded as the very epitome of the narrator system's abstracting tendencies. However, the meanings generated editorially were always, as Gunning puts it, 'immanent'.[87] Mise-en-scène played an important part in establishing the basis for social criticism. Scott Simmon speaks, in relation to *The Song of the Shirt*, of cinematography's 'intimacy', its ability to 'move "setting" forward into a topic'.[88] The more closely one examines the part played by mise-en-scène in these films, the less abstract they seem. The settings thus moved forward constitute an anti-system: a narrative mode producing sense rather than intelligibility.

In attempting to identify in the Biograph 'editorials' a narrative mode whose medium is not parallel editing, I shall endorse the broader argument developed by Ben Brewster and Lea Jacobs, that 'the emergence of much more highly edited scenes in feature films in the 1910s in both Europe and America by no means displaced a situational emphasis on the co-presence in space and time of significantly contrasted characters'. Brewster and Jacobs establish in great detail the continuing importance in cinema of pictorial effects adapted from theatrical models.[89] There is plenty of situational emphasis in the Biograph editorials. I want once again to concentrate, however, on a narrative mode which relied neither on pictorial effects drawn from the theatre, nor on parallel editing.

A Corner in Wheat must count as the ultimate editorial. It interweaves three lines of action: the first concerns a farmer who cannot earn a just price for his crop; the second, a speculator who has cornered the market in wheat; and the third, the urban poor, who can no longer afford the price of a loaf of bread. These lines of action are interwoven by parallel editing alone. On no occasion do the protagonists in one encounter the protagonists in another. In Frank Norris's 'A Deal in Wheat', the story upon which the film is based, the farmer–producer Lewiston ends up as a breadline consumer, thus narrativising the relation between these disparate scenes of American life. Griffith cuts the link. Gunning describes this tour de force of theoretically motivated editing as an anticipation of Eisenstein and Vertov.[90]

A Corner in Wheat develops its 'most basic contrast', Gunning says, in the first three shots, which show 'staunch yeomen farmers' in distress, on the one hand, and capitalism flourishing, on the other.[91]

> 1. (ext./mls) Farmyard partly enclosed by house, to the left, and barn with open door, to the right. Hayrick and cart in background. Farmer in foreground, his Wife on one side of him, Daughter on the other. An Older Man is seated beside the barn, a bag of grain on his lap. The Farmer has a sack of grain open at his feet. Three times, he sinks his hands into the sack, scoops out some grain, then lets it trickle through his fingers. He gestures from the grain to his family. Their livelihood will depend on what he can harvest from it. Shouldering the sack, he summons the Older Man, and they exit past the camera. The camera holds on the two women watching them leave.

> 2. (ext./ls) A ploughed field stretching into the distance. The Farmer and the Older Man move up the field towards the camera, spreading grain. Behind them, a harrow pulled by two white horses turns at the far end of its traverse, guided by a Farmhand. The Farmer and the Older Man exit past the camera, to the left, and then reappear, and move away down the field, spreading grain. The horses perform the same manoeuvre, the Farmhand remaining within shot, as pivot. The whole ensemble recedes.

> Intertitle: The Wheat King. Engineering the great corner.

> 3. (int./mls) The Wheat King in his office, animatedly giving instructions.

No one could doubt the abstractness of the contrast drawn editorially, in these scenes, between farm and office. But does this contrast create 'images with an emblematic and almost allegorical tone' (that is, *abstract* images), as Gunning claims?[92]

What is remarkable about the film's opening shots of farm life is that the actions they depict are complete actions, and possess a rhythm of their own. At the end of the first shot, instead of cutting as the men depart for the fields, Griffith invites us to continue to watch the women watching them depart. That look does not mean anything. Rather, it constitutes a residue of undefined feeling which carries over into (carries us over into) the next shot, of the men at work in the fields. The first shot's central action thematises completeness. The Farmer sifts the grain three times, on each occasion allowing it to run between his fingers before he once again plunges his hands into the sack. He does not edit himself. One could say, as Simmon does, that Griffith has directed the actors playing the farm family into a 'heavy, rhythmic, antirealistic stylization, eliminating extraneous gestures for an archetype of the farmer'.[93] But the rhythm in question seems to me expressive above all of individuality. This is how one person has chosen to conduct himself in adversity. What part does the action of dipping one's hand three times into a sack of grain play in any known 'archetype' of the farmer, or in the staunchness of staunch yeomen?

I would want to say that the act of sifting produces a sense which falls short of intelligibility (of emblematic or allegorical meaning). The purpose of its repetition is to make a particular person present to us for a certain time, a time which is *his* time, not ours (we might prefer to see something else). This, perhaps, is the elusive Bazinian Griffith. Bazin's remark about duration in *Nanook of the North* has some relevance to the farmyard scene in *A Corner in Wheat*, 'antirealistic stylization' notwithstanding. 'Montage could suggest the time involved,' Bazin points out. 'Flaherty however confines himself to showing the actual waiting period; the length of the hunt is the very substance of the image, its true object.'[94] The substance of Griffith's image is that element in the act performed which, even though the project the act sustains is universal and age-old, resists generalisation.

Equally significant, because it takes the edge off the binarism introduced by our first glimpse of the Wheat King in his office, is the fact that this opening sequence involves three shots, not two. In both of the first two shots, the Farmer and the Older Man at some point exit foreground left past the camera (all that differs in this movement is the shot-scale). The visual rhyme, which is not created by editing, since there is no match on action, gives us the sense of that in individual lives which carries over from one place and time to another, and by carrying over creates individuality. 'From these depressing scenes,' the *Dramatic Mirror* reviewer observed, in a passage Gunning does not quote, 'we turn to the affairs of the speculator where the great wheat corner is being arranged.'[95] Depressing *scenes*: farming is revealed in its various aspects as a way of life, before contrast revises it into allegory.

The pattern of contrast editing is at its most intense in a sequence which concerns the lavish dinner party thrown by the great speculator after he has engineered his corner in wheat. Griffith cuts repeatedly from the diners to a bakery patronised by the humble and the destitute (shots 6–10).

> Intertitle: The gold of the wheat.

> 6. (int./mls) A dinner party. An extravagantly laid table. The guests make merry. A place has been left for the Wheat King, who arrives in triumph, and bows to the assembled company. A toast to his triumph. He and his wife touch glasses.

Intertitle: The chaff of the wheat.

7. (int./mls) Bakery. The scene is staged in depth. In the foreground to the right, parallel to the side wall of the set, there is a counter heaped high with loaves of bread, and behind it the Baker (plump, eminently respectable). A placard propped against the near end reads: 'Owing to the advance in the price of flour the usual 5 cent loaf will be 10 cents.' In the background, there is a second counter, parallel to the back wall of the set. An open hatchway frames the Shopgirl tending it. There is a second placard attached to the wall above it: 'The rise in wheat is responsible.' On either side of the hatchway are shelves filled with loaves. A male Shop Assistant occupies the space between the counters. He sweeps the floor, or rearranges the loaves, or chats. During the scene, three customers approach the front counter, three the back, their movements more or less synchronized. The first two customers who approach the front counter are dismayed to find that the price of bread has risen, but pay up anyway; the third, a woman with a young child, cannot afford to pay, and returns the loaf she had chosen.

8. As 6. Further celebration. A ripple of toasting runs down the table from back to front. The Wheat King is in animated conversation with his wife and others.

9. As 7. A line of paupers, arranged diagonally, fills the left-hand side of the frame. The counter behind which the Baker stands, once heaped high with loaves, is now empty. The paupers, all movement suspended in a tableau vivant, stare glumly at this complete lack of provision. Much of the rear part of the shop has been masked by the line, and by other figures in the background to the right; but the two placards are still clearly visible.

10. As 8. The dinner party breaks up. The Wheat King leaves.

Again, I would say that, where the activities in the bakery are concerned, at any rate, as much of the work of definition is done by staging in depth as by contrast edit. Shot 7, for example, might in itself be sufficient to give the lie to David Bordwell's contention that Griffith had 'little recourse to the fine-grained intrashot choreography developed by his contemporaries'.[96]

Equally intriguing, for those who have sought an abstract style in the Biograph films, is the tableau vivant which constitutes shot 9. For Gunning, the tableau vivant 'stands out as a particularly excessive moment in which the frozen gestures of the actors draw attention to the shot as an image pregnant with meaning'.[97] The stasis of the tableau contrasts starkly with the vibrant motion of the diners, thus bringing a theme implicit throughout the film to a 'point of abstraction and dominance'. Griffith, Gunning concludes, has expressed the power of the Wheat King by reducing the people who are the victims of his greed to 'immobility'.[98] He is certainly right, I think, to insist on the image's excess. But might that excess not be, to turn his own formula against him, an excess of mimesis over meaning, rather than an excess of meaning over mimesis? The tableau vivant strikes me as an element in a story told by mise-en-scène, not contrast editing. Its effect depends upon a difference in degree from shot 7 rather than upon a difference in kind from shots 8 and 10. Taken together, shots 7 and 9 unfold like a violently compressed Naturalist novel. They stage a descent down the bottom rungs of the socio-economic ladder, from customers who can pay the extra five cents for a loaf of bread, to those who cannot, at least on this occasion, to those who never could. If there is contrast, in the stasis of shot 9, it is contrast with the feverish activity which had previously filled the shop, even in the hard times depicted in shot 7. The line of men obscures everything in the shop – its potential as a site of encounter, exchange, community – except the two signs announcing the new policy. The stasis has congealed with almost stereoscopic density around the life (the movement, the buzz) in the place.

Brewster and Jacobs report that they have not discovered anything comparable to the tableau in other films of the period, and that they cannot relate it to any 'iconographic tradition' derived from the theatre.[99] The tradition Griffith meant to explore, I think, was literary rather than iconographic. The Naturalist fiction which began to appear in the 1870s added a new pattern to the small stock of curves describing the shape lives take (or adapted an old one from classical and Shakespearean tragedy): the plot of decline, of physical and moral exhaustion.[100] Most nineteenth-century novels divided existence into a long rise stretching to the age of 60, measured in social and moral terms, and a short physical decline. Naturalist fiction envisaged instead a rapid physical rise to the moment of reproduction in the 20s, then a long redundancy accelerated by the emergence of some innate physical or moral flaw. Zola's Rougon-Macquart novels (1871–93) analysed the effects of heredity and environment on the members of a single family, tracing the passage of a genetic flaw down the legitimate line of the Rougons and the illegitimate line of the Macquarts. In each generation, the inherited flaw topples an individual life into a downward spiral of disease, alcoholism, poverty, or madness. This downward spiral was the way in which Naturalist novels, in Europe and America, spoke about individual and social development: among them, Norris's *McTeague: A Story of San Francisco* (1899) and *The Octopus: A Story of California* (1901). Norris was (with reservations) Zola's most prominent American disciple. *The Octopus* supplied Griffith with two elements of his film: the dinner sequence, with its contrast between extravagance and starvation, and the speculator's burial under a load of his own wheat.[101]

In 'A Deal in Wheat', Sam Lewiston, the farmer who sells up when he cannot get a decent price for his wheat, moves to Chicago, where his brother finds him employment. But the decline has already set in. 'Thrown out of work, Lewiston drifted aimlessly about Chicago, from pillar to post, working a little, earning here a dollar, there a dime, but always sinking, sinking, till at last the ooze of the lowest bottom dragged at his feet ...' He ends up on the bread line, homeless and a beggar.

> There was something ominous and gravely impressive in this interminable line of dark figures, close-pressed, soundless; a crowd, yet absolutely still; a close-packed, silent file, waiting, waiting in the vast deserted night-ridden street; waiting without a word, without a movement, there under the night and under the slow-moving mists of rain.

This silent file, waiting without a word, without a movement, is, I believe, the source of Griffith's tableau vivant. Norris understood the bread line as the penultimate stage in the crowd's downward spiral into abject poverty: 'a small platform, as it were, above the sweep of black water, where for a moment they might pause and take breath before the plunge'.[102] So did Griffith. The tableau vivant is not an emblem of the immobility inflicted by capitalist excess. It is, in its congealment, its surplus of presence-effect, a momentary resting-place, a pause before disintegration. It takes hold on us by filling the deep space created by the intricate choreography of the previous scene in the shop with a frieze-like suspension of activity. Griffith, taking a hint from Norris, has developed a counter-narrative.

In *The Usurer* (1910), a moneylender wreaks havoc by calling in loans. One client shoots himself. Another, a widow with a sick child, having seen the child's bed removed from under her, goes to the moneylender's office to plead with him. Unknown to her, he is in the adjoining safe when she arrives; her collapse knocks the door shut. Because the lock of the safe is regulated by a timing mechanism, he cannot escape, and suffocates. Once again, the 'editorial' theme is established by parallel editing, this time between a banquet and scenes of debt-collection. The bailiffs visit the widow first, then the man who will eventually shoot himself (he, too, has a young daughter), and finally a petty-bourgeois couple: they have white-collar jobs, and the obligatory daughter. The usurer has a sister, but no wife. As in *A Corner in Wheat*, Charlie Keil observes, 'a principle of moralising contrast links cause and effect as the protagonist celebrates while his victims suffer'.[103] The most notable cut of all is from the debtor raising a gun to his head to the usurer raising a glass to his lips in toast.

A lot of work is done, too, by mise-en-scène, including pictorial effects adapted from theatre. The apartments in which the three sets of debtors live are carefully differentiated. The widow's has little in it, apart from the truckle bed where her daughter lies sick. The widower's contains a dressing-table with mirror, a carpet, some chairs, and some prints on the wall. The clerk and his wife enjoy not only the privilege of separating home from work, but a good assortment of furniture: a table, some ornate chairs, prints on the walls, curtains across the window (rather than a blind), and above all a glass-fronted cabinet with china on top. The scope of the constituency subject to harassment by the usurer and his minions has no doubt been enlarged in this way so that it might include among its potential future victims members of the new middle-class audience cinema was attempting to attract. Significantly, the middle-class family redeems itself. We see husband and wife separately, in shots 7 and 9, then together at the office in shot 35, then at home with their daughter, in shot 41, one of the longest and most elaborate in the film.

> 41. (int./mls) The apartment. Their daughter asleep in a rocking-chair. The clerk and his wife return from the office. Exhausted, they stand facing the camera, heads bowed in despair. The daughter wakes, and standing between them appeals to them to value what they have. The mutual embrace creates a tableau.

The middle-class family has found strength in its own moral resources: in the power of faith, in childhood innocence. Griffith redeems it at the level of content, by avoiding any further mention of indebtedness, and at the level of form, by the tableau's genteel choreography. The other families don't fare so well. The widower, who has a child, but no moral resources, succumbs to despair; while the widow in effect gets lucky when her fainting fit condemns the usurer to death by suffocation, and his repentant sister subsequently cancels the debt. Cinema's new audience could consider itself handsomely flattered.

But there is some Earth (some real Naturalist dirt, one might say) in the otherwise sanctimonious World created by Griffith's film. It reveals itself in episodes featuring the hapless widower. In *The Usurer*, as in *A Corner in Wheat*, Naturalism proliferates in the pause (the rendered duration) between one 'theoretically motivated' cut and another. The usurer takes his first punitive step against a defaulter immediately after we have been introduced, in shot 9, to the home of the middle-class family. It is taken, not against them, but against the widower. In shots 10–12, Griffith cuts back and forth between a dinner party, during which the usurer presents his sister with a necklace, and the widower's apartment.

> 11. (int./mls) The widower's apartment. A dressing-table with mirror, a carpet, some chairs, some prints on the wall. The usurer's bailiffs, or 'collectors', supervise the removal of furniture from the apartment: the dressing-table, the chairs. One collector gives a contemptuous little kick to the carpet to speed it on its way. A drawer falls out of the table. The widower and his daughter look on helplessly. After the men have left, she makes a consoling gesture towards him, but is rebuffed.

There can be little doubt as to what the contrast means. But the scene in the widower's apartment, a lengthy scene with scope for a great deal of business, cannot altogether be subsumed into that meaning. Nor does reference to pictorial effects adapted from the theatre really help, I think, when it comes to the scene's most telling moment: the physical act of removal. This act is the scene's (and indeed the film's) Earthing: its discovery of the matter in history.

There are few scenes more melancholy, in nineteenth-century fiction and painting, than the enforced sale or removal of household goods. Thackeray made something of a specialism of such clearances, notably in *Vanity Fair*

(1848), where Sedley's bankruptcy leaves him no choice but to sell the contents of the house in Russell Square. 'Old women and amateurs have invaded the upper apartments, pinching the bed-curtains, poking into the feathers, shampooing the mattresses, and clapping the wardrobe drawers to and fro.'[104] Clearance involves a double reduction. It deprives commodities of their past, of the surplus of meaning and value they have acquired through use over time; and it deprives them of their future, because the ruthless scepticism of the bargain-hunters who thumb curtains, prod mattresses, and bang the doors of cabinets is evidence that they have, beyond a certain point, no future; the thumbing and prodding exposes them as the waste-matter they will before very long become. Thackeray despatches the faithful Captian Dobbin to auction to purchase Amelia Sedley's piano, but no act of piety, however gallant, can undo the damage done by matter's exposure as matter.

The Naturalists did not usually bother with the acts of piety. In Zola's *L'Assommoir* (1876), Coupeau and Gervaise, reduced by alcoholism to abject poverty, live in rented accommodation, and thus do not even have any furniture to sell. Gervaise removes handfuls of wool from a mattress, smuggles them out of the building in her apron, and sells them for ten sous each. The mattress-cover follows, then the bolster, and finally the bedstead itself, dismantled and taken away piece by piece. Gervaise, that much more impoverished than the Sedleys, has had to perform clearance's double reduction herself. Throughout the novel, furniture and its removal or dismemberment have mapped her downward spiral into degradation. When Coupeau collapses, a stretcher is brought for him from the hospital, and he is loaded on to it 'like a piece of furniture'.[105] In such moments, narrative itself loses its grip upon meaning, since all it has to reveal is more of the same: more formlessness, more contingency. Matter now shows through everywhere in history.

No furniture at all is removed, or taken apart, or otherwise put at risk, in Charles Reade's celebrated dramatisation of *L'Assommoir*, *Drink* (1879). To be sure, the stage directions indicate a dwindling, with regard to tables and chairs, between the apartment occupied by Gervaise and Lantier in Act 1 and that occupied by Gervaise and Coupeau in Act 6.[106] But there is no equivalent, in the play, to the novel's brutal double reductions, its relentless exposure of contingency. Pictorial effects achieved by the accumulation of realistic detail did play a part in early-twentieth-century Naturalist theatre. In his 1909 production of Eugene Walter's *The Easiest Way*, the story of an actress's descent into prostitution, David Belasco went out of his way to fill the stage with documentary objects, most of which are put to some use.[107] Presumably, though, there was no great enthusiasm among producers for the nightly trashing (twice on Saturdays) of valuable props.

Cinema, by contrast, immediately developed an appetite for double reduction. The American Mutoscope and Biograph Company's *The Suburbanite* (1904) describes the efforts of a pair of careless and increasingly malicious removal-men to deliver furniture to a brand-new suburban villa. One man stumbles, dropping a tub full of crockery; the drawers slide out of a chest carried by the other, and their contents spill out. Wreckage strews the sidewalk. This is not just another fine mess, an impromptu festival of accident; though it is certainly that. The suburban life has been turned inside out, so that anyone passing down the street can see at a glance what it is made of. The removal-men are the agents (even the artists) of inversion. To them, the cherished heirloom and the expensive dinner-set alike are simply *stuff*. Through ineptitude and malice, they make sense (mere sense) out of household goods whose disposition within the new house would have made it (fully intelligible as) a home.

In the Biograph *A Drunkard's Reformation* (1909), an alcoholic father begins to understand the error of his ways when his daughter takes him to a performance of *Drink*. But Griffith himself probably learned as much from Naturalist fiction as he did from Naturalist theatre. The clearance scene in *The Usurer* is the kind of thing Naturalist fiction did consistently well – in Norris's *McTeague*, the sale of household goods ('a pillage, a devastation') represents a point of no return[108] – and Naturalist theatre, as far as I am aware, scarcely at all. The collectors, like the removal-men in *The Suburbanite*, are the agents and artists of a double reduction to matter. Their art lies in the malicious kick aimed at the already threadbare carpet, in the carelessness which allows drawers to slide out of a chest. They, too, make mere sense.

I have drawn attention to moments in Griffith's Biograph films when mimesis exceeds itself by contriving, largely through mise-en-scène, an image which appears nothing other than palpable: Enoch Arden's withdrawal into the climber's unruly bulk when the realisation dawns that he will never reclaim his old life; the frozen bread line; the kick aimed at the carpet, as drawers slide out of the chest. Literature, I have shown, played a part in the design of a counter-narrative capable of articulating contingency. This, then, is a fully Bazinian Griffith: a Griffith whose work recalls Bazin's observation on another film-maker with a taste for the novels of Frank Norris, Eric von Stroheim. 'He has one simple rule for direction. Take a close look at the world, keep on doing so, and in the end it will lay bare for you all its cruelty and its ugliness.'[109]

It is worth noting, however, that the presence-effects which constitute a counter-narrative, in these films, and their claim to immediacy, have been produced diegetically by loss: loss of status, of self-respect, of being. The matter palpably on view, animate or inanimate, is so much *waste*-matter. Each instance of too much presence-effect is configured by an absence-effect: the trace of what has gone missing. These absence-effects speak (mutely) to the founding absence of the human observer whose authority and compassion might have mediated them (might have taken the unbearable edge off the excess of presence). It is the machine's-eye view which, in producing too much presence-effect, too much immediacy, has laid the world bare in all its cruelty and ugliness. The automatism of the mechanically reproduced image became increasingly a preoccupation, for film-makers and writers alike, in the period during and immediately after the First World War. It is to that preoccupation that I now turn.

Notes

1   'Dickens, Griffith, and the Film Today', in *Film Form: Essays in Film Theory*, ed. and trans. Jay Leyda (London: Dennis Dobson, 1951), 195–255, pp. 199–200.

2   Ibid.

3   Eileen Bowser, *The Transformation of Cinema 1907–1915* (New York: Charles Scribner's Sons, 1990), 53–4.

4   'The Formulation of the Classical Style, 1909–1928', in David Bordwell, Janet Staiger, and Thompson (eds), *The Classical Hollywood Cinema: Film Style and Modes of Production to 1960* (London: Routledge, 1985), 157–240, p. 175.

5   'The Assistant Producer', in *Stories* (New York: Vintage Books, 1995), 546–59, p. 548. Nabokov became a keen movie-goer, for courting purposes, in 1915: *Speak, Memory: An Autobiography Revisited* (New York: Quality Paperback Book Club, 1993), 236–7.

6   Tom Gunning, 'The Cinema of Attractions: Early Film, Its Spectator, and the Avant-Garde', in Thomas Elsaesser (ed.), *Early Cinema: Space, Frame, Narrative* (London: BFI Publishing, 1990), 56–67. 'What follows the cinema of attractions', as David Bordwell puts it, 'is not merely a cinema of narrative but a cinema of narrative *integration*, which absorbs cinematic techniques and engaging moments into a self-sufficient world unified across time and space': *On the History of Film Style* (Cambridge, MA: Harvard University Press, 1997), 127.

7   Charlie Keil, *Early American Cinema in Transition: Story, Style, and Filmmaking, 1907–1913* (Madison: University of Wisconsin Press, 2001); Lee Grieveson, *Policing Cinema: Movies and Censorship in Early-Twentieth-Century America* (Berkeley: University of California Press, 2004); Charlie Keil and Shelley Stamp (eds), *American Cinema in the Transitional Era: Audiences, Institutions, Practices* (Berkeley: University of California Press, 2004).

8   'Formulation', 157.

9   Tom Gunning, *D. W. Griffith and the Origins of American Narrative Film: The Early Years at Biograph* (Urbana: University of Illinois Press, 1991), 18; Keil, *Early American Cinema*, 7.

10   'On Suture', in *Questions of Cinema* (Basingstoke: Macmillan, 1981), 76–112, p. 107; 'Film, System, Narrative', in *Questions of Cinema*, 131–44, pp. 134–5.

11   *When the Movies Were Young* (New York: Dover Publications, 1969), 90. First published in 1925.

12   Thompson, 'Formulation', 163–73.

13   The remark is recorded in Lewis Jacobs, *The Rise of the American Film* (New York: Harcourt, Brace, 1939), 119.

14   *The Nigger of the 'Narcissus' and Typhoon and Other Stories* (London: J. M. Dent, 1950), x. For a contrasting view of Griffith's debt to literature to the one advanced here, see Mikhail Iampolski, *The Memory of Tiresias: Intertextuality and Film*, trans. Harsha Ram (Berkeley: University of California Press, 1998), ch. 3. Iampolski finds in Griffith's fondness for poetry evidence of an attachment to an Emersonian or Swedenborgian transcendentalism. For him,

montage creates a 'hieroglyphic stasis', over and above narrative, as a stimulus to 'transcendental vision'.

15 Quoted by Gunning, *D. W. Griffith*, 174.

16 Jesionowski, *Thinking in Pictures: Dramatic Structure in D. W. Griffith's Biograph Films* (Berkeley: University of California Press, 1987); Gunning, *D. W. Griffith*; Simmon, *The Films of D. W. Griffith* (Cambridge: Cambridge University Press, 1993); Paolo Cherchi Usai (ed.), *The Griffith Project*, 8 vols. to date (London: British Film Institute, 1999–2004) – vols 1–7 cover the Biograph period.

17 *D. W. Griffith: American Film Master* (New York: Museum of Modern Art, 2002), 17. First published in 1940.

18 *D. W. Griffith*, 25–6.

19 *When the Movies Were Young*, 66; 'Dickens, Griffith, and the Film Today', 200–201.

20 *D. W. Griffith*, 112–14, 109, 118.

21 Ibid., 135–7, p. 137.

22 Ibid., 233. Gunning is by no means alone in this emphasis. Jesionowski, too, discerns a 'new relationship' with images in Griffith's Biograph films. 'He confronted his audiences, and continues to confront them, with films in which disarmingly "realistic" effects are based on alarmingly abstract construction' (*Thinking in Pictures*, 2).

23 Ibid., 17–18.

24 *Griffith Project*, vol. 1, 143.

25 *Thinking in Pictures*, 42.

26 In this respect, the psychoanalytic emphasis in film theory's account of narrativisation, an emphasis filtered out by recent film history, might once again come into the reckoning. In Heath's view, suture 'states and restates' the productivity or excess it is designed to contain in the very act of containing it: 'Narrative Space', in *Questions of Cinema*, 19–75, p. 53.

27 I draw here on Gunning's valuable account of *The Lonely Villa*: *Griffith Project*, vol. 2, 139–44.

28 Gunning, *D. W. Griffith*, 141; Simmon, *Films*, 29.

29 Grieveson, *Policing Cinema*, 172–86. As my discussion of Lawrence's *The Lost Girl* has shown, the panic surrounding white slavery did not subside with the outbreak of war.

30 *Biograph Bulletin*, 18 August 1908, reprinted in *Griffith Project*, vol. 1, 82–3.

31 In *Suspensions of Perception: Attention, Spectacle, and Modern Culture* (Cambridge, MA: MIT Press, 1999), Jonathan Crary has explored the demand made by 'Western modernity' that human beings should 'define and shape themselves in terms of a capacity for "paying attention"': that is, the capacity to isolate one part of a sensory field from another 'in the interests of maintaining an orderly and productive world' (pp. 1, 17). Hugo Münsterberg, one of Crary's attention-specialists, brought to Harvard by William James in 1892, and author of books like *Psychology and Social Sanity* (1914) and *Psychology and Industrial Efficiency* (1913), was also, as we have seen, a commentator on film. 'Of all internal functions which create the meaning of the world around us,' Münsterberg claimed, 'the most central is the attention': *The Photoplay: A Psychological Study* (New York: Dover Publications, 1970), 31.

32 Brian McHale, *Constructing Postmodernism* (London: Routledge, 1992), 147.

33   *Textbook of Insanity*, trans. Charles Gilbert Chaddock (Philadelphia: F. A. Davis, 1904), 368–9, 373–4, 381–2.

34   *The Standard Edition of the Complete Psychological Works*, ed. James Strachey et al., 24 vols (London: Hogarth Press, 1953–74), vol. 6, 254–6.

35   This is the case I make in *Paranoid Modernism: Literary Experiment, Psychosis, and the Professionalization of English Society* (Oxford: Oxford University Press, 2001). The context I propose there for such investments in paranoia is the transformation wrought by what Harold Perkin has termed the 'rise of professional society'. Paranoia, the psychiatrists maintained, was the professional person's madness of choice. One might want to reconsider, from this point of view, the famous advertisement Griffith placed in the *New York Dramatic Mirror* on 3 December 1913, which does not hold back in the claims it makes for his professional expertise. The advertisement, Richard Schickel remarks, was 'the beginning of a fame unprecedented for a director, but a fame that would soon be *the* precedent for all who would claim to be truly creative artists in the newest art': *D. W. Griffith: An American Life* (New York: Limelight Editions, 1996), 203.

36   *Griffith Project*, vol. 2, 28–9.

37   Ibid., vol. 2, 77–9, 87–9.

38   Ibid., vol. 3, 93–5; vol. 7, 42–5.

39   *Biograph Bulletin*, no date, reprinted in *Griffith Project*, vol. 3, 93–4.

40   *Text-Book of Insanity*, 393.

41   *Moving Picture World*, 3 May 1913, in Griffith Project, vol. 7, 42.

42   *Memoirs of My Nervous Illness*, ed. and trans. Ida Macalpine and Richard A. Hunter (London: William Dawson, 1955); 'Psychoanalytic Notes on an Autobiographical Account of a Case of Paranoia (Dementia Paranoides)' (1911), *Standard Edition*, vol. 12, 1–82.

43   Eileen Bowser mistakenly identifies the subject of the second flashback as the judge: *Griffith Project*, vol. 7, 43.

44   Tom Gunning has remarked on the inventiveness of the latter scene: *D. W. Griffith*, 275.

45   Ibid., 24.

46   *Theory of Film: The Redemption of Physical Reality* (Princeton: Princeton University Press, 1997), 63. First published in 1960. My use of Kracauer's emphasis on the redemption of physical reality has been influenced by Miriam Bratu Hansen's excellent introduction to the Princeton edition of *Theory of Film*, as well as by D. N. Rodowick, 'The Last Things Before the Last: Kracauer and History', *New German Critique*, 41 (1987), 109–39; and Heidi Schlüpmann, 'The Subject of Survival: On Kracauer's *Theory of Film*', *New German Critique*, 54 (1991), 111–26.

47   Ibid., 46–8.

48   'The Evolution of the Language of Cinema', in *What Is Cinema?*, ed. and trans. Hugh Gray, 2 vols (Berkeley: University of California Press, 1967), vol. 1, 23–40, pp. 24–5, 27.

49   For an account of Kracauer's kinship with Bazin, at this time, see Martin Jay, *Permanent Exile: Essays on the Intellectual Migration from Germany to America* (New York: Columbia University Press, 1985), 173–4.

50   'Evolution', vol. 1, 36.

51   *Hollywood: Spaces and Meanings in American Film* (London: Wallflower, 2001), 5.

52   I am not sure that this objection (if it should be considered a valid one) has been met by Philip Rosen's absorbing and authoritative rehabilitation of Bazin: 'History of Image, Image of History: Subject and Ontology in Bazin', in Ivone Margulies (ed.), *Rites of Realism: Essays on Corporeal Cinema* (Durham: Duke University Press, 2003), 42–79.

53   'The Semiology of the Cinema', in *Signs and Meaning in the Cinema*, rev. edn (London: BFI Publications, 1998), 79–106, p. 92. I have also benefited from Mary Ann Doane's discussion of Peirce in *The Emergence of Cinematic Time: Modernity, Contingency, the Archive* (Cambridge, MA: Harvard University Press, 2002), ch. 3. For Peirce, Doane notes, the index, at once sign and not-sign, is 'perched on the threshold of semiosis' (p. 101).

54   *The Skin of the Film: Intercultural Cinema, Embodiment, and the Senses* (Durham: Duke University Press, 2000), 92–3.

55   *Sound Technology and the American Cinema: Perception, Representation, Modernity* (New York: Columbia University Press, 2000), 77, 238.

56   'Temporality, Storage, Legibility: Freud, Marey, and the Cinema', in Janet Bergstrom (ed.), *Endless Night: Cinema and Psychoanalysis, Parallel Histories* (Berkeley: University of California Press, 1999), 57–87, pp. 57, 85. The essay has been reprinted as ch. 2 of *The Emergence of Cinematic Time*.

57   'On Narcissim', *Standard Edition*, vol. 14, 67–102; Trotter, *Paranoid Modernism*, ch. 2.

58   'Temporality', 85.

59   'Evolution', vol. 1, 36.

60   An argument I develop at length in *Cooking with Mud: The Idea of Mess in Nineteenth-Century Art and Fiction* (Oxford: Oxford University Press, 2000).

61   Rick Altman makes a powerful case for the historical significance of adaptations in 'Dickens, Griffith, and Film Theory Today', in Jane Gaines (ed.), *Classical Hollywood Narrative: The Paradigm Wars* (Durham: Duke University Press, 1992), 9–47.

62   Heidegger, 'The Origin of the Work of Art', in David Farrell Krell (ed.), *Basic Writings* (London: Routledge, 1993), 139–212; Jameson, 'The Synoptic Chandler', in Joan Copjec (ed.), *Shades of Noir: A Reader* (London: Verso, 1993), 33–56.

63   'Synoptic Chandler', 49.

64   'Heidegger on the Connection between Nihilism, Art, Technology, and Politics', in Charles Guignon (ed.), *The Cambridge Companion to Heidegger* (Cambridge: Cambridge University Press, 1993), 289–316, pp. 298–301.

65   'Synoptic Chandler', 49.

66   'Origin', 170.

67   *The Movies, Mr Griffith and Me* (Englewood Cliffs, NJ: Prentice-Hall, 1969), 47.

68   *Adventures with D. W. Griffith*, ed. Kevin Brownlow (London: Faber and Faber, 1988), 166.

69   *Art of the Moving Picture*, 57.

70   *Babel and Babylon: Spectatorship in American Silent Film* (Cambridge, MA: Harvard University Press, 1991), 169.

71   *Leaves of Grass*, ed. Jerome Loving (Oxford: Oxford University Press, 1990), 202–4.

72   I draw here on Gerald L. Bruns's analysis of Heidegger's poetics, in *Heidegger's Estrangements: Language, Truth, and Poetry in the Later Writings* (New Haven: Yale University Press, 1989), 39–43.

73   *D. W. Griffith*, 232–6.

74   *Biograph Bulletin*, 28 October 1909, reprinted in *Griffith Project*, vol. 3, 79.

75   Ibid., vol. 4, 68–70.

76   *Poems* (London: J. M. Dent, 1927), 158.

77   *Thinking in Pictures*, 172.

78   *When the Movies Were Young*, 195.

79   Technically, two single-reelers; Part One released on 12 June 1911, Part Two three days later; reissued as a two-reeler on 29 August 1916.

80   'Enoch Arden', lines 1–4, in *Tennyson: A Selected Edition*, ed. Christopher Ricks (London: Longman, 1989), 592.

81   *Griffith Project*, vol. 5, 50–52.

82   The conventions I have used to describe shot-scales in my shot-by-shot analyses conform to those used by Keil, in *Early American Cinema*. Long shot (ls) = human figure shown in totality. Medium long shot (mls) = human figure shown from knees up. Medium shot (ms) = human figure shown from waist up. Medium close-up (mcu) = human figure shown from chest up. Close-up (cu) = the human head only in view (or a small object).

83   'Enoch Arden', lines 244–5, in *Selected Edition*, 598.

84   'The Stereoscope and the Stereograph', in Alan Trachtenberg (ed.), *Classic Essays on Photography* (New Haven, CT: Leete's Island Books, 1980), 72–82, p. 77.

85   Quoted by Gunning, *D. W. Griffith*, 241.

86   Ibid., 134–7.

87   Ibid., 138.

88   *Films*, 33.

89   *Theatre to Cinema: Stage Pictorialism and the Early Feature Film* (Oxford: Oxford University Press, 1997), 200, 29.

90   *D. W. Griffith*, 244; *Griffith Project*, vol. 3, 130–41, p. 137.

91   *D. W. Griffith*, 241.

92   Ibid., 249.

93   *Films*, 38.

94   'Evolution', 27.

95   The review is quoted in full by Schickel, *D. W. Griffith*, 143–4.

96   *On the History of Film* Style, 196.

97   *D. W. Griffith*, 249.

98   *Griffith Project*, vol. 3, 139–40.

99   *Theatre to Cinema*, 76.

100 Philip Fisher, 'Acting, Reading, Fortune's Wheel: *Sister Carrie* and the Life History of Objects', in Eric Sundquist (ed.), *American Realism: New Essays* (Baltimore: Johns Hopkins University Press, 1982), 259–77, p. 271.

101 When a reviewer declared that his play *A Fool and a Girl* (1907) was 'as inartistic as a Zola novel', he took pride in the association: Schickel, *D. W. Griffith*, 86–7.

102 'A Deal in Wheat', in *A Deal in Wheat and Other Stories of the New and Old West* (London: Grant Richards, 1903), 3–26, pp. 22–4.

103 *Griffith Project*, vol. 4, 153–6, p. 154. Keil confusingly refers to the moneylender's sister as a wife, while the cast-list he prints has her as a sister. The moneylender is surely unmarried and childless, in contrast to his fertile, unfortunate victims.

104   *Vanity Fair*, ed. J. I. M. Stewart (Harmondsworth: Penguin Books, 1968), 205. To 'shampoo', in this context, is to prod.

105   *L'Assommoir*, trans. Leonard Tancock (Harmondsworth: Penguin Books, 1970), 379, 329.

106   *Drink*, ed. David Baguley (London, Ontario: Mestengo Press, 1991), 39, 107.

107   Lise-Lone Marker discusses the production at length in *David Belasco: Naturalism in the American Theater* (Princeton: Princeton University Press, 1975), ch. 6. It ran for 157 consecutive performances, and aroused a great deal of comment.

108   *McTeague: A Story of San Francisco*, ed. Jerome Loving (Oxford: Oxford University Press, 1995), 210–17.

109   'Evolution', 27.

4

James Joyce
and the Automatism of the
Photographic Image

The meeting between James Joyce and Sergei Eisenstein, in November 1929, at Joyce's Paris flat, has assumed folkloric status in discussions of the relation between modernist literature and early cinema. Joyce, by this time, was practically blind, though he did his best to conceal the fact. He expressed a keen interest in Eisenstein's films, but he hadn't seen any of them, and he wasn't likely to. They listened to a recording he had recently made of 'Anna Livia Plurabelle'. Eisenstein finally understood the severity of Joyce's blindness when he was leaving the flat, and Joyce fumbled for his overcoat.[1] There was certainly good will on both sides, and admiration. 'What Joyce does with literature', Eisenstein was to observe, 'is quite close to what we're doing with the new cinematography, and even closer to what we're going to do.'[2] Joyce repaid the compliment. Eisenstein, it seems, was one of the few directors to whom he might have entrusted a film of *Ulysses*.[3]

There is enough evidence from letters and memoirs to suggest that Joyce had long made a habit out of movie-going; and he did at least put other people's money where his mouth was by opening the first cinema in Dublin, the Volta, in December 1909.[4] To be sure, his comments on what he had seen at the movies are scattered, casual, and for the most part unspecific. We don't really know which films made a significant impression upon him. Unlike other writers of the time, he did not describe or even allude to movie-going in his work, except in the most oblique fashion. Unlike them, he had nothing to say, in print at least, with regard to cinema as a phenomenon. But it would be fair to assume that he knew what he was talking about.

My aim is to demonstrate that the interest Joyce took in cinema had to do with the automatism of the mechanically reproduced image, and that this interest had a part to play in shaping one of the literary 'automatisms' (or exercises in authorial detachment) he designed for *Ulysses*. I want to set these literary machinations against a certain filmic machination operative, under particular circumstances, in the work of some film-makers, from the transitional era onwards. In order to clear the ground for such an approach, I need first – and drawing upon the account of Griffith's parallel editing developed in the previous chapter – to address the question of 'montage' in *Ulysses*.[5]

Joyce and montage

There is a good deal to be said, in Joyce's case, for analogies established on the basis of montage between literary and cinematic practice.[6] No episode in *Ulysses* has been associated more consistently with montage than 'Wandering Rocks'.[7] The episode takes place in the streets of central Dublin at 3 o'clock in the afternoon. It consists of eighteen short scenes, and a coda, each with its own setting. Its structuring principle is the interpolation into one scene of another which occurs at the same time but in a different place, and which those present are not in a position to witness. Some of the interpolated events clearly belong to other scenes in the episode; others do not. Lee Jacobus has argued – on the basis of Joyce's encounter with Eisenstein, and their presumed common interest in montage – that these interpolations should be understood as 'intercuts'. The interpolations, Jacobus observes, 'appear to be special effects that owe more to the concept of film intercutting than to anything that precedes them in literature'.[8]

In the fifth scene, Blazes Boylan is in Thornton's the fruiterers, at 63 Grafton Street, buying fruit to add to the basket of delicacies he will send Molly Bloom, to sweeten her up for seduction.

> He turned suddenly from a chip of strawberries, drew a gold watch from his fob and held it at its chain's length.
> – Can you send them by tram? Now?
> A darkbacked figure under Merchant's arch scanned books on the hawker's car.
> – Certainly, sir. Is it in the city?
> – O, yes, Blazes Boylan said. Ten minutes.
> The blond girl handed him a docket and pencil.
> – Will you write the address, sir?
> Blazes Boylan at the counter wrote and pushed the docket to her.
> – Send it at once, will you? he said. It's for an invalid.
> – Yes, sir. I will, sir.[9]

The narrative catches a glimpse of what it would be impossible for anyone in Thornton's actually to see: the 'darkbacked figure' of Leopold Bloom scanning the books on display at a bookstall in Merchant's Arch, also in search of a present for Molly, as we discover in scene 10. We might want to regard the glimpse as an 'intercut': a cutaway to some other event happening at the same time in a different place.

D. W. Griffith's 'narrator system', given shape by the Biograph films of 1908 to 1913, and further developed in features such as *Judith of Bethulia* (1914), *The Birth of a Nation* (1915), *Intolerance* (1916), *Broken Blossoms* (1919), and *Way Down East* (1920), was the most widely known and most powerful model of montage practice available at the time when Joyce was writing *Ulysses*. As we have seen, the narrator system produced a new articulation of time and space (in the cross-cut race to the rescue), a new articulation of character (in the disclosure of feeling through the look 'over' the cut), and a new articulation of socio-economic disparity (in connections made without regard to diegesis). Is any of that what happens in 'Wandering Rocks'?

The race to the rescue traditionally cross-cuts between victim, assailant (or assailants), and overdue liberator. Will the liberator, hurtling through billows of dust along obstacle-strewn highways, reach the barricaded victim before the assailants do untold damage to her? Like the *Odyssey*, *Ulysses* has something of the race to the rescue about it, of course. Will Odysseus reach Ithaca before Penelope succumbs to one or other of her suitors? In the fifth scene of 'Wandering Rocks', Bloom and Boylan, both a long way from Ithaca, each buying a present for Molly, each with Molly very much on his mind, are engaged in a race to the rescue. The scene ends with Boylan asking the shop-girl if he can use the telephone, an instrument frequently employed in races to the rescue. Indeed, it has been said that the telephone, which connects two places at one time, provided film-makers with a model for certain kinds of montage practice.[10] But Boylan will not call Molly, when he gets to the phone; while Bloom has no intention of returning to Eccles Street to confront him (quite the reverse).

The purpose of parallel editing was to establish beyond doubt the significance of certain selected actions of certain selected protagonists. It abstracts those actions from their milieux (from any milieu), and sets them exclusively in relation to one another. 'Wandering Rocks' does establish beyond doubt the significance of actions undertaken by Boylan and Bloom with Molly very much in view. And, as parallel editing would require, we do catch further glimpses of Bloom at the bookstall, in scenes 9 and 10; and of Boylan, an anticipatory red carnation between his teeth, in scenes 18 and 19. But these actions are never abstracted from their milieux and set exclusively in relation to one another. Thus, it would make no sense to say of Bloom, as it is necessary to say of the husband in *The Lonely Villa*, or John Davis in *After Many Years*, that his only function is to go away, and then come back again. Even the one-dimensional Blazes Boylan exists in relation to events other than his forthcoming seduction of Molly. Nor does the narrative space defined by 'Wandering Rocks', like that defined in the Biograph races to the rescue, become a zone which assailant and liberator pass through on their way to where the 'victim' (hard to conceive her as such) awaits them. Dublin itself is the main 'character' in 'Wandering Rocks'. The schema Joyce drew up for Carlo Linati in 1920 lists as personae not figures from the *Odyssey*, but rather 'Objects, Places, Forces'. The episode's 'sense', Linati was told, is 'The Hostile Milieu'.[11] Joyce might just conceivably have planted a joke about races to the rescue in 'Wandering Rocks'. But its scenes have not been parallel edited through interpolation in order to generate suspense.

I have so far made rather heavy weather of rebutting claims to discern montage-effects in *Ulysses*. But I feel that the weakness of such claims lies in their failure to specify how montage was used in cinema, and for what purposes, at the time of writing.[12] As far as I am aware, it has yet to be shown convincingly that Joyce used montage techniques either to generate suspense, or to reveal character, or to establish socio-economic disparity. There were of course other uses to which montage was put, in the cinema of the period, whose potential interest to Joyce scholarship may eventually establish. It could also be said that in 'Wandering Rocks' Joyce *anticipated* Eisenstein (though not, surely, Eisenstein's characteristic abstraction).[13] What we cannot say, as things stand, is that montage techniques informed the episode's conception and design. A knowledge of those techniques tells us nothing about the episode's specificity as literature, about the pressures shaping it from within and without. I want now to explore that specificity, by devoting attention to preoccupations and techniques evident not in films exhibited in the 1920s (and the theory behind them), or in films exhibited in 1909, when Joyce briefly ran the Cinematograph Volta,[14] but in films Dubliners could actually have seen in 1904.

Objects, places, forces

The first six episodes of *Ulysses* were written in what Joyce called, in a letter of 1919 to Harriet Shaw Weaver, an 'initial style': they combine third-person, past-tense depiction of events with first-person present-tense enactment of stream of consciousness, and with dialogue.[15] Despite considerable disruption, the initial style survives more or less intact through the next three episodes ('Aeolus', 'Lestrygonians', 'Scylla and Charybdis'); which brings us to the end of what Joyce at one time thought of as the novel's first part. Indeed, the initial style just about survives the tenth episode, 'Wandering Rocks'; but not the eleventh, 'Sirens'. 'Wandering Rocks' was apparently an addition to plans which had seemed firm as late as May 1918.[16] Its eighteen scenes plus a coda sit somewhat uneasily at the centre of the novel's eighteen episodes; they belong neither to the naturalism of its first part, nor to the wholesale experimentation of the second. There is no equivalent adventure in Homer. Odysseus had avoided the Wandering Rocks – that 'Shifting labyrinth between two shores', as the Linati scheme has it – by navigating instead between Scylla and Charybdis.

Stephen Dedalus and Leopold Bloom, with whose thoughts and feelings the initial style has made us astonishingly intimate, do put in an appearance, but not yet in conjunction, and to little local effect. The initial style has somehow mislaid them. It has forgotten about the epic adventure whose resolution will be their coming together. It loses them in a crowd of Dubliners, some of whom have thoughts and feelings with which we become momentarily intimate. These Dubliners do come together, at random, or in pursuit of business or pleasure, but it is the fact of the city, of the city's layout, routines, and ceremonies, rather than the teleology of any adventure they are engaged in, which brings them into relation with one another.

Those wholly lost in the crowd have by that very fact been placed beyond the reach of montage. They do not possess a significance for each other which parallel editing or any other technique could bring out. Early film-makers devised various methods for the extraction of significance from busy scenes.[17] But they may also have felt a certain residual affinity for crowdedness, and what gets lost in it (or emerges momentarily from its depths, only to sink back again). Noël Burch has argued that many of the films made in the major producing countries before 1914 required the kind of 'topographical' inspection which gathers up sets of visual data from 'all corners of the screen' in their quasi-simultaneity, without troubling to distinguish between what contributes to the development of a narrative and what doesn't.[18] This affinity for the throng – for a rhythm of emergence and abrupt dwindling – found expression in some rather unexpected places. Eisenstein, as we have already seen, broke off from an essay in praise of Griffith as the first major exponent of montage in order to recall the passer-by in *Intolerance*: a tall bearded man in a bowler hat who suddenly materialises on the sidewalk (and in the film), thrusting himself between the young man and woman who have fallen into conversation, before striding off down the street (and out of the film). Eisenstein remembered the man's face as mask-like, and he does indeed glare ferociously at no one and nothing in particular. The glimpse identifies the city as a 'hostile milieu'.

That milieu stands forth in the prominence given in 'Wandering Rocks' to figures with no part at all to play in the odyssean adventure. 'Cashel Boyle O'Connor Fitzmaurice Tisdall Farrell, murmuring, glassyeyed, strode past the Kildare street club' (p. 235). We have already encountered Farrell, in 'Lestrygonians', where Bloom, chatting to Mrs Breen, advises her to stand smartly aside:

> – Mind! Let this man pass.
> A bony form strode along the curbstone from the river, staring with a rapt gaze into the sunlight through a heavy stringed glass. Tight as a skullpiece a tiny hat gripped his head. From his arm a folded dustcoat, a stick and an umbrella dangled to his stride.
> – Watch him, Mr Bloom said. He always walks outside the lampposts. Watch! (pp. 151–2)

We don't see enough of Griffith's rapt gazer, in *Intolerance*, to know whether or not he takes a similar view of lamp-posts; he looks like the kind of person who would. In scene 17 of 'Wandering Rocks', Farrell strides up and down the north side of Merrior Square, and then into Clare Street:

> As he strode past Mr Bloom's dental windows the sway of his dustcoat brushed rudely from its angle a slender tapping cane and swept onwards,

having buffeted a thewless body. The blind stripling turned his sickly face
after the striding form.
  – God's curse on you, he said sourly, whoever you are! You're blinder nor I
am, you bitch's bastard! (p. 240)

In *Intolerance*, the young man similarly turns to look after the striding form
which has just buffeted him, in anger or amazement, but does not appear to
find a sour rebuke to match the stripling's. What the rebuke brings out is a
certain blindness or vacancy integral to the malevolence with which these
passers-by address themselves to the task of routine circumnavigation. Each
could be regarded as a 'force' rather than a character. Their force is the force
of the city: of the latitude the city gives, by sheer size and complication, to
chance. For chance is never not brusque, in one way or another.

That brusqueness seems to recall, and might possibly even allude to, the
emphasis on movement in the first films. The city streets had always been,
for film-makers, the main primary source of the movement which was the
new medium's primary topic. Maxim Gorky first saw the Lumière
actualities at a variety show in Nizhni Novgorod in 1896.

> Carriages coming from somewhere in the perspective of the picture are
> moving straight at you, into the darkness in which you sit; somewhere from
> afar people appear and loom larger as they come closer to you; in the
> foreground children are playing with a dog, bicyclists tear along, and
> pedestrians cross the street picking their way among the carriages. All this
> moves, teems with life and, upon approaching the edge of the screen, vanishes
> somewhere beyond it.[19]

Gorky can feel satisfied that the image on the screen teems with life because
it is replete, everywhere, and for the full fifty seconds, with movement.
Previous visual technologies such as the zoetrope and the phenakistoscope
had put movement on display. What struck commentators on the
cinematographic image most forcefully was at once the quantity and the
apparent arbitrariness of the comings and goings it had somehow found a
way to accommodate.[20] All that these comings and goings are required to
do is to take place. They are not required to be meaningful in any very
obvious way (for example, by taking shape as a narrative).

This lack of meaning could have proved, and evidently did prove, a
problem. What would an audience find in a film to amuse and instruct it
once the thrill of so much random movement had worn off? Fortunately,
there was from the beginning one very obvious way in which the image on
the screen might be rendered meaningful. Cinema spread rapidly across the
globe, in the second half of the 1890s; but the key to its seemingly limitless
appeal was the reinvention of localism. The Lumière machine was both
projector and camera. Everywhere the cameramen went, they filmed in the
locality, in the expectation that the locals would duly pay good money to
witness themselves on screen. Exhibitors throughout the world relied on the

potential overlap between the people in front of the camera and the people in front of the screen. Thus, when the Edison Company filmed in Harrisburg, Pennsylvania, in December 1896, the local paper remarked sagely that it would no doubt prove 'strange and novel' for townspeople to 'see themselves pictured the same as in everyday life'; and that they would be able to recognise 'many a well-known personage'.[21]

In Britain, the vogue for local films began in earnest in 1900.[22] 'The most popular Cinematograph Film in a Travelling Show', a 1901 advertisement for the Cecil Hepworth Company claimed, 'is ALWAYS A LOCAL PICTURE containing Portraits which can be recognised.' A film showing workers leaving a factory would always prove far more popular in the town in which it was shot, the advertisement went on, than the 'most exciting picture ever produced'.[23] The vogue for local films lasted until the First World War. In 1912, a standard work on cinema management stated that there could be no two opinions as to the value of such films as a way to fill a hall or a theatre. 'Everyone loves to see himself, or herself, or friends, or children, on the screen.'[24] Recognition, then, was one way in which the movement made visible by the moving image might also be made meaningful. 'Viewer and film', as Tom Gunning puts it, 'share a dialogic relation.'[25] The larger the group of people filmed, of course, the larger the potential audience. So it came about that cameras were forever being positioned outside factory gates.

On 17 April 1896, the *Freeman's Journal* announced a forthcoming exhibition of the 'greatest, most amazing and grandest novelty ever presented in Dublin: The Cinématographe'. Three days later, the cinema arrived in Ireland. The first series of shows, using equipment and films from London's Empire Palace, at Dan Lowrey's Star of Erin Theatre of Varieties, lasted a week. There were severe technical problems. Lowrey arranged for Felicien Trewey, the Lumières' agent in Britain, to bring his apparatus to the Star of Erin, at a cost of £70 a week. Trewey himself acted as operator. The next series of shows, beginning on 29 October, proved an unequivocal success. The run continued until 14 November, with new films brought in for the final week.

As in Paris, and subsequently in London and elsewhere, the film which most impressed the punters was an actuality made in 1895, *Arrival of a Train at La Ciotat Station*. 'To those who witness the exhibition for the first time', the *Freeman's Journal* reported,

> the effect is startling. The figures are thrown upon a screen erected in front of the audience and, taking one of the scenes depicted – that of a very busy Railway Terminus into which the locomotive and a number of carriages dash with great rapidity – the effect is so realistic that for the moment one is almost apt to forget that the representation is artificial. When the train comes to a standstill the passengers are seen hurrying out of the carriages, bearing their luggage, the greetings between themselves and their friends are all represented perfectly true to life and the scene is an exact reproduction of

the life and the bustle and tumult to be witnessed at the great Railway depots of the world.[26]

Cinema had arrived with a flourish. In January 1897, a further run of Lumière actualities at the Star of Erin apparently filled the house to suffocation. There followed six weeks of Professor Jolly's 'Animated Photographs' of local subjects such as traffic on Carlisle Bridge and the 13th Hussars marching through the city. Lowrey reopened the Star of Erin as the Empire Palace, on 13 November 1897, with Lumière actualities again topping the bill. Before long, films were being exhibited throughout Ireland, in variety theatres, in town and village halls, and at fairgrounds.[27] In 'Wandering Rocks', Lenehan and M'Coy stroll down Sycamore Street beside 'Dan Lowry's musichall', more commonly known as the Empire Palace (p. 223).

The first Lumière films of Dublin were made in 1897 by Alexandre Promio. Promio filmed the Hussars exercising and the fire brigade in action. A wonderful street-scene, shot from the north end of O'Connell Bridge looking up Sackville Street towards the statue of Nelson, also survives. As it opens, vehicles including a horse-drawn buggy and a strange mobile box covered in advertisements, manoeuvre (possibly on the cameraman's instructions) in the foreground. Traffic of all kinds provides the requisite 'bustle and tumult'. The passage of a woman cyclist, conspicuous in a white blouse, threads through the scene. Entering from the right foreground, she merges into the traffic, then, as the scene gradually empties, reappears again in the distance. Sackville Street is the setting for events in 'Aeolus' and 'Lestrygonians'. In 'Wandering Rocks', O'Connell Bridge is where 'many persons' observe the 'grave deportment and gay apparel' of Mr Dennis J. Maginni, professor of dancing (p. 226).

In 1901 and 1902, the Blackburn firm run by Sagar Mitchell and James Kenyon, many of whose films have recently been restored to remarkable effect by the National Film and Television Archive, made several Irish actualities for Ralph Pringle, of the North American Animated Photo Company. Pringle included these actualities in an exhibition held in the Antient Concert Rooms in Great Brunswick Street, in Dublin, between 22 December 1902 and 10 January 1903. Among them was a series of films of congregations leaving churches, advertised as *Living Dublin*. Two of these survive: *Congregation Leaving St Mary's Pro-Cathedral* and *Congregation Leaving Jesuit Church of St Francis Xavier* (both 1902). Crowds leaving church were almost as popular among film-makers as crowds leaving factories, and for the same reason: they constituted both topic and audience.[28] The Mitchell and Kenyon films were shot from a raised position opposite the main entrance to each church. People pour out of the building, and down the steps beneath the camera, often pausing to gaze at it, and thus register their presence. The films have no scenic or topical interest, indeed no interest at all beyond the rather limited opportunities they afford for recognition.

One of them, however, does provide an indication of the way in which circles of mutual acquaintance may have overlapped, in Dublin in the 1900s, so that a person in one became a personage in others. In *Congregation Leaving Jesuit Church of St Francis Xavier*, there is a poster on the wall of the church, just about discernible through the crowd. The poster advises that the annual charity sermon in aid of the Convent of Our Lady of Charity, St Mary's Asylum, High Park, Drumcondra, will be given in St Francis Xavier's Church, on 11 January 1903, by the Revd J. Conmee, SJ.[29] Shown at the Antient Concert Rooms on 2 December 1902 and 10 January 1903, the film may well have helped to advertise the sermon. In the 'Lotus-Eaters' episode of *Ulysses*, Leopold Bloom, entering All Hallows, pauses to inspect a notice pinned to the door. 'Sermon by the very reverend John Conmee S.J. on saint Peter Claver and the African mission' (p. 77). The man clearly put himself about a bit. Conmee is the main protagonist in the first scene of 'Wandering Rocks' (pp. 210–15).

Ulysses resembles the films in the *Living Dublin* series to the extent that some readers might once have read it for the pleasure of reading, if not about themselves, then about people known to them, in person or as a personage, or about familiar places and familiar activities. Joyce made no attempt to reproduce the effect of these films in his novel. But he may well have taken an interest in them as a phemonenon. Cecil Hepworth described how he would arrange for an assistant with a stopwatch to time the event he was filming, so that he could judge when it was likely to end, and adjust the rate at which he cranked the camera accordingly.[30] Joyce, as Hugh Kenner puts it, gave 'Wandering Rocks' over to 'a narrator whose grim delight is to monitor with clock and map the space–time whereabouts of more than thirty characters simultaneously'.[31] In the novel, of course, unlike the *Living Dublin* actualities, the person with the stopwatch and the map is as much of a device as the events he thus keeps an eye on. The purposes of that device may have included an exposure of the conventions which precariously held in place the actuality's appearance of bustle and tumult.

That appearance would only accomplish its effect of bustle and tumult if the spectator could be relied upon to respond as though she or he were present at the scene itself, standing where the camera had once stood. The image had to be read, James Lastra observes, as the 'record of an experience of vision'. We don't just view (a part of) the world; we view the world viewed in a particular place at a particular time. It is the frame, Lastra argues, in cinema as in still photography, which validates the image as the record of an experience of vision. The frame enables. It serves as an index of the act of witnessing, because it presupposes a viewer who views the world represented from a place which is part of that world, which only exists in relation to it.[32] But the frame also *dis*ables, because it permits us to see only as a machine sees, not as we would have seen had we in fact been there, a part of that world. There is in fact little, in many of these local films, to interest anyone who fails to spot a familiar face. Even if we do see someone we know, we don't see them, and therefore don't know them, as we would have done had we been there, standing where the camera once stood. What the actuality as a form had somehow to conceal, with the meagre resources at its disposal, was the double absence which constitutes the cinematic image: of human agency, from its capture; and of the viewer, from the scene viewed. The first actualities exemplify Christian Metz's observation that in cinema the self-dramatising participant and the viewer–voyeur are condemned perpetually to 'miss' one another.[33]

The reason why the arrival of trains at stations rapidly became such a popular subject with film-makers may have been that the scene overcame at the level of content a problem which remained insoluble, prior to the establishment of the classical continuity system, at the level of form. The greetings exchanged between the passengers and their friends *performed* the act of mutual recognition upon which exhibitors were relying to connect audience and scene. It was because *Arrival of a Train at La Ciotat Station* had represented the exchange of greetings that the *Freeman's Journal* could describe it as an 'exact reproduction of the life and the bustle and tumult to be witnessed at the great Railway depots of the world'. The exchange enacts the 'dialogic relation' which ought in theory to obtain between any audience and any view. More generally, the exhibitionism prevalent in actualities could be understood as the performance of an ideal dialogic relation.[34] The participants know perfectly well that they themselves are not just an attraction, as they stare at the camera, or tip their hats to it, or wave, but the substance of cinema's contract with its audience.

No performance of an exchange of greetings, however vivid, could conceal completely the lapse in time and space between the image's capture and its reproduction on the screen. Writing in the *New Review* in February 1896, O. Winter struck a more sceptical note, with regard to such scenes, than the contributor to the *Freeman's Journal*. 'If you and I meet an arriving train,' Winter wrote,

> we either compose the scattered elements into a simple picture, and with the directness distinguishing the human vision from the photographic lens, reject the countless details which hamper and confuse our composition, or we stand on the platform eager to recognise a familiar face. The rest of the throng, hastily scanned, falls into a shadowy background.

The camera, by contrast, neither composes a picture nor singles out a known face. It is forced, Winter went on, 'to render every incident at the same pace and with the same prominence, only reserving to itself the monstrous privilege of enlarging the foreground'. 'We cannot follow the shadows in their enthusiasm of recognition.'[35] The automatism of the photographic image brings home to us the double absence from its capture of human instrumentality and of an immediate audience. Hence the emphasis, in some of the commentaries, on the ghostliness of that capture.

'Their smiles are lifeless', Gorky said of the people in the Lumière actualities, 'although their movements are full of living energy and are so swift as to be almost imperceptible.'[36]

If the exchange of greetings at a railway station could not be relied upon to counteract performatively the essential ghostliness of the spectacle, then some other ceremony would have to be found. One reason why parades and processions became so popular as an actuality topic was that the ceremony constituting them was already a performance, with all the parts assigned. What had to be performed, furthermore, was not the haphazard mutual recognition of one person by another, but, more reliably, the mutual acknowledgement on both sides of official status (as monarch and subject, Lord Mayor and citizen, May Queen and fan).[37] The focus of any parade or procession is precisely that interactive co-presence of performer and audience missing from the image's mechanical reproduction. If Mr May, in Lawrence's *The Lost Girl*, had been able to commission a film of the Natcha-Kee-Tawara parading down the main street of Woodhouse in full Red Indian kit, he might perhaps have become a convert to cinema.

Cecil Hepworth was one of a number of film-makers to chronicle Queen Victoria's visit to Dublin in 1900, an event alluded to in 'Wandering Rocks' (p. 244). He filmed her progress through central Dublin in an open carriage from a variety of positions within the enthusiastic crowd lining the streets. There is an ample display of interactive co-presence, as the monarch graciously acknowledges the tribute paid by her loyal subjects in a constant flutter of hats and handkerchiefs. Hepworth included this footage in a 1922 compilation, *Through Three Reigns*. 'There was an Irish Question twenty-two years ago,' an intertitle informs us, 'but when Queen Victoria visited "Dublin's Fair City" the loyal Irish gave her a wondrous welcome.' An equally loyal (British or Irish) cinema audience might well have felt itself transported, by the ceremony's staging of interactive co-presence, to that other place and time of the image's original capture.

It was no coincidence, I would suggest, that Joyce chose to begin 'Wandering Rocks' with Father Conmee receiving (up to a point) the recognition due to a local personage, and end it with the Viceroy and his party receiving (up to a point) the acknowledgement due to the status of Her Majesty's representative in Ireland. The choice indicates that Joyce shared the actuality-makers' concern with the loss of interactive co-presence: a loss as necessary to the mechanically reproduced text as it was to the mechanically reproduced image. For it is not just Dublin which became for the first time the focus of an episode, in 'Wandering Rocks', but, as Hans Walter Gabler has pointed out, the text itself as text. Since 'Wandering Rocks' has no equivalent in the *Odyssey*, its 'substratum' or 'reference base' at any particular moment can only ever be actions described elsewhere in the episode or in the novel as a whole.[38] The episode's coda, which recapitulates the viceregal cavalcade's progress through central Dublin, quite literally takes apart the ceremony of mutual acknowledgement which the actuality-makers relied on to recreate the liveness of a live event.

To a large extent, this anatomisation could be understood as literature's revenge on the blandness of ceremonies of mutual acknowledgement, in life or on film. The range of attitudes shown to the Viceroy and his entourage by characters already well established in the narrative, such as Thomas Kernan, Simon Dedalus, Buck Mulligan, and Blazes Boylan, shows us at the same time what the novel as a form could do to complicate the picture of a 'wondrous welcome' for British rule. Even more thoroughly immunised from wondrous welcome are those characters whose various self-absorptions have been given, in a manner unique to *Ulysses*, a style of their own. 'From Cahill's corner the reverend Hugh C. Love, M.A., made obeisance unperceived, mindful of lords deputies whose hands benignant had held of yore rich advowsons' (p. 242). As all these characters and more rehearse their distinguishing self-absorptions, in a collective gesture which falls well short of full acknowledgement of the Viceroy's social and political status, so the novel rehearses its own methods. The coda to 'Wandering Rocks' is for the most part automatised initial style. The literary machine which turns out the clause heralding Boylan's appearance in it – 'By the provost's wall came jauntily Blazes Boylan . . .' (p. 243) – is quite clearly the same machine as turned out the clause heralding Bloom's appearance in 'Lotus Eaters': 'By lorries along sir John Rogerson's quay Mr Bloom walked soberly . . .' (p. 68). When the writing does depart from the initial style, it is only to announce its own imminent transformation into *écriture*, by previewing future episodes, future styles. 'Above the crossblind of the Ormond Hotel, gold by bronze, Miss Kennedy's head by Miss Douce's head watched and admired' (p. 242).

There is also, however, in this section, a strain of visual automatism: a resolve to view the scene as a machine would view it, without reference to any organising or participant consciousness. This machine cannot distinguish, as a human observer most certainly would have done, between the animate and the inanimate. Thus, the Viceroy finds himself saluted enthusiastically not only by the Queen's loyal subjects, but by the images on hoardings, a schoolboy's upstart collar, and the liquid sewage oozing out of a sluice into the Liffey. All these (non-)gestures have to be taken into account. At the same time, a person's intentions towards the implied observer, or towards the spectacle unfolding before them both, are no longer a guide to what might be thought worth describing in his or her behaviour.

> John Henry Menton, filling the doorway of Commercial Buildings, stared from winebig oyster eyes, holding a fat gold hunter watch not looked at in his fat left hand not feeling it. (p. 243)

The watch exists for us by its absence from its owner's consciousness. A human observer, standing where the implied narrator stood, and caught up in the miniature drama of Menton's response to the cavalcade, would not have thought it worth mentioning. The Joycean machine does. Novels do not ordinarily attend to the intensity with which a character does not see or feel what he holds in his hand. Modernist writing, as Garrett Stewart would say, has revealed itself as neither impressionist nor expressive, but rather 'in some new way strictly technical, a prosthesis of observation in the mode of inscription'.[39]

In these moments of visual automatism, Joyce fashions something very like an actuality, but with the performance of mutual recognition or mutual acknowledgement which ought to cover over the lapse in time and space between production and reproduction of the image unpicked. The smiles on the faces of the Dubliners saluting the cavalcade are as lifeless as those Gorky saw on the faces of the people in the first Lumière actualities, even though their movements, too, are full of living energy. We cannot follow the shadows, Winter might have said of this scene, in their enthusiasm of recognition and acknowledgement. Among them, appropriately enough, is Cashel Boyle O'Connor Fitzmaurice Tisdall Farrell, his gaze furiously blank, like that of Griffith's projectile passer-by, who 'stared through a fierce eyeglass across the carriages at the head of Mr M. E. Solomons in the window of the Austro-Hungarian viceconsulate' (p. 244). The machine cannot not record that ghostly appearance of a gaze, little though it has to do with enthusiasm of any kind. Joyce's visual automatism has reproduced, in its own writerly terms, film's original neutrality as a medium.

I hope I have done enough to suggest that a knowledge of films of the *Living Dublin* kind can illuminate some at least of the scenes which compose 'Wandering Rocks'. One way to think about the elaborate failed ceremonies which begin and end 'Wandering Rocks' might be as a burlesque of the ceremonies of recognition and acknowledgement which gave shape to the kind of film Dubliners were most likely to see, in Dublin, in 1904. But I have not yet been able to address the issue of the interpolations – or 'intercuts', as montage theorists would have it – which structure the episode as a whole. The issue needs to be addressed, first of all, in terms of the individual section, or scene. What is Leopold Bloom doing in the middle of Boylan's purchases in Thornton's? My answer to that question will involve an excursus into the history of what happened to film's neutrality as a medium once cinema became a narrative art.

Mechanical vision

'Shifting labyrinth between two shores', the Linati schema has under 'Technic' for 'Wandering Rocks'. It is hard enough to discern the structure in the most stable and composed of labyrinths, of course, never mind one which won't keep still. The Lumières knew this. Their films set a labyrinth to catch a labyrinth: a framing of the image which allows, as Noël Burch puts it, 'ample space for the development of the action in all directions'.

However, that broad tolerance (that affinity with the throng) was in its own way methodical. According to Burch, indeed, it reveals a 'quasi-scientific attitude'. In a Lumière actuality, he says, the scene unfolds before the camera 'rather like the behaviour of a micro-organism under the biologist's microscope or the movement of the stars at the end of the astronomer's telescope'.[40] Something similar could be said of the scenes which make up 'Wandering Rocks'. And yet the episode's 'Technic' is an automatism which would appear to stretch or to distort, rather than merely to confirm, the rhythm of emergence and abrupt dwindling which structures the Lumière actualities.

The basic unit (indeed the sole unit) of the actuality is the *tableau*. Early French film catalogues use 'tableau' in a sense corresponding more or less to the modern 'shot', and the term has been translated into English as 'scene'. Modern film historians use it to refer to a type of shot (the centred axial long shot, looking at a scene as if at a box set on stage from the centre of the theatre stalls), and to a type of construction based on that shot.[41] Burch speaks of the tableau's 'rigorous frontality'.[42] It consisted of everything which took place in front of the camera until the film ran out. But the technological limitation of early cinema was always already a principle. Because each tableau had its own completeness, which was the completeness of the activities represented, understood as 'life itself', it should under no circumstances be interfered with. No attempt was to be made to cut into it, to dissect it, to take it apart and put it back together again; or to link it with other scenes, and thus declare it incomplete, a mere fragment. Stephen Heath notes the tableau's 'particular fixity', Burch its 'autarchy' (its despotism).[43] That despotism was a declaration of the medium's neutrality as a medium.

The structure of the tableau survived the development of a narrative cinema which set one scene next to another in a syntagmatic chain. The first multi-shot narrative films, from around 1903, were chase films. It was a convention of these chase films that each shot should be held until all the participants, however many of them there might be, had finally disappeared from view. There was to be no stinting on action, on sheer visibility. Every available burglar and policeman passes sweatily through the shot, and away. In fact, the shot is usually held for an instant *after* the participants have all disappeared from view. During that instant, the camera gazes at nothing, or next to nothing: at 'white space'. Actualities are sometimes empty of people, for an instant, until the development of the action in all directions supplies a filler or two. There the automatism is, however, for the most part, of too much. In the chase films, by contrast, it is of too little: the gaze at or into nothing, which no human observer, determined to keep up with the pursuit, would have held for an instant.

The general view is that the establishment in the period 1908–1917 of the 'classical continuity system' put a stop at once to the too much and to the too little through which cinema had been exposed as a machine's-eye view of the world.[44] To begin with, the term 'continuity' designated any effort made to smooth the flow of the narrative. It came to refer to a specific set of guidelines for cutting shots together, whether by scene dissection or by montage. Continuity editing made it possible for the first time to situate the spectator at the optimum viewpoint in each shot, and to keep that viewpoint on the move as the story developed. According to Burch, it ensured 'identification of the spectator-subject with the viewpoint of a mobile camera'.[45] The optimum viewpoint is not that from which an action can be seen in its entirety, but that from which it can be understood in its essence. The first films had been all about seeing an action in its entirety, or near-entirety: the too little as well as the too much. The classical continuity system found all sorts of ways to rule out such excesses of presence- or absence-effect (excesses which made visible, as it were, the lapse in time and space between image and viewing). The 'cut-on-action', for example, which interrupts the perception of an event in order to generate suspense, eliminated the 'white space' surrounding entrances and exits in the early chase films. I want to argue, however, that during and after the establishment of the continuity system, film-makers both within and beyond what one might think of as mainstream or mass-market cinema continued to develop forms of automatic vision which widen rather than conceal the lapse in time and space between image and viewing. They did so, I think, by moving the camera in a particular way.

Panning shots were fairly well established in actualities by 1900, and in dramatic films by 1905: in both cases, their primary function was to keep action within the frame.[46] Tracking shots began as soon as someone mounted a camera on a train; or, in the case of the Lumière actualities shot in Venice, a gondola.[47] In 1904, Hale's Tours made the link explicit by using a railway carriage as a movie theatre, with the audience in raked passenger seats and a screen in place of the view out of the front window. The theatre-carriage shook convincingly as shots taken from a train's cowcatcher were projected on the screen.[48] The purpose of such simulations, and of the relatively rare tracks-in in dramatic films of the period, was, as Burch puts it, to invite the viewer across the threshold into the scene (to cover over his or her absence from it).[49] By 1911, when Hale's Tours closed down, other kinds of invitation had become standard issue: notably close-ups and montage. On the whole, though, with the exception of tracking shots on a chase and the like, camera movement remained a relatively small part of the stylistic repertoire, at least in Hollywood, until late in the silent era.[50]

Indeed, film-makers in the silent era distinguished quite explicitly between tracking shots which follow people around, in some way, with the camera on a carriage moving beside or in front of them, or on a vehicle moving beside or in front of another vehicle containing them; and those in which the camera moves in relation to a static or partly static scene. During this period, the latter would almost invariably have been condemned for drawing attention to the act, or the techniques, of filming.[51] Hence, no doubt, their rarity.

Significant use of lengthy tracking shots on a static or partly static scene began with Giovanni Pastrone's *Cabiria*, in 1914. So great was the reputation of this film that the tracking shot on a static or partly static scene became known as a 'Cabiria movement'. Their primary function was to make the best possible use of the vast three-dimensional sets built at the Italia Company's studios in Turin. Pastrone said that he had sought to heighten yet further the impression of relief by installing curved rather than straight tracks.[52] Such movements were often regarded as an alteration to the world in view rather than to the method of viewing it. 'Scenes are slowly brought to the foreground or moved from side to side,' reported the *New York Dramatic Mirror* on 13 May 1914, 'quite as though they were being played on a movable stage.' By this method full value could be given to deep sets; and, more importantly, characters 'brought close' to the audience 'without any break'.[53] These tracking shots were understood as a subtly disguised invitation across the threshold.

They have, as Barry Salt puts it, an 'intensifying function'.[54] They do not simply bring the characters close to the audience without any break. They are often wonderfully expressive. They capture the feeling immanent in the narrative space they describe. I'm thinking in particular of a scene in *Cabiria* in which the Roman hero Fulvius Axilla and his faithful sidekick, the strongman Maciste, having rescued the child Cabiria from the high priests of Moloch, conceal her in the attic of an inn in Carthage. Fulvius is asleep on a bed at the left of the frame, while on the right Maciste has Cabiria on his knee, and mends her clothing. As Fulvius gets up and moves towards a shuttered window in the centre of the back wall, the camera tracks to the right around a post in the centre of the room, to move in on Maciste and Cabiria (he is now combing her hair). Fulvius is at this point concealed behind Maciste and Cabiria, but the camera moves beyond them to bring him into view, peering out through a gap in the shutter, and a trap-door, where it halts. The trap-door is raised: the innkeeper has brought food and drink, and after a brief altercation climbs up into the room. As the innkeeper moves off to the left, the camera tracks back and to the left, around the central post, to resume its original position. This scene could perfectly well have been shot from a static camera: there is no need (or almost no need) for the camera to move at all. But the gentle curving movement forward throws a watchful embrace around the anxious care the two men have bestowed on the child. It beautifully expresses tenderness. Indeed, it *is* tender: the care taken to shoot the scene in this particular way enacts the care Fulvia and Maciste have bestowed and will continue to bestow on Cabiria. The characters have been brought close to us in a more than physical sense.

My point is that tracking shots towards or away from a person or an object were no sooner in use than they became expressive in a variety of ways. The same could not be said of another kind of tracking shot to be found here and there in early cinema: the lateral movement sideways across a static or partly static scene. Like the track-in and the track-out, the lateral track had an antecedent in actualities shot from a train; with the camera positioned at the window of one of the carriages, rather than on the cowcatcher or in the guard's van. It was this effect of movement *across*, of traversal, which particularly fascinated film-makers: an effect at its most acute with the camera kept at (more or less) a 90-degree angle to the scene. The lateral tracking shot thus maintains the 'rigorous frontality' of the tableau; or extends it sideways.

Such shots are an extreme rarity in *Cabiria*, and they have no obvious expressive function. On one occasion, Fulvius and the innkeeper come out through the door of the inn and turn to their left (our right). The camera pans to keep them in view, and tilts, so that we only see them from the waist down, and then, in excess of any narrative obligation, tracks to the right. All the additional movement reveals is a stretch of paved road, as the lower halves of the two characters dwindle further and further into the distance: 'white space', in short. The emptiness on which the shot concludes, like that incorporated into successive shots in the chase films, speaks only of automatism: the camera's inveterate attentiveness to something in the scene which a human observer would almost certainly remain unaware of.

The lateral tracking shot is the least anthropomorphic of camera movements: human beings do not ordinarily move sidewards while looking to the front. We think of a tilt or pan as comparable to the turning (up or down, right or left) of a person's head.[55] By contrast, the term used to describe a lateral track – crabbing – rather significantly lacks any reference to the human. It's often a virtuoso movement (this, we think, is something the director has called for); and to that extent draws attention to itself. But what it draws attention to, in the final analysis, is not so much the skill and imagination with which it has been accomplished as the camera's status as a machine. It *expresses* little or nothing because it expresses a machine (a machine's movement, a machine's-eye view). At issue here is a fundamental departure from the human (from the way in which human beings see the world). 'Whenever camera movements depart from "natural" lines of sight or of movement,' Raymond Durgnat remarks in the course of a discussion of films by René Clair and Max Ophuls, 'the spectator becomes vaguely conscious of a certain uneasiness, or of exhilaration.'[56] Tracks in and out often produce exhilaration. Uneasiness is more likely to attend the crab-like deviation from natural lines of sight and movement which is the lateral tracking shot. Such shots might be thought to represent one of the ways in which cinema continued to work on its automatism.

To the best of my knowledge, the first significant lateral tracking shot in narrative cinema occurs in George Loane Tucker's *Traffic in Souls* (1913). It shows the villainous organisers of a vice ring, who have been brought to justice by the good work of the policeman hero and his adventurous fiancée, in their cells awaiting trial. *Traffic in Souls* was among the first feature-length films to be produced in America. Ben Brewster has argued that its 'transitional character' lies in 'the way it cobbles together available devices from one-reel cinema and elsewhere to construct something qualitatively new'.[57] The 'something qualitatively new' was a narrative film which went to great lengths to establish the plausibility of the coincidence (that the heroine should find employment as the villain's secretary) on which the plot turns. Among the 'devices' adapted from one-reel cinema is the quasi-documentary treatment of episodes of white slavery, including the abduction of Swedish immigrants fresh off the boat from Ellis Island, and, I think, the lateral track.

As Brewster points out, the function served by this solemn track along the line of villains is that of an emblematic shot. In its pure form, as in the medium close-up of a cowboy bandit pointing a gun straight at the camera which could be used either to begin or to end Edwin S. Porter's *The Great Train Robbery* (1903), the emblematic shot does not represent a development in the story, but rather indicates its theme or general nature. Brewster compares it to the opening and closing closer shots of the Lubin one-reeler *Bold Bank Robbery* (1904), which show the villains in a drawing-room in expensive suits and in gaol in convict garb respectively.[58] Like those shots, it is set apart (by the track rather than by a closer shot-scale), and it does indicate a theme: criminals brought to justice, or perhaps criminals brought to justice *by cinema itself*.[59] However, unlike them, it also constitutes a development in the story. It assembles the known villains, and readies them for justice (it is diegetically motivated). In that respect, it might be compared to what Tom Gunning calls the 'apotheosis endings' of films like the Pathé *A Policeman's Tour of the World* (a handshake between detective and thief, over an image of the globe around which their game of cat-and-mouse has taken them).[60] Except that it isn't an ending. Further sequences follow: the chief villain, released on bail, returns home to find his wife dead of a heart attack and his daughter driven mad by shame and grief; he himself, as we learn from an insert of a newspaper in a rubbish bin, subsequently commits suicide; and the detective asks his boss for leave to go on honeymoon.

The lateral track along the line of villains may well derive from the emblematic shot or the apotheosis, but it does not deliver the 'particular fixity' of tableau space which is the foundation of the allegorical meaning they propose. The shot's departure from natural lines of sight or of movement is a departure from, or one might even say *within*, allegorical meaning. In departing from natural lines of sight and movement, in departing from what might otherwise become allegory, the shot draws attention to two aspects of the no-longer-tableau space traversed. First, the space it creates is mechanically demarcated: a row of cells, with warders stationed at regular intervals between them for further emphasis. Secondly, the space contains a gap, or absence, at its centre: a single empty cell. The shot seems like a commentary on space, or on the ways in which space might be imagined, as well as on the nature and inevitability of justice. Lateral tracking shots extend the tableau's 'rigorous frontality' to one side or the other. But that movement somehow prises open the tableau (the continuity of space-time it manifests, its repletion with presence-effect) in the process of extending it. The lateral tracking shot should perhaps be considered as a dis-tension rather than an ex-tension of the tableau: a departure from it which pulls it sideways in order to reveal it as a mask. But to speak of it as an unmasking may be to attribute to it an expressive capacity it does not lay claim to, even in a film as dedicated to moral uplift as *Traffic in Souls*.

The traversal of a mechanically demarcated space, and the consequent revelation of a gap or absence within it, clearly distinguishes the lateral tracking shots in *Cabiria* and *Traffic in Souls* from the railway panoramas of the actuality-era. We have to do now not with the apparently artless capture of a succession of landmarks or scenic effects, but with an enquiry by mechanism into mechanism itself. Lateral tracking shots remained a rarity throughout the silent period. But the use to which they were put was, I hope to show, remarkably consistent. What follows is by no means an exhaustive survey of the lateral tracking shot in silent cinema. My aim, rather, is to explore the use to which the device was put in four exemplary films: Griffith's *Intolerance* (1916), Abel Gance's *Napoléon* (1927), King Vidor's *The Crowd* (1928), and Carl-Theodor Dreyer's *Vampyr* (1932). *Vampyr* is strictly speaking not a silent film, but it comes close to being silent, in accordance with the world it depicts; and it was conceived to some extent within the conventions of silent cinema.

Cabiria certainly left its mark on *Intolerance*, whose Babylonian scenes incorporate extravagant tracking and crane (or elevator) shots. Griffith seems to have kept something in reserve for 'Babylon's last bacchanal', a celebration which takes place shortly before the city is overwhelmed by Cyrus's army. As Karl Brown recalled, the scene began with a full shot of the entire set. The shot 'continued inward and downward, until it ended with a close-up of the king and his Princess Beloved admiring one another to the rhythm of our great crowd of dancing girls, dancing without music but in perfect cadence'.[61] The camera's movement is in fact inward, downward, and *across*, and includes a track to the right which follows the movements of some dancers who dance along the broad steps leading up into the temple. As far as I am aware, this is the only lateral tracking shot in *Intolerance* (though there are one or two pans which are quite hard to distinguish from tracks). Given that the shot lasts for rather less than ten seconds, it would be absurd to make great claims for its significance in relation to the film as a whole. But it is nonetheless worth noting that the steps along which the dancers dance are demarcated by vertical stripes. The dancers dance across, or against, that pattern. The fluidity of their movements is enhanced by the exactitude of a pattern it cannot altogether obliterate. The shot is, in its very small way, an enquiry into mechanism. To say that is already to risk saying too much about it.

The lateral tracking shot continued to crop up in films aspiring to the status of epic or historical saga.[62] Carl-Theodor Dreyer's *Leaves from Satan's Book* (1919), one of the longest silent films made in Denmark, emulates *Intolerance* in drawing parallels between stories set in four different historical epochs (the link being God's promise to Satan to lift a thousand years from his sentence for each soul he fails to seduce). At one point during the French Revolution episode, a lateral track follows Marie Antoinette as she is transferred from one prison to another. As David Bordwell has shown, Dreyer's early films are characterised by their construction of a shallow and consistently stable tableau space. 'Viewed as a long shot, usually from a straight-on angle, the tableau presents a unified, closed organization.' The shot which accompanies Marie Antoinette in her passage from one doorway to another simply extends the tableau, without in any way disrupting the spatial decorum it exemplifies.[63]

'Moving laterally and at a constant speed,' Bordwell remarks of this shot, 'Dreyer's camera will have none of the sudden flights of German or French Impressionist camera movement of the period.'[64] The shot is notable for happening at all. However, those 'sudden flights', in French and German cinema, were soon to create a new context for the use of the lateral tracking. According to Barry Salt, the initial *Cabiria*-induced enthusiasm did not last long. Not until 1923, and then only in France and Germany, was there a further 'explosion of camera mobility'. Salt singles out for mention a trilogy of films by Lupu Pick: *Scherben* (1921), *Sylvester* (1923), and *Der Letzte Mann* (1924).[65] In the event, of course, *Der Letzte Mann* (*The Last Laugh*) was to be directed not by Pick, but by F. W. Murnau. It does indeed contain some very inventive tracks on a more or less static scene. By the end of the silent era, then, crabbing was just one among a wide variety of 'flights' the camera might suddenly take, and indeed was expected to take. This new expectation provides the context for a more complex understanding of the aesthetic and political function of camera movement. It should be possible to say more about the function of the lateral tracking shots used by Gance, in *Napoléon*, and Vidor, in *The Crowd*, than it was about those used by Pastrone, Griffith, and Dreyer. Whereas Dreyer's shot preserves the tableau of which it is an extension, Gance and Vidor were determined to pull the tableau apart: to turn it inside out.

From the beginning of his career, Gance had subjects of universal significance in mind. The time had come, he declared in 1917, to make the 'great popular epic of the cinema', the new *Chanson de Roland*. *The Birth of a Nation*, the cinema's first *chanson de geste*, was his model. Like Griffith, he could be said to have worked through melodrama (and *in* melodrama) towards epic: the subject's universal significance was to be understood as the outcome of the struggle between good and evil which shapes the individual life. Gance's films of the 1920s combined the exposition of narrative space through mise-en-scène with radical experiment at the level of the image. Composition in depth absorbs the spectator's look into melodrama's 'ideal space', a laboratory for the passions, and thus into narrative. Devices such as the close-up and the track in and out further manipulate that look, coaxing it into identification with one or more of the protagonists. In an illuminating account of the politics of style in these films, Norman King has argued that the spectator's absorption into 'story-experience' amounts to an 'effacement' of the film as performance, as discourse (as commentary on the action, as direct address to the audience).[66]

There is, however, a counter-tendency, which complicates the melodrama. For the spectator's look at the scene is mediated, as often as not, by a look or relay of looks already in place within it. Our identification is not directly with a protagonist, but with an intra-diegetic observer who looks at the protagonist. Such mediations change the status of the image, King notes, 'impelling it towards spectacle'. In *Napoléon*, Bonaparte is consistently observed within the frame by family, companions, friends, aides, camp-followers, allies, and enemies. He is the supreme object of the mediating look (its supreme fiction). We identify not with him, but with those who look on, as we do, at the spectacle which is Bonaparte, and always from below. Like those who gaze awe-struck within the frame, we are not capable either of his deeds or of his vision. The spectacle permits us to glimpse 'an order of things', King observes, 'a potential in which we can imaginatively participate, a sense of unity in which we momentarily share' – but only as a looker-on summoned to adore both its supreme object, and its creator.[67]

The mediating look creates a certain distance, as well as an absorption, and through that distance the film can be apprehended as discourse: as itself, perhaps, the ultimate spectacle. Mediation, King argues, 'is a passage from one direct look to another, from into the frame to at the frame, from melodrama to epic and from hero to author'. Cinematic spectacle – the rapid editing, the superimpositions, the triptychs – arrests the spectator's look at the surface of the image. In the film's finale, or apotheosis, as Bonaparte stands on the heights of Montezemolo envisioning a glorious future for himself and for France, the images, although narratively ascribed to him, assume a force and momentum of their own. They culminate in the maelstrom and the tricolour, here and now in the auditorium, inviting an applause which prolongs the 'sense of unity' they have encouraged us to envision. The development they round off has been from spectacle within the image to the image itself, or rather the flow of images, as spectacle: through mediation, through hypermediation, to a new and otherwise inconceivable immediacy. Gance always hoped to show the film on an immense screen to audiences of 20,000 or more, all of one heart and mind. His radical populism had created a politics of spectacle as the stimulus to, and foundation of, change.[68]

I want now to look more closely at the episode of Bonaparte's return to Corsica to reawaken national feeling, which exemplifies in miniature the process described by King, the working through and in melodrama towards epic; but also includes a superb lateral tracking shot whose exact function within that process it is not at all easy to establish. Bonaparte's arrival at the family home and reunion with his mother after an absence of twelve years takes place within melodrama's ideal space, within the tableau. Sunshine and a swarm of bees greet this return to origins. The reunion scene is beautifully composed in depth: Bonaparte lingers on the threshold, while his sister Elisa approaches their mother, to prepare her for the meeting. Thereafter, an insistent relay of adoring looks, from members of the family, and from the shepherd Santo Ricci, spiritual mentor and representative of the people, re-establishes Bonaparte not only as a surrogate father and the head of the family, but as Corsica's saviour. The sequence, King observes, functions as 'melodrama bonded into epic'.[69] At its climax, a flame burns in superimposition on Bonaparte's face, confirming his status as a man of destiny (and the film's status as spectacle).

There is as yet, however, no guarantee of Bonaparte's political supremacy in Corsica. Pozzo di Borgo, secretary to the Corsican leader Paolo, who plans to deliver the island to the British, whips up hatred against him. The camera tracks in *Cabiria*-style as Paolo prepares to sign a warrant for Napoleon's arrest, dead or alive, and then out again once the treacherous deed has been done. Melodrama's ideal space continues to absorb the spectator. Then the scene changes to the Moulin du Roi inn, a hotbed, an intertitle advises us, of political dissent. We see the exterior of the inn: a harmonious scene, meticulously composed in depth, with groups of people seated at tables; a woman who makes her way in leisurely fashion across the forecourt, exchanging courtesies. In its summery bucolic drowsiness, the scene recalls Bonaparte's approach to the family home. A lateral tracking shot reveals to us the inn's interior. The camera moves sideways (on a dolly, I suspect, rather than a track), at a slightly oblique angle, across a space divided into three compartments. In the foreground, or fore-grounds, political dispute rages. But the shot also traverses, apparently without paying it any attention, a wealth of everyday activity: a man grooms a horse in the stable we glimpse at the rear of the first compartment; one woman places mugs on a shelf, another loaves of bread on a kind of rack which divides the second from the third. Cut to a shot of the entrance: some soldiers bustle in, and proceed to nail the warrant for Bonaparte's arrest to the wall.

After an interlude during which Bonaparte's brothers set off for Calvi to seek help from the French authorities, the action returns to the Moulin du Roi. This time there are harangues rather than debate. Speaker after speaker declares allegiance to a variety of powers. Suddenly, Bonaparte, who has been seated in disguise among the rival factions, rises to declare that Corsica's true fatherland is France, and that he himself represents the fatherland. Pozzo orders the soldiers to seize him, but they are quelled by an imperious look: an eagle's head superimposed on his, in extreme close-up, the film's spectacle superimposed on that of the charismatic deliverer. The scene closes, after a further harangue, with Bonaparte encircled by rapt looks: the rapt looks, not of friends and sympathisers, this time, but of those who moments before had been implacably hostile. Melodrama, meticulously composed in depth, can render political conflict, and its basis in divergences of habit, creed, and temperament, in the gravitational field of a home, a family, a culture. Epic alone, an epic of utterance ('A man will come who will unite all the hopes of the nation and then . . .'), and of the image, produces a resolution.

The lateral track is by no means the least notable of the shots which make up the Corsican episode of *Napoléon*. It is notable not just in its own terms, but because it does not fit in with the process I have described. It does not belong to melodrama, because it disrupts the idyllic tableau established by the preceding shot of the inn's exterior. It pulls the idyll apart to expose the antagonisms concealed deep within it, turns it inside out. But it does not belong to epic, either: to an epic of utterance, an epic of the image. It does not establish that arena where Bonaparte's magnetism will subsequently prevail. The later scene at the inn, the scene which represents the triumph of the image, is shot from a different angle and on a different scale. More radically, the lateral track runs counter to (runs alongside, one might say) the relay of looks which has been throughout the film the basis for the production of spectacle: the production of Bonaparte as a spectacle, the production of the film itself as above all spectacular.

The tracking shot renders a look from nowhere, from beyond the lines of sight and movement natural either to a viewer positioned within the frame, or to the viewer of the film: an anti-look or a non-look, this, in a film which at once personalises and politicises the look. The shot turns the idyllic–personal inside out to reveal political conflict; and it turns political conflict inside out to reveal the quotidian. Its machine's-eye view corresponds to, and thus brings into view, that which is merely habitual (or automatic) within the spectacular clash of passions which occupies the foreground of the scene, and which 'human' observation, by expressive camera movement, or no movement at all, might well have overlooked.

If there was a politics to which this machine's-eye view could contribute, it was, surely, that of a critique of mechanisation in general. So it does, I think, in a reasonably straightforward fashion, in Vidor's *The Crowd*. Vidor, of course, like Gance, made something of a specialism of melodrama bonded into epic. The stunning success of *The Big Parade*, released in November 1925, had shown that the formula was excellent box-office.[70] However, neither *The Big Parade* nor its equally ambitious successor, *The Crowd*, could be said remotely to subscribe to a politics of spectacle. *The Crowd* articulates a disillusionment increasingly felt in America in the mid- and late-1920s at once with mass-society and with the rugged individualism put forward as its antidote and transcendence.[71] John Sims Sr conceives of a Napoleonic destiny for the son born on 4 July 1900. 'There's a little man the world's going to hear from all right,' he announces. But despite displays of initiative as a boy and as a young man making his way in New York, John Jr is not destined either to oppose or to transcend the crowd.

The camera cranes up the façade of a skyscraper, and then down on to and over a dense grid of desks: the office as production line. A plaque on John Jr's desk informs us that he is No. 137. These high-angle shots, of which there are several in the film's first section, are informative. They tell us what modern mass-society looks like, and feels like, when laid out for our inspection. But they also breed, or express, a certain complacency. 'Look at that crowd!' John Jr declares, gazing down at the sidewalk from the top of the bus where he is seated with his girlfriend Mary. 'The poor boobs ... all in the same rut!' 'Cut out the high hat John!' his friend Bert advises. But he doesn't. The next minute he is pouring scorn on a sandwichboard man dressed as a clown ('I bet his father thought he would be president!'). Mary inadvertently ejects her chewing-gum into the open window of a car below. The view from above (intra-diegetic or extra-diegetic) forever stops short of analysis, because it takes its own superiority for granted.

Capitalism's indifference to suffering is revealed not by a high-angle shot, itself always already in some measure indifferent, but by a lateral track. When John returns to work after his daughter has been killed in a traffic accident, the camera tracks across the grid of desks, following him and some of his colleagues, who make unsympathetic remarks or look pointedly at their watches. It ends up square on to the aisle which divides the room into two. John has taken up his place at a desk immediately to the left of the aisle; in an earlier scene, he had hurried down it to the telephone to be told that he had become a father. The lateral track has not simply followed the clerks to their desks. It halts on white space, on a gap or a blankness in the scene which the camera, unlike a human observer in the same position, cannot ignore, and which makes palpable that observer's absence from the scene, as witness and source of sympathy. Its automatism has exposed the indifference which constitutes the system: to the audience, and, it would seem, to John himself. It really has cut the high hat. Unable to concentrate on the job, and severely reprimanded for shortcomings, he quits. It will take all of melodrama's resources to restore him to his family, and the prospect of a modest happiness.

The lateral tracking shot was never more than a rarity, in films of this period, though there are several other examples which could usefully be adduced, including some from genres other than epic and melodrama. A more exhaustive survey would, I suspect, confirm the link proposed here between the shot's departure from natural lines of movement and sight and a preoccupation with automatisms of one kind or another. How appropriate, for example, that when a machine-gun begins to traverse, in Lewis Milestone's *All Quiet on the Western Front* (1930), the camera, rather than panning to the right as the weapon itself does, instead tracks laterally to the right away from it along the trench, keeping pace with the injury and death it deals out. However, none of the films I have so far discussed, *Napoléon* included, amounts to anything like a theory of cinema as mechanical art. I want now to consider the possibility that Dreyer's *Vampyr* did amount, if not to a theory, then to an overt reflection on cinema as a mechanical art. *Vampyr* invites the kind of enquiry which might lead us back, in a roundabout way, to 'Wandering Rocks', and Leopold Bloom's absent presence at the purchases made by Blazes Boylan in Thornton's.

There was a curious collusion, in the 1920s and early 1930s, between inventive cinema and vampirism. Two of the greatest directors of the silent era, F. W. Murnau and Carl Dreyer, made films about blood-sucking: *Nosferatu* (1922), and *Vampyr* (1932). Why vampires? A possible answer is that vampirism allowed film-makers and writers caught up in the modern and its many sciences of becoming to return to ontology, the science of being. It may have encouraged them to take a new and knowingly archaic look at life and death, at existence as such. In *Ulysses*, Stephen Dedalus writes a vampire-poem (p. 47); in T. S. Eliot's *The Waste Land*, the subject of my next chapter, bats with baby faces whistle and beat their wings in violet light, while someone (or something) crawls head downward down a blackened wall.[72] Vampires (the undead) are a zero: neither a thing nor a no-thing, but rather a relation between the two, between existence and non-existence, between plus and minus. Living people are vampire plus, dead people are vampire minus.

Vampyr, unlike *Nosferatu*, includes a great deal of very ingenious, and very inhuman, camera movement in relative independence of the action. In the village of Courtempierre, there is a vampire, Marguerite Chopin, who apparently died unrepentant, and now returns to prey upon the living. She has two (already vampirised) henchmen: the village doctor, and an army veteran with a wooden leg. Their next target is the local chatelain and his two daughters, Léone and Gisèle. The vampirologist Allan Gray happens to be staying at the village inn, and the chatelain seeks his help. On his first night at the inn, Grey follows the shadow of the one-legged veteran along the river-bank to an abandoned warehouse which serves as vampire HQ. How does Dreyer reduce us, as spectators, to the zero embodied, or dis-embodied, by the vampire?

When Gray enters the warehouse, a shot/reverse-shot schema estab-lishes him as our representative in the scene: the dominant point of view, the source of the natural lines of sight and movement which will penetrate and unfold its enigmatic space. Gray ascends to the first storey, or almost to the first storey: he looks out from the staircase through a kind of embrasure, at floor-level. The veteran's shadow rejoins its body, which has been sitting all the while on a bench in a meditative pose. Hearing a sound (a cry for help?), the veteran stirs, reaches for his crutch. As he rises, and moves to our right, the camera pans with him, and frames him leaning over a balustrade speaking to someone below. Cut back to Allan Gray, who leans forward through the embrasure, twisting his head to the left (our right).

As he does so, the camera tracks laterally to the right, away from him, in the direction of his gaze but at a 90-degree angle to it, along a wall marked off by further embrasures, across a gap between parts of the building, down which we gaze momentarily.

Once across the gap, the camera pans to the right, picking up a vivid shadow-dance. Still moving, it rapidly becomes immersed in the dance. The movement ends with a vertiginous look down at the ground floor, where Marguerite Chopin appears, to wave her stick up at the dancers, and yell '*Ruhe!*' She has come to order her henchmen to kill the chatelain.

Two by now familiar features of the lateral tracking shot distend the tableau of Allan Gray's cautious look out through the embrasure (not to mention the shot/reverse-shot schema which brought him into the building, and thus fully into the investigation): the movement is along a façade marked off mechanically into units or segments; and it traverses a gap, an empty space. It is these features, I have argued, which bring home to us the shot's automatism, and consequently our own absence from the scene.

We return to Allan Gray, who starts to explore the building further. The camera goes with him; or, rather, in his proximity, since it now moves in relative independence of him. It does not appear to know more about the place than he does, but it does not express him either (his curiosity, his apprehension). It has departed from his line of sight and movement; departed, one might add, for ever. According to David Bordwell, the significance of the extraordinarily fluid camera-work which accompanies Gray's subsequent investigations at the nearby chateau is that camera time and space are no longer congruent with narrative time and space. If *Vampyr* can be considered a 'major film', Bordwell argues, it is because Dreyer understands that the camera need not be subservient to narrative causality, as it was, by 1932, in classical Hollywood cinema; and that a film can 'foreground' its active role in the construction of narrative space. Never more so than in the celebrated scene in which Gray dreams that he is witnessing his own funeral from inside the coffin. Bordwell quotes Roland Barthes's comment that the spectator of this scene can no longer take up a position, because he or she has only a dead man to identify with: 'the tableau has no point of departure, no support, it gapes open.' The seeing but dead subject, Bordwell adds, is 'the contradictory limit of that representational system which stabilizes space around the pivot point of the observer'.[73] Noël Burch has distinguished between three distinct camera roles or 'attitudes' in *Vampyr*: subjective, objective, and 'authorial'. The purpose of the subjective and objective functions is self-evident. The purpose of the authorial function, responsible for the shots to which Barthes and Bordwell have drawn attention, is to emphasise the fact that there is someone behind the camera who knows what is going to happen. According to Burch, such shots establish the presence of 'sheer artifice' in the film.[74]

It may be, however, that the limit we have reached here is that not of representation, but of the theories of representation developed with regard to literature and cinema during the 1970s. According to those theories, the artifice of a cinema which foregrounds camera-work or a literature which foregrounds writing presses a 'representational system' committed to driving illusionism into contradiction. Artifice works on the representational system from the outside or the inside in order to 'undermine' it. It has to be conceived as an excess, a negation, an impossibility. 'The tableau', Barthes says, 'has no point of departure, no support, it gapes open.' There is much in these arguments that accords with the view I have put forward here. But to my mind the lateral tracking shot, at any rate, should be understood as the product not of an author-function, but of a machine-function, or even a vampire-function. The lateral tracking shot is a movement across and in zero. What it opens up is not an impossibility, or a contradiction, but the coincidence (literally, the falling together into one space and time) of life and death. To see automatically, as a machine sees, is to see death in life, to see life if not from the point of view of death, then from the point of view of not exactly being alive; or as a vampire might see it. That might mean seeing less life than one had expected, as when the death of John Sims's daughter, in *The Crowd*, produces yet more death, in the indifference and hostility his mourning arouses in his co-workers; or more life than one had expected, as when a crossing of the interior of the Moulin du Roi, in *Napoléon*, brings the quotidian fully into view for the first time.

Vampyr theorises the camera as a machine-function by proposing an archaeology of cinema. I don't think Dreyer meant to undermine Hollywood, or illusionism in general, or the concept of narrative. I think he meant to invoke, by revisiting Sheridan Le Fanu, as Murnau had revisited Bram Stoker, the ghostliness of cinema's origin. In *Vampyr*, cinema, which had always drawn the life out of people in bringing them alive, produced a new (and very old) understanding of life's relation to death. Dreyer moved his camera into and across zero; and thus brought film back, once again, to its original neutrality as a medium. Did Joyce, whose Stephen Dedalus was also not averse to revisiting Bram Stoker, conjure up any comparable movement in the actuality footage of an ambiguously 'living' Dublin which constitutes 'Wandering Rocks'?

The will-to-automatism

The lateral tracking shot, a shot called for by the director – called for as a departure from natural lines of sight and movement – might strike us as willed, or even wilful. It insists upon, and relentlessly 'brings out', the automatism always already there in the actuality's fifty seconds of unwavering attention to all of whatever happens to be going on in front of the camera. Where its use is concerned, we have perhaps to speak of a will-to-automatism, a determination to view the world, for however brief an interval, as a machine would view it. The lateral tracking shot forces us to acknowledge that the world has been viewed attentively, but with some other kind or quality of attention than the kind or quality we ourselves would have brought to bear on it, had we been there in person. It does so both because it moves obliquely, like a crab, and because its topic is absence and/or mechanism.

The use of the lateral tracking shot in (some) films of the silent era could serve as a model for the process whereby modernist literature at once mechanised itself and made mechanism its theme. Hugh Kenner has argued that, evolving as it did during the 'second machine age' (roughly, the period between 1880 and 1930), modernist literature began to develop 'parallel technologies' of its own: mechanisms which, like the aeroplane or the linotype press, had nothing to hide, since each moving part was visible, and yet challenged comprehension. For Kenner, *Ulysses* is at its most radical when it dispenses with the idea of the storyteller, forcing us to confront the 'technology of print', and make what we can of it. The 'congruity' insisted upon in *Ulysses* is that between the modern city and the mechanism of the book. 'Dublin's tram system, in 1904 the world's most extensive, gets Stephen Dedalus from Dalkey to Sandymount, and Leopold Bloom from the baths to Sandymount, both by 11 a.m., Bloom again from Sandymount to Holles Street by 10 p.m.'; if it were not for these regulated movements, and the 'sightings' they give rise to, there would have been no story.[75] The movements are at once narrative method, and theme. The noise made by the generator which provided electricity for the tram system catches Stephen's attention, in scene 13 of 'Wandering Rocks'. 'The whirr of flapping leathern bands and hum of dynamos from the power-house urged Stephen to be on. Beingless beings' (p. 232).

Mechanism, of course, had become second nature, to the city-dweller, by 1904. Joyce had to go somewhat further out of his way than the odd tram-ride in order fully to mechanise literature. He had to make the humanly impossible at once his method and his theme. Stephen's brief commentary on the power-house occurs immediately after one of the many interpolations which constitute the episode's primary structural device. 'Two old women fresh from their whiff of the briny trudged through Irishtown along London bridge road, one with a sanded umbrella, one with a midwife's bag in which eleven cockles rolled' (p. 232). The old women, who exist so vividly for us, are absent from the scene of Stephen's meditation. No third term or synthetic space arises out of the juxtaposition of these two images or scenes (Stephen in central Dublin, the women in Irishtown), as it would in montage practice. Interpolation negates. It enforces upon us the humanly impossible: what Stephen could not have seen, what no mere storyteller would have thought it worth mentioning.

Between 11 June 1921, when the first *placards* of *Ulysses* were pulled, and 30 January 1922, three days before the official publication date, Joyce added material which amounts to roughly 30 per cent of the present text. Among the things he added at proof-stage were the interpolations in 'Wandering Rocks'. These bookish devices exhibit a will-to-automatism.[76] For the episode's Art or Science, the Linati schema has 'Mechanics'. Joyce's use of interpolations could be compared to the use of lateral tracking shots by directors such as Gance and Dreyer in one respect: it represents a departure from the natural lines of sight and movement which construct narrative space in fiction before *Ulysses*, and in *Ulysses* itself before 'Wandering Rocks'.

We left Blazes Boylan at the fruiterer, arranging to have his basket sent to Eccles Street. This is how the scene begins:

> The blond girl in Thornton's bedded the wicker basket with rustling fibre. Blazes Boylan handed her the bottle swathed in pink tissue paper and a small jar.
> – Put these in first, will you? he said.
> – Yes, sir, the blond girl said, and the fruit on top.
> – That'll do, game ball, Blazes Boylan said.
> She bestowed fat pears neatly, head by tail, and among them ripe shame-faced peaches.
> Blazes Boylan walked here and there in new tan shoes about the fruitsmelling shop, lifting fruits, young juicy crinkled and plump red tomatoes, sniffing smells.
> H.E.L.Y's. filed before him, tallwhitehatted, past Tangier lane, plodding towards their goal. (p. 218)

The scene bristles with presence-effect, with objects and actions which demand attention both from Boylan and from the narrator whose job it has hitherto been to describe in detail whatever occupies the consciousness presiding over any scene or event. The process by which Boylan selects items for the basket is the process by which the narrator selects items for description. Each description of an item has the colour of the purpose which Boylan has invested in that item. The peaches could scarcely appear anything other than 'ripe' and 'shame-faced'. Indeed, there is a kind of collusion of colour, of colourfulness, of gold and pink, between Boylan and the shop-girl, and between them and the narrator. Meanwhile, the H.E.L.Y.'s sandwichboardmen pass by in the background, on the street outside. Boylan may or may not notice them. Their presence in the background raises the question of who notices what, from where, and why. And their mechanical passage and lack of colour are rather strikingly at odds with the glowing gold and pink complicity. Ultimately, however, they do not disrupt the initial style, because they are part of what Boylan could have seen. They belong in the tableau.

In 'Crapy Cornelia', James had quite explicitly invoked a cinematic effect in order to explain the dashing of White-Mason's hopes of a rather more durable, though no less gold and pink, complicity. On first glance, Mrs Worthingham's unwelcome visitor strikes White-Mason as 'comparatively black – very much as if that had absolutely, in such a medium, to be the graceless appearance of any item not positively of some fresh shade of a light colour or of some pretty pretension to a charming twist'. The medium constituted by the brilliance of Mrs Worthingham's person and wealth is the basis for the vision White-Mason projects of a durable complicity, or marriage. The visitor's 'dingy presence', obscured at first by the 'whole rosy glow' of Mrs Worthingham's manner of life, will soon grow and grow like images in the cinematograph until it in turn obscures both the brilliant medium and the brilliant vision based upon it.[77] Cornelia Rasch's advance upon White-Mason, registered as only a machine would register it, demonstrates his constitutive absence from the 'whole rosy glow' of the scene of marriage. That advance unsettles White-Mason far more decisively than the sandwichboardmen could ever have unsettled Blazes Boylan. Joyce, however, goes further than James in the direction of the machine's-eye view.

In 'Wandering Rocks', the 'darkbacked figure' of Leopold Bloom scanning books on the hawker's car under Merchant's Arch intrudes its dinginess on the whole rosy glow shed by Blazes Boylan's complicity with the shop-girl in Thornton's. Except that there is no actual looming, in this case, no advance of one protagonist on another, no monstrous disruptive enlargement. The rosy glow just gets rosier.

> Blazes Boylan rattled merry money in his trousers' pocket.
> – What's the damage? he asked.
> The blond girl's slim fingers reckoned the fruits.
> Blazes Boylan looked into the cut of her blouse. A young pullet. He took a red carnation from the tall stemglass.
> – This for me? he asked gallantly.
> The blond girl glanced sideways at him, got up regardless, with his tie a bit crooked, blushing.
> – Yes, sir, she said.
> Bending archly she reckoned again fat pears and blushing peaches.
> Blazes Boylan looked in her blouse with more favour, the stalk of the red flower between his smiling teeth.
> – May I say a word to your telephone, missy? he asked roguishly. (pp. 218–19)

The blush has spread from the peaches to the woman who reckons them again in order to display herself again. The scene culminates in an eroticised version of the kind of performance of mutual recognition (in this case, of a kindred spirit) which the makers of the first actualities had so eagerly sought after. No surprise, then, that the carnation should feature prominently, in the coda to 'Wandering Rocks', in Boylan's response to the viceregal cavalcade. 'His hands in his jacket pockets forgot to salute but he offered to the three ladies the bold admiration of his eyes and the red flower between his lips' (p. 243). In this instance, the carnation performs the duty, not of recognition, but of acknowledgement: Boylan is turned on by the *status* of the ladies in the cavalcade.

But then it didn't quite work like that, in the first actualities. The mere performance of recognition or acknowledgement could never conceal completely the lapse in time and space between the capture of an image and its reproduction on the screen. It could not repair the loss entailed in the image's mechanical reproduction. A similar 'lapse' afflicts the initial style, which had promised so much by way of recognition and acknowledgement. Who suffers the loss entailed in the *text*'s mechanical reproduction, in 'Wandering Rocks'?

Boylan could not have seen the darkbacked figure from the interior of Thornton's, and there is nothing to suggest that the thought of Bloom crosses his mind. Unlike the parade of sandwichboardmen along the pavement outside the shop, which he might or might not have taken account of, the apparition of the darkbacked figure is in no sense *for* him. The protagonist whose constitutive absence from the scene that apparition establishes is the narrator: the masterful exponent, in the first nine episodes of *Ulysses*, of a style whose main purpose is to describe only what matters, at a given moment, to a presiding consciousness. Boylan presides, in Thornton's. The fruit matters to him. The blond girl matters. The telephone matters. Even the sandwichboardmen might conceivably matter, as a counterpoint to his sense of wellbeing. Bloom does not matter. For Bloom to matter, one would have to conceive the book in which these incidents are recounted as a neutral recording medium, rather than as a representation of what they might mean to a presiding consciousness (either that which presides within the scene or that which presides over it, as narrator). In 'Wandering Rocks', the narrator expressed by the initial style gives way to a new principle of organisation. 'It is not the voice of the storyteller,' Kenner explains: 'not a voice at all, since it does not address us, does not even speak.' The actions this new principle performs, such as interpolating a glimpse of Bloom into Boylan's deliberations about fruit, are performed, Kenner goes on, in complete disregard of our presence.[78] The scene in Thornton's is storytelling's last hurrah. Our narrative appetite has been re-aroused by the possibility of a further twist in the tale: it could be that Boylan's flirtation with the blond girl will distract him, immediately or at a later date, from his pursuit of Molly. The new principle which interrupts this furtive blossoming of story could not care less about such titillations. Its job is simply to record, as a machine would, as the proper recovery of literature's original neutrality as a medium would require, the fact of Bloom's concurrent absorption in the books on the hawker's car.

Kenner's understanding of city and book as parallel technologies leads him to the conclusion that both are 'haunted' by the 'shades' of people.[79] 'Beingless beings' is Stephen's term for the power-house dynamos. The thought could also refer, beyond his consciousness, to the two old women we have just glimpsed trudging through Irishtown along London Bridge Road. These two beings have been rendered even more beingless by their presence, courtesy of the book's automatism, in a scene from which they are absent. Bloom, similarly, has been interpolated as an absence into a scene dedicated to another's presence, a scene which would not be a scene at all (an incident in the narrative) unless he were absent from it. We are back in the 'kingdom of shadows' in which cinema began, and to which Joyce seemed at times intent on returning literature. Darkbacked Bloom and crapy Cornelia have rejoined the grey faces which struck Maxim Gorky. In one case, it is the protagonist who feels the loss this absent presence entails; in the other, it is the very principle upon which narrative fiction before *Ulysses* had been based. The interpolations in 'Wandering Rocks' are the product of a will-to-automatism determined to reproduce in literature that which is most nearly automatic in a modern understanding of existence as such. Joyce did not make cinema out of literature by means of montage. He interpolated cinema (cinema as it had been, in 1904) into literature. He lodged cinema's grey ghostliness among literature's pink and gold expressions of narrative desire.

The stimulus to that will-to-automatism came from a specific visual technology. In his Paris notebook of 1903, Joyce had reflected on the status of the photograph.

> Question: *Can a photograph be a work of art?*
> Answer: A photograph is a disposition of sensible matter and may be so disposed for an aesthetic end but it is not a human disposition of sensible matter. Therefore it is not a work of art.[80]

Cinema, likewise, as Joyce knew very well, is not a human disposition of sensible matter. By the time he came to write 'Wandering Rocks', however, he no longer supposed that the human disposition was the only appropriate basis for a work of art. The basis for the episode's narrative method is a decidedly inhuman disposition. What Joyce sought to emulate in cinema, if anything, was its automatism.

Notes

1   Richard Ellmann, *James Joyce*, rev. edn (New York: Oxford University Press, 1982), 654. See also Sergei Eisenstein, *Immoral Memories: An Autobiography*, trans. Herbert Marshall (Boston: Houghton, 1983), 214; Marie Seton, *Sergei M. Eisenstein: A Biography* (New York: Grove Press, 1960), 149; Gösta Werner, 'James Joyce and Sergei Eisenstein', trans. Erik Gunnemark, *James Joyce Quarterly*, 27 (1990), 491–507.

2   Léon Moussiac, *Sergei Eisenstein*, trans. Sandy Petrey (New York: Crown Publishers, 1970), 148.

3   Seton, *Sergei M. Eisenstein*, 149.

4   Ellmann, *James Joyce*, 300–303, 311. There are useful summaries of the biographical evidence concerning Joyce's interest in cinema in Alan Spiegel, *Fiction and the Camera Eye: Visual Consciousness in Film and the Modern Novel* (Charlottesville: University of Virginia Press, 1976), 71–80; and Thomas L.

Burkdall, *Joycean Frames: Film and the Fiction of James Joyce* (London: Routledge, 2001), 1–8.

5   The term most often used, as I have indicated, to bring Joyce into relation with cinema: Burkdall, *Joycean Frames*, 8–17. Nicholas Andrew Miller, taking a very different approach, has used the 'historical moment' of the first showings of *The Birth of a Nation* in Dublin to reflect not only on the development of Irish cinema, but on the 'Lestrygonians' episode of *Ulysses*: *Modernism, Ireland and the Erotics of Memory* (Cambridge: Cambridge University Press, 2002), ch. 4.

6   See, for example, Keith Cohen, on an incident in the 'Lotus Eaters' episode of *Ulysses*, in *Film and Fiction: The Dynamics of Exchange* (New Haven: Yale University Press, 1979), 198–203; or R. Barton Palmer, on the 'Oxen of the Sun' episode, in 'Eisensteinian Montage and Joyce's *Ulysses*: The Analogy Reconsidered', *Mosaic*, 18 (1985), 73–85; or William V. Costanzo, on punning in *Finnegans Wake*, in 'Joyce and Eisenstein: Literary Reflections of the Reel World', *Journal of Modern Literature*, 11 (1984), 175–80. The latter has the virtue of addressing work still in progress at the time of the meeting with Eisenstein.

7   Robert Humphrey, *Stream of Consciousness in the Modern Novel* (Berkeley: University of California Press, 1955), 50; Edward Murray, *The Cinematic Imagination: Writers and the Motion Pictures* (New York: Frederick Ungar, 1972), 130–31; Craig Wallace Barrow, *Montage in James Joyce's 'Ulysses'* (Madrid: Studia Humanitatis, 1980), 100–116; Richard Pearce, *The Novel in Motion: An Approach to Modern Fiction* (Columbus: Ohio State University Press, 1983), 46; Spiegel, *Fiction and the Camera Eye*, 170–74; Cohen, *Film and Fiction*, 153–6.

8   'Bring the Camera Whenever You Like: "Wandering Rocks"', Cinema Ambulante, and Problems of Diegesis', in Clive Hart et al. (eds), *Images of Joyce*, 2 vols (Gerrards Cross: Colin Smythe, 1998), vol. 2, 526–38, p. 531.

9   *Ulysses*, ed. Jeri Johnson (Oxford: Oxford Univesity Press, 1993), 218. References will henceforth be included in the text.

10   Eileen Bowser, 'Le Coup de téléphone dans les primitifs du cinéma', in Pierre Guibbert (ed.), *Les Premiers ans du cinéma français* (Perpignan: Institut Jean Vigo, 1985), 218–24; Tom Gunning, 'Heard Over the 'Phone: *The Lonely Villa* and the De Lorde Tradition of the Terrors of Technology', in Annette Kuhn and Jackie Stacy (eds), *Screen Histories: A Screen Reader* (Oxford: Oxford University Press, 1998), 216–27.

11   The schemata Joyce provided for Linati, and for Stuart Gilbert, are reprinted in the Oxford edition of *Ulysses*, 734–9.

12   Detailed discussions of montage in particular scenes in 'Wandering Rocks' frequently conclude with an explicit invocation of film theory, rather than film history. Spiegel invokes dialectic (*Fiction and the Camera Eye*, 173); Cohen, the *actants* of narrative theory (*Film and Fiction*, 156); Jacobus, the Lacanian principle of suture ('Bring the Camera', 535). Burkdall relies explicitly on film theory from the outset: *Joycean Frames*, xii.

13   'Dialectical montage, the conjunction of opposing perspectives, represents Joyce's widest application of the montage concept', Spiegel concludes, with reference to scene 16 of 'Wandering Rocks', 'an application on the largest scale which no longer results in specific visualized effects but which still may be considered a generalized principle of the cinematographic manner' (*Fiction and the Camera Eye*, 173). The word 'still' has a lot of work to do, in this sentence.

14 Keith Williams, commenting on an exhibition of some of the films featured at the Cinematograph Volta, notes that the programme 'provided neat confirmation of Joyce's interest in cinema's ambiguous capacity for vernacular "magic realism"', suggesting what trick films and early cartoons may have contributed to his avowed technic of "Vision animated to bursting point" in the style of "Circe"': 'Cinematic Joyce', *James Joyce Broadsheet*, 57 (2000), 3. On Joyce and the genre of trick film, see Thomas L. Burkdall, 'Cinema Fakes: Film and Joycean Fantasy', in Morris Beja and David Norris (eds), *Joyce in the Hibernian Metropolis: Essays* (Columbus: Ohio State University Press, 1995), 260–69.

15 *Letters*, ed. Stuart Gilbert and Richard Ellmann, 3 vols (London: Faber, 1957–66), vol. 1, 129.

16 Ibid., vol. 1, 114. See Hugh Kenner, *Ulysses* (London: George Allen and Unwin, 1980), 63.

17 See, for example, David Bordwell's highly informative discussion of staging in depth, in *On the History of Film Style* (Cambridge, MA: Harvard University Press, 1997), ch. 6.

18 *Life to Those Shadows*, trans. Ben Brewster (London: BFI Publishing, 1990), 154.

19 'The Lumière Cinematograph', in *The Film Factory: Russian and Soviet Cinema, 1896–1939*, trans. Richard Taylor, ed. Taylor and Ian Christie (London: Routledge & Kegan Paul, 1988), 25–6.

20 James Lastra, 'From the Captured Moment to the Cinematic Image: A Transformation in Pictorial Order', in Dudley Andrew (ed.), *The Image in Dispute: Art and Cinema in the Age of Photography* (Austin: University of Texas Press, 1997), 263–91, p. 273.

21 Stephen Bottomore, 'From the Factory Gate to the "Home Talent" Drama: An International Overview of Local Films in the Silent Era', in Vanessa Toulmin, Patrick Russell, and Simon Popple (eds), *The Lost World of Mitchell and Kenyon: Edwardian Britain on Film* (London: BFI Publishing, 2004), 33–48. The Harrisburg paper is quoted on p. 34.

22 Vanessa Toulmin, ' "Local Films for Local People": Travelling Showmen and the Commissioning of Local Films in Great Britain, 1900–1902', *Film History*, 13 (2001), 118–37.

23 Quoted by Tom Gunning, 'Pictures of Crowd Splendor: The Mitchell and Kenyon Factory Gate Films', in *Lost World*, 49–58, p. 52.

24 Quoted by Bottomore, 'From the Factory Gate', 34.

25 'Pictures of Crowd Splendor', 53.

26 Quoted by Kevin Rockett, 'The Silent Period', in Rockett, Luke Gibbons, and John Hill, *Cinema and Ireland* (London: Croom Helm, 1987), 3–50, p. 4.

27 Rockett, 'Silent Period', 4–5.

28 Bottomore, 'Factory Gate', 35. There were also, it would seem, turn-of-the-century versions of the wedding video. Edith Wharton's Lily Bart notices that during the 'sylvan rites' attending the Van Osburgh marriage the 'agent of a cinematograph syndicate' has set up his apparatus at the church door: *The House of Mirth* (Harmondsworth: Penguin Books, 1979), 106. First published in 1905.

29 The text of the poster is hard to make out. I have relied on the sharp eyes (and no doubt the patience) of Robert Monks: 'The Irish Films in the Mitchell and Kenyon Collection', in *Lost World*, 93–102, p. 95.

30 *Animated Photography: The ABC of the Cinematograph* (London: n.p., 1897), 97.

31 *Ulysses*, 63.

32 Lastra, 'Captured Moment', 266–9.

33 *Psychoanalysis and the Cinema: The Imaginary Signifier*, trans. Celia Britton, Annwyl Williams, Ben Brewster, and Alfred Guzzetti (Basingstoke: Macmillan, 1982), 63.

34 Tom Gunning, 'The Cinema of Attractions: Early Film, Its Spectator, and the Avant-Garde', in Thomas Elsaesser (ed.), *Early Cinema: Space, Frame, Narrative* (London: BFI Publishing, 1990), 56–67, p. 57.

35 Article reprinted in Colin Harding and Simon Popple (eds), *In the Kingdom of Shadows: A Companion to Early Cinema* (London: Cygnus Arts, 1996), 13–17, p. 14.

36 'The Lumière Cinematograph', 25.

37 See John Widdowson, 'Mitchell and Kenyon: Ceremonial Processions and Folk Traditions', in *Lost World*, 137–49.

38 'Joyce's Text in Progress', in Derek Attridge (ed.), *The Cambridge Companion to Joyce* (Cambridge: Cambridge University Press, 1990), 213–36, p. 228.

39 *Between Film and Screen: Modernism's Photo Synthesis* (Chicago: University of Chicago Press, 1999), 281.

40 *Life to Those Shadows*, 18.

41 Ben Brewster and Lea Jacobs, *Theatre to Cinema: Stage Pictorialism and the Early Feature Film* (Oxford: Oxford University Press, 1997), 38.

42 *Life to Those Shadows*, 16.

43 Heath, 'Narrative Space', in *Questions of Cinema* (Basingstoke: Macmillan, 1981), 19–75, p. 39; Burch, *Life to Those Shadows*, 150.

44 The authoritative account is David Bordwell, Janet Staiger, and Kristin Thompson, *The Classical Hollywood Cinema: Film Style and Mode of Production to 1960* (London: Routledge, 1985).

45 Burch, *Life to Those Shadows*, 91.

46 Jon Gartenberg, 'Camera Movement in Edison and Biograph Films, 1900–1906', *Cinema Journal*, 19 (1980), 1–16; Barry Salt, *Film Style and Technology: History and Analysis*, 2nd edn (London: Starwood, 1992), 46–7.

47 For the relation between railway travel and early cinema's 'phantom rides', see Charles Musser, 'The Travel Genre in 1903–1904: Moving Towards Fictional Narrative', in *Early Cinema*, 123–32; Lynne Kirby, *Parallel Tracks: The Railroad and Silent Cinema* (Exeter: University of Exeter Press, 1997).

48 Raymond Fielding, 'Hale's Tours: Ultrarealism in the pre-1910 Motion Picture', in John L. Fell (ed.), *Film Before Griffith* (Berkeley: University of California Press, 1983), 116–31.

49 *Life to Those Shadows*, 39.

50 Kristin Thompson, 'The Formulation of the Classical Style, 1909–1928', in *Classical Hollywood Cinema*, 155–240, p. 229.

51 Salt, *Film Style and Technology*, 82.

52 Burch, *Life to Those Shadows*, 181.

53 'Feature Films of the Week: *Cabiria* the Best Yet', reprinted in George C. Pratt, *Spellbound in Darkness: A History of the Silent Film*, 2nd edn (Greenwich, CT: New York Graphic Society, 1973), 124–6, p. 126.

54 *Film Style and Technology*, 82.

55 David Bordwell and Kristin Thompson, *Film Art: An Introduction*, 6th edn (New York: McGraw-Hill, 2001), 224.

56 *Durgnat on Film* (London: Faber, 1976), 54.

57 'Traffic in Souls: An Experiment in Feature-Length Narrative Construction', *Cinema Journal*, 31 (1991), 37–56, p. 50.

58 Ibid., 46; and, on emblematic shots in general, Burch, *Life to Those Shadows*, 46; and Brewster and Jacobs, *Theatre to Cinema*, 54.

59 For an informative account of the film's social and political context, see Lee Grieveson, *Policing Cinema: Movies and Censorship in Early-Twentieth-Century America* (Berkeley: University of California Press, 2004), ch. 5.

60 'Temporality of the Cinema of Attractions', 48. See also Phil Rosen, 'Disjunction and Ideology in a Preclassical Film: *A Policeman's Tour of the World*', *Wide Angle*, 12 (1990), 20–37.

61 *Adventures with D. W. Griffith*, ed. Kevin Brownlow (London: Faber, 1973), 170.

62 Kristin Thompson reports that Lois Weber directed an intricate tracking shot for a battle sequence in *The Dumb Girl of Portici* (1915): the camera tracks to the right along a row of pillars, past the action, then diagonally backwards and to the left, away from the pillars ('Formulation of the Classical Style', 229).

63 *The Films of Carl-Theodor Dreyer* (Berkeley: University of California Press, 1981), 43, 50.

64 Ibid., 50.

65 *Film Style and Technology*, 157.

66 *Abel Gance: A Politics of Spectacle* (London: BFI Publishing, 1984). Gance's declarations of intent are cited on p. 125.

67 Ibid., 193, 196.

68 Ibid., 201, 205, 213.

69 Ibid., 193–4.

70 Thomas Schatz, *The Genius of the System: Hollywood Filmmaking in the Studio Era* (New York: Pantheon Books, 1989), 36–9.

71 Martin Rubin provides a context for the feelings of disillusionment in 'The Crowd, the Collective, and the Chorus: Busby Berkeley and the New Deal', in John Belton (ed.), *Movies and Mass Culture* (London: Athlone, 1996), 59–92.

72 *Complete Poems and Plays* (London: Faber and Faber, 1969), 73. The emergence of cinema in the 1890s had of course coincided with the flourishing of a 'decadent' literature of vampires, mummies, ghosts, and strangely deteriorating people called Gray, in which Eliot, Joyce, and their contemporaries were steeped.

73 *Films of Carl-Theodor Dreyer*, 105, 109. Barthes's comment occurs in 'Diderot, Brecht, Eisenstein', in *Image – Music – Text*, ed. and trans. Stephen Heath (London: Fontana, 1977), 69–78, p. 77.

74 'Carl-Theodor Dreyer: The Major Phase, in *In and Out of Synch: The Awakening of a Cine-Dreamer* (Aldershot: Scolar Press, 1991), 70–92, pp. 79–80, 83.

75 *The Mechanic Muse* (Oxford: Oxford University Press, 1987), 10, 69, 72, 76, 11.

76 For an illuminating attempt to explain the gratuitousness of the interpolations as an enactment of the 'gift motif' evident in 'Wandering Rocks' (the coin Molly Bloom flings to the one-legged sailor, the book her husband buys her), see Vincent Sherry, *James Joyce: Ulysses*, rev. edn (Cambridge: Cambridge University Press, 2004), 64–72. Sherry adds, however, that by the second half of the episode, 'Joyce's method of gratuitous intrusion seems to become the most predictable and perfunctory of mechanisms' (p. 69).

77 'Crapy Cornelia', in *The Jolly Corner and Other Tales*, ed. Roger Gard (Harmondsworth: Penguin Books, 1990), 221–48, p. 226.

78 *Ulysses*, 65. David Hayman has proposed that we should call this new narrative consciousness 'the Arranger': *Ulysses: The Mechanics of Meaning* (Englewood Cliffs, NJ: Prentice-Hall, 1970).

79 *Mechanic Muse*, 76.

80 'Aesthetics' (Paris Notebook), in *Occasional, Critical, and Political Writing*, ed. Kevin Barry (Oxford: Oxford University Press, 2000), 102–5, p. 104.

5

T. S. Eliot

On 24 April 1915, T. S. Eliot wrote to his cousin Eleanor Hinkley from Merton College, Oxford, where he was at that time a student. He reported that, as a diversion from his studies, he had been 'to a few music-halls, and to the cinema with a most amusing French woman who is the only interesting acquaintance at my boarding house'.[1] The point of this latter expedition was presumably the amusing French woman, rather than the cinema. Of her, alas, we hear no more. But there is sufficient scattered reference to the cinema, in Eliot's letters, essays, and poems, to suggest an enduring preoccupation, and one with definite consequences for his development as a writer.

The recent intensification of interest in literary modernism's relation to cinema, on the one hand, and Eliot's relation to popular culture, on the other, has created a curious blind spot. Enthusiasts for cinema's formative effect on modernist writing have on the whole felt that there is little or nothing to be done with Eliot; while critics who place great emphasis on Eliot's endorsement of popular forms such as music hall argue that it strengthened yet further his already powerful 'aversion to cinema'.[2] On both sides, the tendency has been to quote his remarks about cinema at their most dismissive, and in isolation.[3] Eliot has been cast as the mandarin High Modernist who remained, in this one respect at least, a mandarin High Modernist. I shall argue in this chapter that, contrary to common belief, he does not fit the part.

Eliot, I believe, proved as alert to cinema's example as any of his contemporaries; indeed, a good deal more so than most. I have already noted Hugh Kenner's insistence on his affinity with technologies ranging from the alarm clock through the telephone to, conceivably, the cinema (above, p. 4).[4] I want now to propose that he might be understood as the poet not only of the new machines, but of the newly mechanical behaviour – or behaviour reconceived as mechanical – to which their pervasiveness had given rise.

> So the hand of the child, automatic,
> Slipped out and pocketed a toy that was running along the quay,
> I could see nothing behind the child's eye.[5]

To be the poet of the alarm clock and the child's self-impelling hand meant to write poems which partook in some measure of the automatism which was their topic: poems which knew what it felt like to behave, and perhaps even to want to behave, as if automatised. 'Portrait of a Lady' enlists the reader in just such an exercise: 'You have the scene arrange itself – as it will seem to do ...' (*CPP* 18). The scene's seeming self-arrangement: that, perhaps, for Eliot as for Joyce, is where cinema came in.

In advancing that proposition, I shall once again seek to extend and refine Garrett Stewart's understanding of the 'cultural commonality' between 'automated image projection' and 'the depersonalized verbal techniques of a Modernist stylistic "apparatus"'. I have already identified problems in Stewart's methodology (above, pp. 6–8): that it cannot conceive of an author, or author-function, in literature; and that it takes account only of avant-garde cinema. A further problem arises when the 'communality' envisaged is between the photographic image and a poetic text. Stewart identifies modernist style exclusively with a certain 'signifying over and above the signified': that is, with verbal drift, or skid, with phonemic 'congealment' and 'knotted lexicality' (the latter in regard to a poem by Emily Dickinson). Modernist style, however, has various dimensions. Eliot's poetry does not lack for congealment and knotted lexicality, of course; but it may be that he found his enabling automatism in prosody rather than in verbal drift and skid. For Eliot, I shall suggest, regular metre and rhyme were neither an encumbrance nor an expressive support, but precisely a framing device; in Stewart's term, a 'prosthesis of observation' (as they had been for Dickinson).[6]

The aim of this chapter is to demonstrate that our understanding of Eliot's poetry will be enhanced by a definition of its informing will-to-automatism which takes full account, for the first time, of his commentary on cinema. The parallel histories in play, here, are those of the development of Eliot's poetry up to and including *The Waste Land* (1922), and of the emergence during the same period of a fully narrative cinema (that is, of character-driven story films capable of absorbing a diverse mass audience into a self-sufficient world unified across space and time). In my view, the only way to establish the relation between those histories is through an examination of Eliot's evolving commentary, in poems, essays, and letters, on cinema. Eliot did not write cinematically. But there is a history to his changing view of the medium which can usefully be compared to the history of the ways in which the medium itself changed, during the silent era, as well as to the history of his own attempts to change literature.

The early poems

Cinema appears first in the poems, rather than in letters or essays; and it appears by way of a shared terminology of the screen, and of images that flicker on the screen. The view these poems propose is of consciousness as a space, or event, or drama, of projection. Thoughts or feelings can only be known as they hang in the distance between an internal source of illumination and a configured surface belonging to the world outside. They can only be known technologically.

Or so 'The Love Song of J. Alfred Prufrock', Eliot's hallmark early poem, completed in the summer of 1911, would have us believe. As the poem begins, a question arises, or might arise, during the course of an urban expedition the speaker means to undertake (has already undertaken?) with a nameless (probably male) companion. To pose the question directly would be to be overwhelmed by it.

> Oh, do not ask, 'What is it?'
> Let us go and make our visit.
>
> (CPP 13)

Prufrock's prim rhyme nips curiosity in the bud. The visit, coming quick and tart upon the companion's (possible) question about a question, meets it, in sound if not in sense, before it has fully arisen; and so prevents, or postpones, the damage its arising might do. The visit, of a kind Eliot himself had made often enough as an undergraduate at Harvard, is (or would be) to a room where women come and go, where there is music, and tea, and cakes and ices.[7] Prufrock, it has often been said, behaves, or imagines himself behaving, as though he were in a story by Henry James, 'Crapy Cornelia', whose protagonist strikingly fails, under comparable circumstances, to propose to the woman of his dreams.[8] The purpose of the visit is to relieve him, through ordeal by embarrassment, of any remaining thought of an overwhelming question. For the one person who cannot be admitted, who will never make his presence felt there, is the person Prufrock would have to be if he were to pose the question: a prophet, Lazarus come from the dead.

The space Prufrock enters at once in anticipation and in memory is a space of pure speculary. 'Prufrock', Maud Ellmann notes, 'sees himself *being seen.*' He sees the bald spot on his head as it might appear from the point of view of the women who have gathered at the top of the stair to observe an ungracious departure. He has been estranged, Ellmann adds, by the eyes which 'fix' him in a 'formulated phrase', to the exteriorities of language and space.[9] Does he even show up? 'He is not there yet when we hear him speaking,' Hugh Kenner observes: 'he will never be there, or will perpetually return there – it does not matter.' He will never be there as the person he would like to be, Lazarus come from the dead; but he will always be there, in his own absence, through memory and anticipation. He may consider defying whatever 'automatism' propels him repeatedly, in memory or in anticipation, 'through these streets, through that door, up those stairs'.[10] But he needs it more than it needs him.

The trouble is that the automatism does not work; or does not work as Prufrock would like it to work, for all the embarrassment it causes him, as a shield against overwhelming questions. For this visit undertaken automatically poses a question even more overwhelming, in its sheer immediacy, than anything that might have arisen on an expedition through argumentative streets. The question is sexual arousal, and the sense of self it generates, on the spot, at the time (*which* time no longer matters). Prufrock has been, or will be, or let us risk saying is, aroused by the arms of the women who come and go:

> Arms that are braceleted and white and bare
> (But in the lamplight, downed with light brown hair!) ...

(CPP 15)

What finally puts him at the scene, in the picture, is his attention to bodily texture: the film of light brown hair on a white arm. In describing the body, Victorian writers had for the most part confined themselves to that which was most expressive about it: its overall shape; or its most characterful component, the face; or a particular feature (eyes, nose, mouth). Edwardian writers chose instead to describe the flesh between features. The focus of the new eroticism in literature was on the body as body, rather than as an expression of soul. The down on a woman's body looms large as a provocation to and emblem of male desire in novels by Arnold Bennett, D. H. Lawrence, May Sinclair and others.[11] The story Prufrock now finds himself in is a story by Bennett or Lawrence, rather than by Henry James. Eliot had brought himself bang up to date.

The intensity of Prufrock's arousal produces or is produced by an intensification in the verse. By comparison with its sparse and evenly paced predecessor ('and white and bare'), the line describing the hair on the women's arms seems positively swollen: the repetition of in lamplight/light and the internal rhyme on 'downed' and 'brown' fill it from within with sameness of sound, with emphasis. In this moment of absolute fixation, the poem dwells on the inexpressive body, and also on that in its own formal procedures which foreshadows and outlasts expression: on technique, on poetic matter. It is characteristic of Eliot, however, that he should have embedded the moment of absolute fixation in a parenthesis. The ear hears the conjoining rhyme, the eye sees the disjoining brackets. So Prufrock's arousal is at once overwhelming and ghostly. He must be reckoned most fully present only when absent. The automatism propelling him, in memory or in anticipation, through that door, up those stairs, observes as he would not actually have observed, had he been there himself, in his own person, with an overwhelming question to hand. The couplet describing what the prosthesis or automatism has seen or will see in his place exemplifies the disembodiment of perception by technique.

The circle of illumination within which the light brown hair on a white arm appears in alluring close-up might make us think of the cinema. Such close-ups of the body's less expressive stretches played an important part in some of the earliest narrative films. G. A. Smith's *As Seen through a Telescope*

(1900) begins with a long shot of an elderly man brandishing a telescope, while a woman and a younger man wheeling a bicycle advance up the street towards him. As the telescope settles on the pair, Smith cuts to a medium close-up of the woman's foot resting on a pedal, isolated within a circular vignette. The young man has knelt down to tie her shoelace. She gradually raises her skirt, revealing an expanse of stockinged ankle and leg, which her companion proceeds to caress. As the long shot resumes, the elderly voyeur seats himself contentedly, at the peep-show's conclusion, only to receive a punitive cuff from the young man, who has caught him looking, as the couple pass. By severing foreground from background, the close-up induces a change of medium rather than scale, a metamorphosis. The expanse of ankle and leg on display is an object as much of touch as of sight. Like Prufrock, the elderly man has been made present (has been presented to desire, has shown up) in and through his absence, in and through a prosthesis. The erotic effect of Smith's film lies in what visual technologies see that the human eye cannot; that of Eliot's poem in what poetic technique renders that other forms of representation cannot. Eliot's prosodic circle of illumination and Smith's close-up both achieve effects comparable to those achieved by the stereoscope's grasp of the haptic-contingent (above, pp. 39–41).

'The Love Song of J. Alfred Prufrock' is indeed a love song: the love song of a voyeur equipped with a telescope, or a movie camera, or a page or two in a modern novel. Once body-hair has posed its overwhelming question, there is no way back, for Prufrock. He cannot undo the knowledge his automatism has given him. What remains is to make sense of experience: whether the experience has been of sunsets, and sprinkled streets, or of novels, teacups, and trailing skirts. After all this, Prufrock laments, and so much more,

> It is impossible to say just what I mean!
> But as if a magic lantern threw the nerves in patterns on a screen: . . .
>
> (CPP 16)

There is technique, here, and technology. The odd swerve of 'But as if . . .' at the beginning of the line gets the figure of the magic lantern going. A colon at its end keeps that figure oddly in suspension, at once the product of and contained by a shift or warp in the stanza's rhetorical development. A rhyme conjoining lines of unequal length into a couplet holds it all together, in some fashion: technique exposed as technique, as mechanism. Rhyme itself is the configured surface, the screen, on which a pattern appears which might or might not 'say' just what one means.

Walter Benjamin was to seize eagerly on Baudelaire's description of the person routinely suffering the shocks and strains of modern urban experience as a 'kaleidoscope equipped with consciousness'. Light pours into a kaleidoscope pressed up against the eye from outside, from the world beyond. Benjamin took from Baudelaire's figure its preoccupation with passivity. He imagines a pedestrian forever on the alert for traffic signals, for the cautionary light shone at him or her through pieces of coloured glass. 'Thus technology', he concludes, 'has subjected the human sensorium to a complex kind of training.' Cinema, in which 'perception in the form of shocks' has been established as a 'formal principle', would complete the training.[12] One could say that Eliot's figure presents the modern man or woman as a magic lantern equipped with consciousness. His interest in technology does not, however, entail a comparable techno-determinism.

The magic lantern's light source is internal rather than external. A beam of light, shone through hand-painted or photographic glass slides, takes shape on the screen positioned in front of and at a certain distance from the projector. Two aspects of Eliot's development of the magic lantern as a figure for the way the mind works are worth noting. First, he stresses the force of projection: the image *thrown* onto or against the screen. There can be no doubting the power of the mind's internal light source. Eliot's magic lantern has been equipped with a rather more active consciousness than Baudelaire's kaleidoscope. Secondly, the nerves thrown violently onto the screen have at least been thrown onto it in a pattern. The shape the beam of light has taken is intelligible. The patterned image solicits interpretation. It might even amount to what Eliot was to call in his 1919 essay on *Hamlet* the 'objective correlative' or 'formula' for a particular emotion.[13]

In this respect, the history of the magic lantern, a mainstay of the Victorian entertainment industry, and one of cinema's most significant precursors, can help to explain Eliot's emphasis. Some features of lantern showmanship, such as musical accompaniment, and the commentary provided by a narrator or lecturer, carried over into early film presentation.[14] It seems likely that, given the presence of a narrator or lecturer, the relationship the magic lantern spectator maintained with the images on the screen was, as Noël Burch puts it, 'an *exploratory* one'; a relationship also characteristic of the first film shows.[15] The magic lantern coexisted with the moving pictures for a decade or more after 1895. So Eliot's reference to it, in 1911, was slightly archaic; and no doubt with intent. Prufrock finds himself in the predicament Eliot was to describe in 'The Dry Salvages' (*CPP* 186). He has had the experience (of sunsets and sprinkled streets, of novels, teacups, and trailing skirts), but missed the meaning. The magic lantern – the kind of technology, genteel and old-fashioned, with which Prufrock feels at home – intervenes. It cannot restore meaning to experience. But its automatism has created a pattern, there, on the screen, for exploration, which Prufrock alone would have been incapable of creating.

It is possible that Prufrock is rather too much at home with his old-fashioned technology. His vision of mermaids riding the waves, or lolling in seaweed drapes in chambers beneath them, has something of the magic-lantern show about it. Perhaps Prufrock had been to see (Eliot himself could not possibly have done) the dances presented at the Palace Theatre by a lady calling herself La Pia. The performance, we learn from a report in *The Times*, is 'considerably heightened by a shimmering background of glistening tinsel ribbons and the artful aid of many-coloured lights in combination with clever cinematograph and magic lantern illusions'. Two of La Pia's dances apparently brought the 'opposing elements' of fire and water into play with 'quite extraordinary realism'. In the fire dance, drapery and streaming hair sucked by a 'furious draught' coalesce into flame. In the water dance, a cinematograph turns the whole of the back of the stage into a tossing sea. The waves submerge La Pia, but each time she comes up again unharmed.[16]

The third of the 'Preludes', dated July 1911, describes a woman who, dozing, watches the night reveal the sordid images of which her soul is constituted 'flicker' against the ceiling (*CPP* 23). When Prufrock wistfully remarks that he has seen the moment of his greatness 'flicker' (*CPP* 15), the flickering is that of a candle, or lamp. Here, by contrast, it is the images which flicker, not a light source; the flickering is mechanical. The *OED*'s first citation for 'flicker' in its cinematic sense – a succession of changes in a picture occurring when the number of frames per second is too small to produce reliable persistence of vision – is from H. V. Hopwood's *Living Pictures* (1899). 'There is little doubt but that a continual rattle impinging on the ear', Hopwood complained of early projection systems,

> tends to intensify irritation caused to the eye by flicker on the screen, and it is towards the minimising or concealment of this same flicker that attention is at the present time most strenuously directed. This objectionable phenomenon is traceable to the fact that the picture is periodically cut-off from view, a state of affairs which, of course, does not obtain in natural vision. It must be remembered that though persistence of vision ensures the continuance of one image until such time as another is received, yet the impression does not continue in its full strength, and the general result is therefore a perpetual increase and decrease in the brilliancy of the picture as perceived by the eye. Furthermore, the decrease of light is progressive, but every fresh view is presented in full brilliancy.[17]

The flicker, or perpetual increase and decrease in the brilliancy of the picture projected, is one mark of cinema's automatism: a 'state of affairs' which 'does not obtain in natural vision'. It is unlikely that such an effect would allow for an 'exploratory' relationship between viewer and projected picture. There does not seem to be a great deal of pattern, in Eliot's poem, to the sordid images thrown violently onto or against the ceiling. In this case, projection offers little relief from, and indeed exacerbates, the woman's irritability. One thinks of Leopold Bloom, in *Ulysses*, desperate, like the elderly man in *As Seen through a Telescope*, for a glimpse of a woman climbing into a carriage ('Watch! Watch! Silk flash rich stockings white. Watch!'), and thwarted when a tramcar slews between. Again, the perpetual

increase and decrease in brilliancy engenders (and expresses) irritation.
'Flicker, flicker: the laceflare of her hat in the sun: flicker, flick.'[18]
References to visual technology, in the early poems, enabled Eliot to
define the 'exteriorities of language and space' (in Ellmann's phrase) which
constitute social subjectivity. Indeed, to imagine consciousness as an event
or drama of projection was to grasp the implication of one exteriority in the
other: to find space in language. Spatial prepositions (across, against, along,
among, behind, by, under, upon) play an important part in these poems.
The most interesting spatial preposition of all is 'across', which Eliot uses to
indicate both the distance between viewer and scene, and the distance from
one side of the scene to the other. 'Interlude in London' was based on a visit
Eliot made to London, from Paris, in April 1911. In the hotel, he told Eleanor
Hinkley, 'one looked through the windows, and the waiter brought in eggs
and coffee ...'[19] The speaker of the poem rather more complicatedly
laments that he must live 'across the window panes'.[20] He looks out
through a window into the world beyond; but that world might also seem
to have spread itself out, as it quite often does in Eliot's early poems, from
one side of the frame to the other. The panes are transparent; and they form
a screen. So it is, too, after a fashion, in 'Interlude: in a Bar', of February
1911, which also concerns a space of projection. Across – on the other side of
– the room, shifting smoke settles around 'forms' which pass through or
clog the brain. Yet that other side also functions as a flat surface, a kind of
screen. The walls 'fling back' the scattered streams of a life which appears
'Visionary, and yet hard': at once 'immediate' and 'far', like a projected
image (*IMH* 51). How very few there are, observes the speaker of the fourth
and last poem in the 'Mandarins' sequence of August 1910, who see their
'outlines' on the 'screen'. Christopher Ricks glosses 'on the screen' by
reference to the *OED*'s first cinematic citation, from a 1910 issue of
Moving Picture World: 'People ... like to see on the screen what they read
about.'[21]

Eliot's enquiry into 'across' continued in a fragment beginning 'Oh little
voices of the throats of men' which he enclosed, together with 'The Love
Song of St Sebastian', in a letter of 25 July 1914 to Conrad Aiken. On 30
September 1914, he told Aiken that the stuff he had sent 'is not good, is very
forced in execution, though the idea was right'.[22] As Ricks points out, there
is throughout the fragment 'some likeness to *The Waste Land*'.[23] An
(elderly?) man describes how he has searched the world 'through dialectic
ways', among the living and the dead, but found only appearance, 'unreal,
and yet true'. He then falls into a doze, like the woman in the third
'Prelude', while plumes of lilac sweep across the window panes, and
shadows crawl across the floor. He, too, seems to have been taken up into,
or construed as, a space of projection. Eliot sought not just to come to terms
with, but to explore fully, to articulate in and as the poem itself, the power
of images thrown technologically onto a screen: images visionary and yet
hard, unreal and yet true, like those in an early film.

Bergson

The context usually proposed for the interest these poems take in the relation between consciousness and matter is that of contemporary philosophy in general, and Henri Bergson in particular.[24] The arguments Bergson put forward for the authenticity of immediate experience, most colourfully in *Creative Evolution* (1907), had placed him at the centre of a fierce philosophical debate with wide-ranging implications for the status of religion and science in modern societies. Eliot graduated from Harvard in January 1910, and in October that year left for Paris, to study at the Sorbonne and attend Bergson's weekly lectures at the Collège de France. He had already written the first part of 'Prufrock', the second part of 'Portrait', and the first two 'Preludes'. The completion of these poems had to wait until he could claim to have begun to get to grips with Bergson's ideas. He was later to confess that his only 'real conversion, by the deliberate influence of any individual', had been a 'temporary conversion' to Bergsonism.[25] In October 1911, he returned to Harvard to undertake a doctorate in philosophy. By that time, it would seem, the first flush of enthusiasm was over. In an essay written for one of his Harvard courses, most likely in 1912 or 1913,[26] Eliot mounted a substantial critique of the doctrines developed not only in *Creative Evolution*, but in earlier works such as *Time and Free Will*, *Matter and Memory*, and *An Introduction to Metaphysics*.

Eliot's main target was the absolute distinction Bergson had drawn between the internal world of consciousness, which engenders and is defined by freedom, and the external world of matter, where all is necessity.[27] According to Bergson, consciousness, which operates in real time, or duration, takes shape as an interpenetrative multiplicity; possessing neither quantity nor extension, it eludes measurement. Matter, by contrast, product of a merely 'numerical' multiplicity, possesses nothing except quantity and extension; it invites, and is made known by, measurement. It inhabits clock time, rather than real time; extension, rather than intensity. The terms appropriate to an understanding of consciousness and matter, Bergson wrote in *An Introduction to Metaphysics*, are those supplied by 'intuition', on the one hand, and by 'analysis', on the other. Intuition – 'the kind of *intellectual sympathy* by which one places oneself within an object in order to coincide with what is unique in it and consequently inexpressible' – eschews symbols, and has no point of view. Analysis, by contrast, is 'translation, a development into symbols, a representation taken from successive points of view'; and space both its object and its medium.[28] Language is 'spatialised', Bergson argued in *Time and Free Will*, in that it demands that we establish between our ideas 'the same sharp distinctions, the same discontinuity, as between material objects'.[29]

Of course, the assimilation of thought to things through analysis had abundant practical uses. The danger Bergson saw was that the very effectiveness of such methods might lead to the treatment of non-spatial phenomena (such as states of mind) as though they were spatial. Analysis can never capture the interpenetrative multiplicity of immediate experience. 'The inner life', Bergson declared in *An Introduction to Metaphyics*, 'is all this at once: variety of qualities, continuity of progress, and unity of direction. It cannot be represented by images.' To be sure, one could, in investigating the inner life, 'solidify duration once it has elapsed, divide it into juxtaposed portions and count all these portions'. Such an analysis would, however, be accomplished 'on the frozen memory of the duration, on the stationary trace which the mobility of duration leaves behind it, and not on the duration itself'. Intuition alone can grasp immediate experience, Bergson argued, through the development of 'supple, mobile and almost fluid representations' which 'mould' themselves to its 'fleeting forms'.[30]

Eliot's major criticism was that the absoluteness of these distinctions could never be sustained in practice. Bergson, he was able to point out, frequently uses the spatialised language of magnitude, number, and point of view, even when describing the immeasurable intensity of states of mind: for example, in the account of intuition's 'forms', and of the 'representations' which 'mould' themselves to those forms. How could one *not* use such language? Eliot's Bergsonian poems further spatialise the necessary spatialisation of any thought about thought itself. It seems very likely that Prufrock's 'overwhelming question' is one to which intuition alone could provide an answer. However, no sooner is it broached than it produces a spatial figure of speech which itself spaces out intuitionist discourse. In the third 'Prelude', the protagonist's dawn vision, immeasurable though it may be in its intensity, could scarcely be said to have obliterated the nightmare thrown against the ceiling: a pattern made not by duration itself, but by the stationary traces it has left behind, by their irritating flicker. 'Rhapsody on a Windy Night', often regarded as in some degree Bergsonian, is a poem about the sheer resilience of the practical intellect, and of the quantifiable life it has built for itself.[31]

In *An Introduction to Metaphysics*, Bergson's preferred metaphor for analysis had been the photograph, or succession of photographs. An analytic account of movement in space will amount, he proposes, to 'so many snapshots', each constituting a point of view on movement, rather than movement itself, a 'clumsy imitation'.[32] But he did not hold back for much longer from the opportunity to engage with a visual technology capable of producing an altogether less clumsy imitation of movement in space. By 1907, in the long concluding chapter of *Creative Evolution*, the cinematograph had become the way in which he thought about analysis in general. 'Suppose', he pondered, 'we wish to portray on a screen a living picture, such as the marching past of a regiment.' Photographs of individual marchers projected in rapid succession on to the screen would never 'make movement'. If the photographs are to make movement, to appear 'animated', to capture the 'suppleness and variety of life', there must be movement *in* them. In cinema, of course, the apparatus itself supplies the movement.

> It is because the film of the cinematograph unrolls, bringing in turn the different photographs of the scene to continue each other, that each actor of the scene recovers his mobility; he strings all his successive attitudes on the invisible movement of the film. The process then consists in extracting from all the movements peculiar to all the figures an impersonal movement abstract and simple, *movement in general*, so to speak; we put this into the apparatus, and we reconstitute the individuality of each particular movement by combining this nameless movement with the personal attitudes. Such is the contrivance of the cinematograph. And such is also that of our knowledge. Instead of attaching ourselves to the inner becoming of things, we place ourselves outside them in order to recompose their becoming artificially.

Bergson concluded that 'the mechanism of our ordinary knowledge is of a cinematographical kind'. Science, he went on, is no more capable than 'ordinary knowledge' of attaching itself to the inner becoming of things: 'it always considers moments, always virtual stopping-places, always, in short, immobilities.' Real time, 'regarded as a flux, or, in other words, as the very mobility of being', eludes the grasp of science and ordinary knowledge alike.[33]

According to Bergson, then, the cinematographic 'analysis' of movement in space is the opposite of intuition: it cannot capture inner becoming. This argument poses something of a dilemma for film theory, which has on occasion wanted to claim that the thing cinema is best able to do is to capture inner becoming, or *durée réelle*. Gilles Deleuze founded a widely influential theory of cinema on the thesis Bergson put forward in *Matter and Memory* (1896): that movement understood as a physical reality in the external world was inextricable from the image understood as a psychic reality in consciousness. Deleuze argues that Bergson's objection was to cinema as he knew it in 1907. The films made during the industry's 'primitive' phase were ones in which 'the image is in movement rather than being movement-image'. Bergson does indeed seem to have felt that the main shortcoming of the films then made was the viewer's externality to the scene viewed. Mercifully, Deleuze adds, cinema did not remain 'primitive' for very long. 'The evolution of the cinema, the conquest of its own essence or novelty, was to take place through montage, the mobile camera and the emancipation of the view point.' The advent of the continuity system, we might say, transformed the shot from a spatial into a temporal category. Thus, cinema would 'rediscover that very movement-image of the first chapter of *Matter and Memory*'.[34]

What makes Bergson's critique of cinema an inconvenience from the point of view of film theory is what makes it interesting from the point of view of the history of early cinema and of literary modernism. Bergson understood that the film-makers of the era had not yet found a way to bridge the gap between movement in the apparatus and movement in the image on the screen. Until they did, the viewer would always remain absent from or external to the scene viewed. The critique, far from being overhasty, is in fact very shrewd. Bergson regarded both intuition and analysis as definitively human activities. But his passionate advocacy of intuition as that which gives value to life alerted him, as different priorities might not have done, to the limitations of forms of knowledge not conducive to 'the kind of intellectual sympathy by which one places oneself within an object in order to coincide with what is unique in it and consequently inexpressible'. Bergson understood cinema's automatism: we see what a machine has seen, not what a human being equipped with intellectual sympathy stood in the same place at the same time would have seen.

Eliot was profoundly interested, both as a poet and as a student of philosophy, in intuition's failure: in those cinematographic forms of knowledge which, unable to grasp the *durée réelle* in which consciousness most fully exists, instead map the space around it. The third poem in a sequence called 'Mandarins', written in August 1910, imagines an elderly philosopher in 'obese repose':

> The cranes that fly across a screen
> Pert, alert,
> Observe with a frivolous mien –
> Indifferent idealist,
>   World in fist,
>   Screen and cranes.

(IMH 21)

In the manuscript, Eliot added the phrase 'attentive intuitionist' to his description of the philosopher, before deleting it. It is the philosopher's idealism, or faith in the power of intellectual sympathy, which encourages him to grab the world in his fist: rather as Prufrock would squeeze it into a ball in order to roll it towards an overwhelming question (*CPP* 15). The poem appears to suggest that the world is not that easily squeezed. The cranes in flight across the screen might well be Bergson's marching men: a rapid succession of images of individual beings in motion which yet fail to 'make movement'. The cranes on the screen have a 'mien', but no meaning; if they do have a meaning, for the attentive intuitionist, he seems unlikely to divulge it. An intervening rhyme, itself pertly alert at the stanza's tautly sprung hinge, defines them for us as observers rather than observed (observers with attitude, at that). The world's indifference to the philosopher is a good deal more colourful than his indifference to it. The stanza uncoils cinematographically down and across the page, fitting its own trajectory as poetic and linguistic enquiry (snapshots of the process of thought) into that of birds in two-dimensional flight: *écran* is the French for screen, and a word savoured by Jules Laforgue, whose work the poem echoes.[35] The stanza describes intuition. It performs analysis.

The poem's conclusion may take hints from both Bergson and Laforgue, but its melancholy is that of 'Prufrock' and 'Portrait of a Lady'.

> And what of all that one has missed!
> And how life goes on different planes!

(IMH 21)

It seems fair to say that a characteristic concern with lost opportunity has been fed through Bergson's understanding of the inherent spatiality of analysis, which itself took shape from his understanding of cinema. Eliot, while he regrets what has gone missing, and what might conceivably be restored through the purposeful exercise of intuition, finds rather more to admire than Bergson had ever done in the automatism analysis automatically renders: a frivolous mien on a frivolous screen; an evening spread out against the sky, like a patient etherised upon a table; or a soul stretched tight across it (*CPP* 13, 23). Intriguingly, the idea of the screen as the plane on which a certain kind of life 'goes', survives into the fourth and last poem in the 'Mandarins' sequence. This poem, as we have already seen, offers one further thought, a thought not indicative of 'spleen'. How very few there are, the speaker muses, who see their 'outlines' on the 'screen'. Eliot's thought would seem to be a thought at once about the power and about the infrequency of self-recognition. As we saw in the previous chapter, it was a thought never far from the minds of the first film-makers.

Bergson regretted the cinema, and its compelling performance of the viewer's externality to the scene viewed; an externality lethal to intuition. But it is worth noting that he also regarded the denaturing artifice produced by any form of analysis as the foundation of comedy. Comedy is a view from outside: a view which does not attempt recognition, or acknowledgement; a view in which intellectual sympathy has been disabled. 'The attitudes, gestures and movements of the human body are laughable', Bergson wrote, 'in exact proportion as that body reminds us of a mere machine.'[36] His theory of laughter made no reference to cinema, but it demonstrates (to the point of savouring) externality's usefulness. Unlike Wyndham Lewis, for example, Eliot does not appear to have shown any great interest in that theory.[37] But one could argue that his poems develop the tendency in Bergson's thinking it exemplifies rather more assiduously than they develop the idea of intuition. The human body did remind him on occasion of a machine. Like Bergson, he understood that it quite often takes a machine to know one; that visual technologies bring out the mechanism in attitudes, gestures, and movements.

Eliot on cinema

On 27 November 1914, five months before his visit to the cinema with the amusing French woman, Eliot described to Eleanor Hinkley an intervention in a recent debate at Merton College. The topic of the debate had been 'the threatened Americanisation of Oxford'. Eliot's contribution was to point out 'frankly' to those present 'how much they owed to Amurrican culcher in the drayma (including the movies) in music, in the cocktail, and in the dance'.[38] He seems to have regarded the Americanisation of Oxford as an opportunity rather than a threat. This brief manifesto has understandably gone down well with those who argue that throughout his career Eliot was, as David Chinitz puts it, 'productively engaged' with a variety of forms of popular culture. It has gone down well, that is, except in so far as it expresses considerable enthusiasm for the movies. Chinitz, for example, uses it to substantiate his thesis that Eliot discovered the rhythms and cadences which shape some of his early poems in American popular music circa 1911. 'It is "Amurrican culcher ... in music, in the cocktail, and in the dance" that gives Eliot's poetry its distinctive resonance.'[39] Critics have been in altogether too much of a hurry, as Chinitz has been in this instance, to drop 'drayma (including the movies)' from the catalogue of forms of popular culture with which Eliot can be said to have engaged productively. He himself had a fair amount to say about the movies.

The letter of 27 November 1914 to Eleanor Hinkley goes on to describe in vivid fashion further developments in the 'great ten-reel cinema drama, EFFIE THE WAIF', which Eliot had begun to sketch out for her two weeks previously, on 14 October 1914.

> MEDICINE HAT, Wyoming, Christmas Eve. Spike Cassidy, the most notorious gambling house proprietor in the county, (ever since the early death of his wife, his only good influence), returns from the saloon, where he has won all the money and shot a man, to find a small bundle on his doorstep. He stops and stoops. A feeble cry from the bundle – it squirms, it is warm, it is alive! He takes it tenderly in his arms.

Reformed by the 'sweet insidious influence of the child', Spike becomes mayor of Medicine Hat, and the richest man in the county. But there is a 'canker in the rose': Spike's ex-partner, Seedy Sam, now a ruined and desperate man, who reappears with his son Peter, a 'comic simpleton'. Already it is clear than no melodramatic stone will be left unturned in this bold excursion into Amurrican drayma. The serial-style action of *Effie the Waif*, chronicled in a succession of letters, piles continent upon continent and protagonist upon protagonist: Effie's mother, Gwendoline (or Guendolyne), Lady Chomleyumley; a Prussian spy making plans of the Medicine Hat gas-works; Early Bird, an 'Indian Maiden'; Pegoon, an 'Irish lass', daughter of Mrs Flaherty who runs the hash house; and many, many more.[40]

As Susan McCabe points out, these letters demonstrate that Eliot was thoroughly familiar with the narrative conventions of popular cinema.[41] It is significant that the narrative conventions he chose to burlesque should above all have been those of that quintessentially American genre, the Western. In the period immediately before the First World War, the 'fictitious Wild West of cowboy-and-Indian films' became the 'American subject par excellence', hugely successful both at home and abroad.[42] One mark of that success was the delight commentators such as Eliot took in the energy with which an American myth had been squeezed out of reckless narrative hybridity. According to an article in *The Times* of 28 January 1915, the war had by no means diminished the Western's popular appeal. '"Cowboys is off," we had been told by an experienced friend, but if the term cowboy includes anyone who wears a sombrero and jack-boots and goes at full cinema gallop across the stage airily letting off his carbine with one hand, then he is not off.' The writer goes on to describe, without naming, an 'admirable drama' which 'combines Wild West and Red Indians, soldiers and fighting, gambling in high life, spies, bribes, and plans with all the delicious and hilarious relief that belongs to a runaway carriage and a comic coachman'.[43] There were many such.

Eliot's burlesque captures precisely the racial stereotyping which had underwritten the cowboy's emergence in fiction and film as the embodiment of white supremacy. Thus, there is to be a battle between Pegoon's thirty-one cowboy admirers and the thirty-one 'Mexican "greaser" admirers' of the dancer Paprika ('Huge eyes and a stiletto. Easily offended'). Like many Westerns, *Effie the Waif* includes 'good' as well as 'bad' Indians. For example, the heroine of Kay-Bee's *The Invaders* (1912), a Sioux chief's daughter named Sky Star, rejects a suitor already accepted by her father, and falls for a railway surveyor. When the Sioux decide to attack the surveyors, she rides off to alert the garrison of a nearby fort, and, despite suffering a serious fall, accomplishes her mission; she dies of her injuries. In *Effie the Waif*, Early Bird, the daughter of Oopaloompah, chief of the Boozaways, is engaged to Night Hawk, but throws him over on the appearance of Wilfred Desborough, scion of one of Harlem's oldest families, who has come west to make his fortune. 'Later, she is killed while saving W.'s life.'[44]

These letters to Eleanor Hinkley also make it clear that Eliot had an acute understanding not only of the narrative conventions of popular cinema, but also of the techniques it favoured. He meant to visualise a series of scenes rather than merely to tell a story. Early on, as Wilfred Desborough proceeds westward up the Erie on a canal boat, 'he turns and gazes at the Statue of Liberty disappearing on the horizon (not strictly accurate geography, but a fine scene)'.[45] The kind of reverse-angle cutting Eliot envisages here – a shot of Desborough, on the canal boat, turning, followed by a shot of the Statue of Liberty – proved hard to accomplish in the studio, and in fact found its first consistent use in Westerns such as *The Loafer* and *The Shotgun Ranchman*, which Arthur Mackley made for Essanay in 1912.[46] Its effect is to create a synthetic space: to superimpose the 'fine scene' on 'geography'. 'It became apparent', as Lev Kuleshov was to observe in *Art of the Cinema* (1929), 'that through montage it was possible to create a new earthly terrain that did not exist anywhere.' Kuleshov describes an experiment he undertook in the early 1920s, in Moscow, in which the two protagonists are seen greeting each other even though the streets they walk down were miles apart. 'They clasp hands, with Gogol's monument as a background, and look – at the White House – for at this point, we cut in a segment from an American film, *The White House in Washington*. In the next shot they are again on the Boulevard Prechistensk.'[47] Kuleshov would have got the joke in *Effie the Waif*. Eisenstein, whose disjunctive and polemical use of montage has most often been associated with modernism, might not have done.

There was experiment in cinema long before the emergence after the war of the avant-garde film-makers whose work has understandably attracted the attention of literary scholars. Westerns were often remarkably inventive. Richard Abel comments, as the trade press did at the time of the film's release, on the virtuosity of the battle-scenes in *The Invaders*.[48] Furthermore, the virtuosity had dramatic purpose.

As the Sioux warriors plan their attack on the railwaymen, Sky Star sits in a wigwam. She leans to her right (screen left), listening intently. Outside, in a space which bears no direct relation to the wigwam, a warrior gestures extravagantly to his left (screen right), in what we assume to be the direction of the surveyors' camp. Cut to Sky Star, who recoils to her left (screen right), and then, in a gesture which mimics that of the warrior, but substitutes fear and tenderness for hostility, reaches out to her left (screen right) in the direction of the threatened white men, before glancing back horror-struck to her right (screen left). This sequence establishes Sky Star in a quasi-abstract space expressive less of the topography of the Sioux camp than of the painful split in her own allegiances. Westerns like *The Invaders* were certainly melodramatic, but it was possible to look at them, as Eliot evidently did, and even to admire them, from a technical point of view.

Eliot's eye had evidently been caught by other cinema-tricks as well. At one point in *Effie the Waif*, Lady Chomleyumley travels to India, the scene of Effie's abduction, where she interviews a faquir.

> After a lot of hocus pocus, he produces a crystal sphere into which she gazes. The next reel of course shows what she saw in the sphere: the whole history of the foul abduction of her husband and her babe from their station in Kashmeer, with the aid of a monkey, a cobra, and a man-eating tiger. I shall elaborate this later; the point is that she is finally shown Effie in her present position in the act of spurning Peter (Effie is going to be awfully good at spurning before she gets through).[49]

Lengthy flashbacks of the kind Eliot has in mind here came into fashion around 1910. By 1914, the device was capable of considerable complexity. In *The Family Record*, successive flashbacks reveal the histories of a man and woman long separated; in *The Man That Might Have Been*, flashbacks revealing the episodes from the hero's life contrast with reverie concerning what he 'might have been' if his dead son were still alive. The fashion for lengthy flashbacks lasted until around 1917.[50] Such scenes quite often began with an insert shot of a letter referring to a past incident, followed, possibly after a cut back to the letter's meditative recipient, by a dissolve straight into shots of the incident referred to. Eliot's choice of the crystal sphere as transitional object was by no means implausible.

Of equal interest is his plan to cut from Gwendoline at the crystal sphere to 'Effie in her present position in the act of spurning Peter'. Cross-cutting between parallel events was a technique perfected by D. W. Griffith in the films he made for the Biograph Company between 1908 and 1913. In some of those films, as in the scenario for *Effie the Waif*, the cut is psychologically motivated, a product of one character's strong feeling for another; and the space thus created a 'space of the imagination' where gestures meet in a 'phantom embrace'.[51] Eliot's emphasis on Effie's 'position' in a particular 'act' shows him thinking in precise terms about the way in which the cut from one strand of the narrative to another might be effected. His understanding of film technique was thoroughly up to date, and a good deal more sophisticated than that shown by cinephile writers such as Franz Kafka.[52] What interested him, above all, it would seem, was the construction of a 'new earthly terrain that did not exist anywhere': a narrative space made in and by a machine.

Eliot's cinematic ambitions soon evaporated, even in the letters to Eleanor Hinkley, which increasingly fell back on other kinds of *jeu d'esprit*, notably the theatrical skit, and on accounts of 'cubist teas' and the like.[53] By this time, cinema's transformation into a mass-medium dedicated primarily to narrative fiction was more or less complete. In October 1917, A. R. Orage, editor of the *New Age*, writing as R. H. Congreve, reflected on the future of the cinema.

> I have recently been to a cinema exhibition, and I was not a little surprised by the contrast it presented with the moving pictures I saw some ten or eleven years ago. Then, I remember, the exhibition was extremely crude but surprisingly interesting for the length, at any rate, of half an hour. One saw scenery photographed from a moving train, rivers from source to mouth, panoramas of cities and the like. It was a vivid geography lesson. In the cinema of to-day, to judge by my recent experience, one seldom sees any of these instructive things. The programme is designed to amuse, to thrill, to interest, but never to instruct.

While remaining certain that cinema would never 'command the attention of the intelligent as a form of art', Orage thought that it had its uses as a medium of mass entertainment, and as a popular alternative to the drama and the novel.[54] Such were the terms in which Eliot began to think about the cinema again, in the years after the First World War, when he sought to establish himself as a poet and critic by forging an alliance of 'high' and 'low' art against mass culture.

In the 'London Letters' Eliot began to contribute to *The Dial* in 1921, cinema features on occasion as the epitome of mass culture.[55] The high–low alliance he hoped to forge against this menace, as a poet and critic, was primarily with music hall. The essay in memory of Marie Lloyd published as the last of *The Dial* 'London Letters' in December 1922, and then in a shorter version in *The Criterion* in January 1923, an essay unremittingly hostile to cinema, was in effect a manifesto for the new alliance. The tone of these 'London Letters', and of the 1937 essay on 'Religious Drama: Mediaeval and Modern', so different from that of his intervention in the debate at Merton College, has understandably led to comparisons with the critique of mass culture mounted by Theodor Adorno, F. R. Leavis, and others.[56] However, the interest of Eliot's view of cinema lies in the evolution of its responsive detail rather than in the broad thrust of a polemical stance taken once and for all.

In 'The Romantic Englishman, the Comic Spirit, and the Function of Criticism', published in Wyndham Lewis's journal *The Tyro*, in April 1921, Eliot worried about the expression of national life in myth; or, rather, about the lack of its expression as myth in contemporary theatre. 'The myth', he explained, 'is imagination and it is also criticism.' The figure of the 'Romantic Englishman' fashioned in literature from Shakespeare to Chesterton had been larger than life, and by that token a mirror in which the (white male) English reader could observe a version of himself, warts and all. In Eliot's view, the theatre no longer offered 'comic purgation' through myth. It was only in the music hall, he maintained, and 'sometimes in the cinema', that opportunities still arose for the 'partial realization' of a mythic figure. Music hall exhibited the 'fragments' of a 'possible English myth'. Both the strength and the weakness of the cinema lay in the breadth of its appeal. 'Charlie Chaplin is not English, or American, but a universal figure, feeding the idealism of hungry millions in Czecho-Slovakia and Peru' (*AWL* 142–3).[57] Chaplin, a product of the English music hall, appears to be disqualified by his subsequent allegiance to Hollywood, rather than by a lack of mythic status.

A year later, in the first issue of his new journal, *The Criterion*, Eliot returned briefly to Chaplin. Chaplin's 'egregious' merit, he now thought, was to have 'escaped in his own way from the realism of the cinema', and thus 'invented a *rhythm*'.[58] Rhythm more appropriately describes a feature of ritual performance than a feature of narrated myth. In ritual performance, rhythm produces catharsis. Eliot continued to think of rhythm as what set Chaplin's performances apart from the 'realism' of cinema and theatre alike. In 1933, he was still berating contemporary drama for its failure to satisfy the need for ritual. It was the rhythm so utterly absent from modern drama, he explained, which made Massine and Charlie Chaplin the 'great actors' they were, and the juggling of Rastelli more 'cathartic' than any performance of *A Doll's House*.[59] During this period, Eliot did not dismiss cinema out of hand. He wanted to find something in it which might yet transform it from within.

So, it is worth noting, did Ezra Pound. Between 1917 and 1919, Pound supplemented his meagre income by reviewing art exhibitions for the *New Age*. The set of 'Art Notes' for 26 September 1918 took as its topic two films recently released by the Hepworth Company, *The Refugee* and *Tares*. Cinema, Pound declared, is no more and no less than photography, and therefore not an art. Like photography, it does not permit that process of 'selection and emphasis' which constitutes art as art. It is therefore matter for the drama critic, and only of interest in so far as it sets itself apart from the realism of photography and theatre alike. This does happen, Pound went on, even in a sensational melodrama like *The Refugee*, in the odd moment of 'admirably acted pantomime'.[60] Pantomime was for Pound what rhythm was for Eliot: a fragment of myth or ritual which held the personal and the impersonal in productive (and possibly even cathartic) tension.

What made that tension more productive in music hall than it would ever be in cinema, in Eliot's view, was the co-presence of performer and audience. Since both parties to the collaboration were palpably there in the flesh in the same place at the same time, there could be no knowledge of a role (as artist, as spectator) which was not also knowledge of a person. Marie Lloyd's 'moral superiority' as a performer was based on 'her understanding of the people and sympathy with them, and the people's recognition of the fact that she embodied the virtues which they genuinely most respected in private life'.[61] In the music hall at its best, the mutual recognition constitutive of local community could not be distinguished from a mutual acknowledgement of role or status (as artist, as spectator). The result was a myth expressive of national life. In the cinema, on the other hand, unlike the music hall or the theatre, performer and audience never coincide: for one party to be present, the other must be absent. This failure to coincide was an important theme in Walter Benjamin's 'The Work of Art in the Age of Mechanical Reproduction', first published in 1936, and of a radio address Eliot gave to sixth-form students in the same year. The cinema, Eliot explained, 'gives an illusion not of the stage but of life itself'.

> When we see a great music-hall comedian on the stage ... we feel that he is conscious of his audience, that a great deal of the effect depends upon a sympathy set up between actor and audience, and we like to feel that some of his gags are spontaneous and were not thought of the night before. But when we see Laurel and Hardy, it is not Laurel and Hardy acting for *us*, it is Laurel and Hardy in another mess.[62]

Cinema's gags have all been thought of the night before (or more likely several nights before). Laurel and Hardy's latest mess has been mechanically reproduced; they act not for us, but for any audience anywhere at any time. No prospect, then, of a performance expressive of national life.

In assembling Eliot's remarks about cinema in poems, letters, and essays, I have sought to demonstrate the fascination he felt for its automatism. He regarded that automatism as disabling, in so far as the machine came between performer and audience, denying them co-presence, and as enabling, in so far as the machine made it possible to see what the human eye alone could not have seen: the pattern thrown on a screen, a 'new earthly terrain', a rhythm in excess of mimicry. His own art was not a mechanical art. But it may be that he continued to interest himself in the automatisms one machine in particular had so profoundly clarified. The work he had embarked on, in the years immediately after the First World War, when he evidently thought long and hard about cinema, was a difficult long poem. Before examining *The Waste Land*, I need briefly to take account of a further possible reason for such curiosity, a reason bound up with difficulty itself.

No definition of literary modernism would be complete without some reference to Eliot's remark, in an essay of 1921 on 'The Metaphysical Poets', that the modern poet had no choice but to be difficult.

> Our civilization comprehends great variety and complexity, and this variety and complexity, playing upon a refined sensibility, must produce various and complex results. The poet must become more and more comprehensive, more allusive, more indirect, in order to force, to dislocate if necessary, language into his meaning. (A brilliant and extreme statement of this view, with which it is not requisite to associate oneself, is that of M. Jean Epstein, *La Poésie d'aujourd'hui*.)[63]

Jean Epstein was a leading avant-garde film-maker and film theorist. On 8 September 1921, Eliot wrote to Richard Aldington thanking him for 'the Epstein book', which he had found 'most interesting': 'I disagree with some important conclusions, but it is a formidable work to attack, and therefore very tonic.' Epstein had made his chosen writers (Aragon, Cendrars, Apollinaire) a 'more serious affair, to be tackled in earnest'.[64]

According to Epstein, the primary characteristic of the work of the most significant contemporary poets was that it required as much effort in the reading as in the writing.[65] In (or by) that effortfulness, it did justice to a world whose complexity would otherwise elude description. The most startling claim Epstein made in *La Poésie d'aujourd'hui* was that poetry and film had much to learn from each other's example. Theatre was dead, because no actor could compete with a screen-image which rendered the slightest tremor visible, and dramatic. In cinema, simply to be, to walk, run, stop in one's tracks, turn round, was to be devoured by an audience greedy for spectacle. Epstein concluded that for mutual support cinema and the new poetry should align (*superposer*) their aesthetic strategies. The basis for that alignment lay in certain qualities of the cinematic image: qualities produced by the difference between the way a machine sees and the way a human being sees.

Cinema had become through its systematic use of close-ups a 'theatre of the skin': a look into the world, that is, rather than at it. That shift from one plane to another (Eliot had wondered at 'how life goes on different planes' in the third poem of his 'Mandarins' sequence) unsettles the spectator's equilibrium as no event in theatre had ever done, or ever could do. Equally unsettling, Epstein thought, was the image's suggestiveness. 'On the screen, the essential quality of the gesture is not to complete itself.' Such incompletion seemed more appropriate to poetry than to theatre. Then there was of course the rapidity with which one image succeeded another. 'Details jostle one another to make a poem, and in a film images cut together form a mixture, a dense entanglement.' Epstein even hoped that such jostlings might provide an education in speed of response. 'After a few Douglas Fairbanks, I'm knackered, but I don't feel boredom.'[66] In these and other respects, Epstein felt, cinema and the new poetry had a great deal to learn from each other. Eliot, it would appear, did not agree. But there can be little doubt that Epstein made him think again, in September 1921, after he had drafted the first three sections of *The Waste Land*, about what it took to be modern.

The Waste Land

Cinema, as Stanley Cavell put it in *The World Viewed*, is characterised twice over by automatism. In the first place, it removes the 'human agent' from the 'task of reproduction'; in the second, it mechanically defeats our presence as spectators to the reality reproduced. 'I am present not at something happening, which I must confirm, but at something that has happened, which I absorb (like a memory).' *The World Viewed* was originally published in 1971, amid developments in cinema worldwide whose common obsession with technique, with the medium's ample capacities, has since come to be regarded as in some sense 'modernist'. Modernism, understood as an art or literature which breaks decisively with the past, or thinks that it has broken with the past, was on Cavell's mind. He argued that the automatism in any medium is that in it which leads us to believe that the work of art to which it gives rise is 'happening of itself'. In a tradition, the successful writer is the one who knows how to activate the medium's automatisms; or, we could say, reverting to a terminology I have used in previous chapters, the one who knows how to reactivate the medium's original neutrality as a medium. A medium which remains neutral, as a medium, could be said to 'happen of itself'. Is that still possible, literary modernism asks, for literature? And, if so, what would neutrality look like, after so much art? 'The modernist artist', Cavell argues, 'has to explore the fact of automatism itself, as if investigating what it is at any time that has provided a given work of art with the power of its art as such.'[67]

My argument has been that Eliot's understanding of the automatisms in literature developed in parallel with his understanding of cinema as a medium automatic through and through. When he wrote the poem which became *The Waste Land*, he was every bit as uncertain of the worth of the project as Cavell supposes the modernist should be. The drafts reveal the extent and vigour of his efforts to 'activate' the poetic automatisms of regular metre and rhyme. For example, the original opening of 'The Fire Sermon' consisted of a lengthy passage describing the morning routine of Fresca, a wealthy socialite, written in imitation of Alexander Pope.[68] Pound cut this, on the grounds that there was no place for such imitations in a modern poem. But Eliot continued to believe that the poem might still, on occasion, happen, or appear to happen, by itself. He continued to explore the fact of automatism. Monumental though the commentary on *The Waste Land* now is, relatively little account has been taken of the persistence in it of regular metre and rhyme. My aim in this final section is to examine the coincidence of the poem's appeal to literary tradition, made apparent to ear and eye by regularity of metre and rhyme, with what Eliot took to be most mechanical (most denatured) in a newly homogeneous mass society.

Cinema does appear in *The Waste Land*; in the manuscript, at any rate, if not in the final version. We are introduced to the 'close' or 'sweating' rabble which 'sees on the screen' (that is, can 'identify', 'know', or 'recognise') a 'goddess or a star'; and in 'silent rapture' worships from afar.[69] This is cinema as Eliot had presented it in the essay on Marie Lloyd: a homogenising mass-medium, a machine for the manufacture of passivity. However, his reference to it in the draft of an ambitious long poem is by no means casual. The reference occurs during the imitation of Pope. It would have been inserted into the account of Fresca's brilliant career as a celebrity, which arises out of, or rises above, the meticulous, unsparing description of her morning routine (breakfast, toilet, bath). Those who witnessed her emergence onto the 'varied scene' of fashionable society (the stage, the turf, boxing peers), we are told, were as comprehensively struck by her 'supernatural grace' as Aeneas had been by that of his mother, when the goddess made herself known without warning, or as the sweating rabble is by that of the film-star whose image saturates the screen.

The double simile affords Fresca a double apotheosis: first, mock-heroically, as Venus; then, by mere extrapolation, since a celebrity is already a star on a smaller scale, as Norma Shearer or Constance Talmadge. Eliot's purpose is not to cut Fresca down to size, any more than Pope's purpose in *The Rape of the Lock* had been to cut Belinda down to size. It is, rather, to understand the basis of her appeal. Hence his hesitation in defining what an audience does – identify, recognise, know – when it sees a star on the screen. Aeneas's response to his mother clearly combines recognition of her as a person with acknowledgement of her divine status. The cinema audience acknowledges a star's divine status, as the medium's creation, but also recognises, or would like to recognise, a certain individuality: the individuality of a being which must be assumed to undergo elsewhere (off-screen) a routine involving breakfast, bath, and toilet. Eliot's interest in Fresca is an extension of his interest in Chaplin's ability to transcend realism, and thus create myth. That transcendence was in his view merely automatic: a product of the photographic machine's capacity to isolate and endlessly reproduce the 'rhythm' of a particular performance. But he did not dismiss it out of hand. In fact, he wanted some of it for his poem. For Fresca's apotheosis does indeed rise above, as well as arise out of, the banal insistence on beverages. Both, however, have been produced by the same literary automatism.

My suggestion is that in such selective usage regularity of metre and rhyme acts (on ear and eye alike) as a kind of frame. In cinema, as in still photography, the frame both enables and disables. On the one hand, it serves, as James Lastra has noted, as an index of the act of witnessing, because it supposes a viewer who is part of the same world as the activities represented.[70] On the other, it permits us to see only as a machine sees; not as we ourselves would have seen had we in fact been there, a part of that world. Literature, of course, is not indexical. But the heroic couplet, as Pope used it, as Eliot uses it, does powerfully indicate, by its segmentation of event, by parcelling narrative out into glimpse or sound-bite, the presence of an observer. But which observer? Or *what* observer, we should perhaps ask, since the morning routine does not seem to have been witnessed in person. Eliot sees Fresca as literary tradition had already seen her, as Pope saw Belinda. The frame both enables and disables. The scene it presents is, as Eliot said of the image on the screen, visionary, and yet hard; unreal, and yet true. There is, perhaps, a certain neutrality to it.

Eliot evidently agreed with Pound that the Fresca passage added up to rather too much automatism. But the poem as a whole methodically departs from and returns to regularity of metre and rhyme. Indeed, the process evident in the Fresca passage – whereby the very exactness (and exactingness) of the measure taken of the mechanical modern bourgeois or petty-bourgeois life provokes a wild rhetorical flourish, an antic gesture – creates a pattern within it. The pattern first becomes evident in the Unreal City passage which concludes 'The Burial of the Dead' (*CPP* 62–3). As Eliot's notes make clear, the unreality of the crowd of commuters flowing across London Bridge is an effect already there in Dante (mediated, perhaps, by James Thompson), and in Baudelaire.[71] The opening lines of the passage at once acknowledge the power of that effect and outdo it by their virtuosity, as Christopher Ricks has shown.[72] Eliot makes his own uncanniness, or makes uncanniness his own. The lines which follow seem by comparison rather *too* canny in their mimesis of the routines of the commuting life.

> Sighs, short and infrequent, were exhaled,
> And each man fixed his eyes before his feet.
> Flowed up the hill and down King William Street,
> To where Saint Mary Woolnoth kept the hours
> With a dead sound on the final stroke of nine.
>
> (*CPP* 62)

The sighs are from Dante. But they rapidly give way to a dull pedestrian beat which is that both of office-workers heading for the office and of the verse itself, which has eased obediently back into iambic pentameter. An iambic up-and-down captures the office-workers' steady progress up the hill and down King William Street. A rhyme bolts two syntactically separate units of description together. Such cast-iron regularity could scarcely fail to produce, as though automatically, its own tribute to mimesis. 'With a dead sound': the double iambic foot (two stressed syllables after two unstressed) creates, by varying a pattern forcefully established, a dead sound of its own. The author of these lines is an automatism of technique engendered, or so it would appear, by the automatism of (some kinds of) modern experience. Iambic pentameter functions here, and to more precise effect than in the Fresca passage, as the frame which both enables and disables.

The exercise of technique has dulled the poem's engagement with literary tradition down to a description which merely documents: to 'footage' of the kind which constitutes many an early film of London bridges and streets. The crowd thus captured was often thought to consist of automata, or ghosts. 'Their smiles are lifeless,' Maxim Gorky had said of the people in the very first Lumière films, 'although their movements are full of living energy and are so swift as to be almost imperceptible. Their laughter is silent, although you see the muscles contracting in their grey faces.'[73] Visionary, and yet hard; unreal, and yet true. The makers of these documentary or 'actuality' films had sought to provoke in the urban crowd they filmed gestures of recognition or acknowledgement (of another person, of the camera itself) which would override the lifelessness. Eliot does something similar, in burlesque. As the automatised description of Fresca's morning routine produces by reaction a simile comparing her celebrity to that of a goddess or film-star, so the automatised description of a commuter's morning routine produces by reaction the hearty welcome the speaker affords a well-known face which is also that of a mythic personage. 'There I saw one I knew, and stopped him, crying: "Stetson!"' The line balloons beyond pentameter, beyond that which might be thought to happen of itself. It expands into antic improvisation. The speaker reminds Stetson that they fought together at Mylae, during the first Punic War, and slyly enquires whether the corpse he planted last year in his garden has sprouted yet (*CPP* 63). 'Some poetic devilry is at work in the closing lines of "The Burial of the Dead",' Grover Smith remarks, 'an instance of the "skits" to which Eliot confessed.'[74]

So who was Stetson? The Stetson was a hat with a broad brim and high crown customarily worn by cowboys. The *OED* cites various contemporary catalogue entries promoting the J. B. Stetson 'Boss of the Plains' sombrero hat. On 15 March 1921, *The Times* announced that the John B. Stetson Company had just opened new showrooms in New Bond Street.[75] Stetson might be regarded as the last gasp of the energies which had gone into *Effie the Waif*. If Venus returns as a screen-goddess, the soldier from Mylae returns as a cowboy: he is at once a person met on the street, and a figure from classical legend, and that figure's reincarnation on the screen. In this case, however, the figure is male rather than female. Because his automatism is so aggressively larger than life, in its way with corpses, Stetson provokes a certain devilry, as Fresca would never have done. Eliot finds in him and his imputed deeds a rhythm or pantomime exceeding realism. His appearance on the screen has provoked an overwhelming question, a question to which there is no answer.

The poem's most extensive and most savage commentary on the homogenisation of modern urban middle-class or lower-middle-class experience takes the form of a scene in 'The Fire Sermon' set during the 'violet hour' at the end of the working day, when a house agent's clerk seduces a typist in her apartment. As Lawrence Rainey points out, it was an innovation, on Eliot's part, to put a typist into a 'serious' work of literature; hitherto typists had featured only in light verse, and in genre and realist fiction.[76] In a story first published as 'The Common Round' in the *New Age*, in 1917, and then in revised form as 'The Pictures' in *Art and Letters*, in 1919, and as 'Pictures' in *Bliss and Other Stories* (1920), Katherine Mansfield drew together typing, cinema, and one or two other preoccupations which were to surface in *The Waste Land*. Miss Ada Moss, a resting actress, wakes up cold and hungry in a 'Bloomsbury top-floor back', as a 'pageant' of 'Good Hot Dinners' of the kind favoured by Eliot's Lil and Albert passes fantasmatically 'across the ceiling'. Ada aims to fortify herself at once against her landlady's violent demands for rent, and against the 'common round' she will have to make of the theatrical agencies, with a cup of tea at an ABC, where the waitress boasts that her man is just back from the army, as brown as mahogany; he has brought her a brooch from Dieppe. The common round, with its perpetual prospect of uncommonness in the shape of a part in a play or a film, is all that stands between Ada and these cockney tormentors. At the North-East Film Company, a 'beautiful typist' (the 'Cinema Typist', in the original version) appears at the top of the stairs on which the applicants wait and dismisses them all brusquely. At the Bitter Orange Company, there is a form to be filled in: ' "Can you aviate – high-dive – drive a car – buck-jump – shoot?" read Miss Moss.' Looking good in a Stetson would no doubt have been a plus. At the end of the ordeal, Ada's only feeling is of relief. ' "Well, that's over," she sighed.' She allows herself to be picked up and taken home by a 'stout gentleman'.[77]

Mansfield sets lower-middle-class aspiration, and the moral laxness it induces, against a robust proletarian acceptance of life as it is and always has been; as Eliot was to do in *The Waste Land*. Eliot reinforced the contrast by framing Lil's tale in free verse barely distinguishable from prose, and the clerk's seduction of the typist in stately quatrains. Technique's automatism, listlessly sort-of-rhyming 'at once' with 'response', 'defence' with 'indifference', superbly renders her capitulation (*CPP* 68). In this case, mythic apotheosis does not emerge from within the scene, provoked by automatism, but surrounds it from the outset in the shape of Tiresias, its perpetual witness. Tiresias, Eliot said, is a 'mere spectator', and yet the most important 'personage' in the poem. What he *sees*, in fact, is its 'substance' (*CPP* 78).

Victorian poetry had prepared Tiresias for Eliot as the figure of the blind seer 'outside of death and birth', to whom knowledge always comes 'before' the event, or 'afterward', in Algernon Swinburne's version, but never during it; never at the time, never in the moment. The knowledge, when it came, was of misconduct. 'I, Tiresias the prophet, seeing in Thebes/ Much evil ...'[78] Eliot's Tiresias, however, has been updated by association with the violet hour at the end of the working day, when the 'human engine' awaits release like a taxi throbbing in readiness. 'I Tiresias, though blind, throbbing between two lives ...'(*CPP* 68). There may even be an echo here of Epstein's defence of difficulty in modern literature. Among the thoughts stirred in him by a line from Blaise Cendrars's *Dix-neuf poèmes élastiques* – 'J'ai des pommettes électriques au bout de mes nerfs' ('I have electric cheek-bones at my nerves' ends') – are 'que rien ne donne mieux l'impression de nervosité qu'un moteur trépidant' (*trépider* is to throb, quiver, or vibrate, with anxiety, with ardour).[79] The throb in the 'moteur trépidant' of the clerks and typists waiting for work to end is a throb in Tiresias, too; and, I would say, in the engine of technique, of the quatrains which render what he will see and has already seen.

There is a throb in the scene's spatiality, a spatiality projected by and for Tiresias, a spatiality built into the very terms of that projection. Tiresias maintains that he has foresuffered all 'Enacted on this same divan or bed'. In English, the determiners (or specifying agents) 'this' and 'that' are ranged along a scale of proximity. The former refers to things which are close (in time or space) to the speaker, things which bear some relation to him or her; the latter refers to things which are distant from and bear no relation to the speaker. (I talk about 'this' table if I happen to be leaning on it at the time, 'that' table if it stands at the far end of the room.) 'This' carries associations of intimacy, 'that' of strangeness, of the unknown. When the prophet in the desert is beckoned in under the shadow of '*this* red rock', in 'The Burial of the Dead', we feel, for a moment, that we might conceivably be in the vicinity of or the approaches to a source of redeeming knowledge; rather less so, perhaps, when Madame Sosostris hesitates over '*this* card'. In 'A Game of Chess', by contrast, we find ourselves in an enclosed room, listening to 'that noise', which might or might not be the wind under the door, but which is in any case radically unfamiliar. In the poem's first section, we edge towards a tantalising but ultimately sterile knowledge; in the second, we edge away from a threat to the very possibility of knowledge.[80]

Tiresias throbs between an intimate foreknowledge of what has been enacted on *this* same divan or bed, and the typist's separation of herself from its enactment: 'Well now that's done ...' She absents herself from a sense of occasion, smoothing her hair 'with automatic hand', putting a record on the gramophone.[81] Tiresias, by contrast, wants intimacy, the intimacy of arousal. He may not share Prufrock's fondness for body-hair, but he does unmistakably linger over the undergarments piled on the divan (*CPP* 68–9). For a moment, vision closes in on touch. Like Prufrock, Tiresias has put himself in the picture, gendered male, in and through a description of arousal.[82] Ellmann quite rightly calls him a Peeping Tom.[83] But the divan has as little to offer by way of redeeming knowledge as the red rock or Madame Sosostris's blank card. Tiresias, like Prufrock, is a visitor before and after the event, automatically. He throbs, within the automatisms of language itself, between his own urgent *this* and the typist's listless *that*; between the desire for presence and the desire for absence. To that extent, we might speak of him as a magic lantern or even a camera-projector equipped with consciousness.[84] For cinematic experience is uniquely both of *this* (the lived moment, utterly absorptive) and of *that* (an event which took place somewhere else some time ago). In cinema, this is always already 'that', and that 'this'. *The Waste Land* struggles subsequently to disarm the throbbing automatisms of perception and behaviour compulsively repeated in 'The Fire Sermon'. In its final movement, it attempts to separate out decisively 'that' sound high in the air from 'this, and this only': from a knowledge which redeems.

Ezra Pound and John Rodker

In 1928, Ezra Pound provided for the final issue of *The Exile* a set of editorial notes, or 'Data'. One of these notes had to do with cinema. 'The machine film, the "abstract" or Gestalt film now exists,' Pound declared. The machine film was the product of twelve years of 'research' conducted independently of literature and the visual arts, he went on, though with some overlap (for example, Jean Epstein's collaboration with Blaise Cendrars). In March 1923, in *The Dial*, Pound had praised the montage sequences of machinery in motion in Abel Gance's film of that year, *La Roue*, though he gave most of the credit to literature, and to contemporary abstract art. 'Thanks, we presume, to Blaise Cendrars, there are interesting moments, and effects which belong, perhaps, only to the cinema. At least for the sake of argument we can admit that they are essentially cinematographic.' In 1928, he felt able to look back charitably on a 'noble effort' ruined by a 'punk sentimental plot'.[85]

Even in retrospect, Robert Wiene's *The Cabinet of Dr Caligari* (1920), abjectly imitative of contemporary art, seemed to Pound a complete failure. However, he went on to argue that German culture had subsequently absorbed the 'real art movement since 1900', thus producing a properly abstract cinema. In Walter Ruttmann's *Berlin: City Symphony* (1927), he maintained, 'we have at last a film that will take serious aesthetic criticism'. It would be sheer snobbery not to acknowledge that such a film was 'on parity with the printed page'. European cinema, at any rate, had finally earned his approval. America, by contrast, ignoring the real art movement since 1900, had fallen behind. '*The* American film', Pound had regretfully to report, 'is *The Thief of Bagdad*, a bed-time story told for a child of the desert '[86]

It was Pound who introduced the young American cameraman Dudley Murphy to Fernand Léger, thus helping to bring about one of the most properly abstract films of the decade, *Ballet mécanique* (1923).[87] Indeed, Léger was eager to credit Pound and Murphy with a 'technical novelty' of which he had made considerable use: an optical prism held over the lens in such a way as to shatter the image into overlapping and interpenetrating forms.[88] The novelty was the outcome of experiments Pound had undertaken with Alvin Langdon Coburn in the production of multiple-image photographic portraits by means of an instrument known as a 'vortoscope'. Some of these were exhibited at the London Camera Club in 1917.[89] Pound, too, more or less knew what he was talking about when it came to abstract cinema. Even so, it is hard to disagree with Michael North's conclusion that by 1923 his own work was 'far too advanced' to receive any 'significant impetus' from his relatively brief association with cinema.[90] However, there does seem to be something vortoscopic about his celebrated description of the 'radiant world' known to medieval philosophers, where 'one thought cuts through another with clean edge': 'magnetisms that take form, that are seen, or that border the visible, the matter of Dante's *paradiso*, the glass under water, the form that seems a form seen in a mirror, these realities perceptible to the sense'.[91]

The most striking claim Pound made in his *Exile* essay was that the success of films like *Berlin: City Symphony* 'should flatten out the opposition (to Joyce, to me, to Rodker's *Adolphe*) with steam-rolling ease and commodity, not of course that the authors intended it'.[92] This new abstract cinema might yet create an audience for the new (or newish) abstract literature. John Rodker's *Adolphe 1920* had been appearing in *The Exile*, and was published in book form in 1930. It is a text preoccupied with cinema. At one point, the protagonist treats himself to a session with some kind of mechanical peep-show, most likely a mutoscope. The mutoscope was a motion picture device consisting of a series of photographs mounted on a cylinder. Mutoscopes showed a wide range of 'films', but the most popular tended to involve young women in various states of undress. 'Mutoscope pictures in Capel Street: for men only,' Leopold Bloom recalls in the 'Nausicaa' episode of *Ulysses*. 'Peeping Tom. Willy's hat and what the girls did with it. Do they snapshot those girls or is it all a fake? *Lingerie* does it.'[93] Rodker's protagonist, lacking Bloom's interest in the way things work, rapidly becomes absorbed in the 'prospects of some approaching revelation'. He slips a coin into the machine.

It began to mutter. Where its heart was, a woman rose from a chair, smiled, patted her elaborate hair, unhooked a shoulder-of-mutton blouse, a petticoat or two, stood self-consciously for a minute in lace-edged drawers, laced boots and black stockings, smiling a timid 1890 smile. Wondering, fearful of losing it, he thought he could not bear her smile to fade, yet suddenly the eyes were dark, and he was with his thoughts. She too in that darkness, from which for a moment he had called her. A coin brought her back: as though gratefully she shyly reappeared, went through all her senseless gestures, smiled and smiled. And darkness again, heavy, inevitable. That room, that sofa, filled his brain with warm shapes and comforting light, and the woman moved amicably through it.[94]

Ulysses was in a number of respects *Adolphe 1920*'s most significant point of departure. It would be possible, nonetheless, to see in this passage an elaboration not only of Bloom's curiosity about Willy's hat and what the girls did with it, but of the scene revealed to another modernist Peeping Tom. Tiresias, too, pores over lingerie. He, too, brings back over and over again out of the darkness an event in a room, on a sofa. If Prufrock is a magic lantern equipped with consciousness, then perhaps Tiresias is a mutoscope (rather than a camera-projector) equipped with consciousness. Both make their visits with the aid of technology's throbbing engine. Those visits articulate Eliot's will-to-automatism.

My argument here has been that Eliot's affinity with cinema went a great deal deeper than any belated discovery of montage technique in his poems would suggest. Eliot got to grips with cinema in a way that Pound, for all his vortoscopic enthusiasms, never did. It is worth noting that Rodker was a part of Eliot's circle in the years leading up to *The Waste Land*. His Ovid Press published *Ara Vos Prec* in 1920. The closest parallel (in fact, the only parallel) I can think of to Stetson's appearance in 'The Burial of the Dead' is Rodker's 'Wild West Remittance Man', a poem which peppers the boredom of English offices and drawing-rooms with baroque gun-slinger fantasy; it was published in the *Little Review* in July 1919, and then in *Hymns* (1920).[95] Furthermore, on 10 July 1922, Eliot wrote to Rodker, asking him to contribute a 3,000-word article on the cinema to *The Criterion*.[96] Had it been written, that article might have altered literary modernism's relation to cinema fundamentally. Even in its absence, we should acknowledge the inventiveness of the uses Eliot made in his work of movie-going. We still owe a debt to the amusing French woman.

Notes

1 *Letters*, ed. Valerie Eliot, vol. 1 (London: Faber and Faber, 1988), 97.
2 David Chinitz, *T.S. Eliot and the Cultural Divide* (Chicago: University of Chicago Press, 2003), 210. See Ronald Schuchard, 'In the Music Halls', in *Eliot's Dark Angel: Intersections of Life and Art* (Oxford: Oxford University Press, 1999), 102–18; Sebastian D. G. Knowles, ' "Then You Wink the Other Eye": T. S. Eliot and the Music Hall', *American Notes & Queries*, 11 (1998), 20–32; Barry Jameson

Faulk, 'Modernism and the Popular: Eliot's Music Halls', *Modernism/Modernity*, 8 (2001), 603–21; Chinitz, *Cultural Divide*, ch. 3.

3 For example, Marjorie Perloff, *21st-Century Modernism: The 'New' Poetics* (Oxford: Blackwell, 2002), 40.

4 *The Mechanic Muse* (Oxford: Oxford University Press, 1987), 25, 34.

5 'Rhapsody on a Windy Night', in *Complete Poems and Plays* (London: Faber and Faber, 1969), 25. References will henceforth be included in the text as *CPP*.

6 *Between Film and Screen: Modernism's Photo Synthesis* (Chicago: University of Chicago Press, 1999), 285, 266, 286, 284, 288.

7 Conrad Aiken, 'King Bolo and Others', in Tambimuttu and Richard March (eds), *T. S. Eliot: A Symposium* (London: Frank Cass, 1965), 20–23, pp. 21–2.

8 Lyndall Gordon, *Eliot's Early Years* (Oxford: Oxford University Press, 1977), 47.

9 *The Poetics of Impersonality: T. S. Eliot and Ezra Pound* (Cambridge, MA: Harvard University Press, 1987), 69.

10 *The Invisible Poet: T. S. Eliot* (London: Methuen, 1959), 21.

11 David Trotter, *The English Novel in History, 1895–1920* (London: Routledge, 1993), 201–2.

12 'On Some Motifs in Baudelaire', in *Illuminations*, trans. Harry Zohn (London: Fontana, 1973), 157–202, p. 177. Benjamin's essay, first published in 1939, begins where the first section of *The Waste Land* ends, with Baudelaire's salutation of the *'hypocrite lecteur'*.

13 'Hamlet', in *Selected Prose*, ed. Frank Kermode (London: Faber and Faber, 1975), 45–9, p. 48.

14 Ian Christie, *The Last Machine: Early Cinema and the Birth of the Modern World* (London: BBC Educational Developments, 1994), 90. See also Laurent Mannoni, *The Great Art of Light and Shadow: Archaeology of the Cinema*, trans. Richard Crangle (Exeter: University of Exeter Press, 2000), ch. 11.

15 *Life to Those Shadows*, trans. Ben Brewster (London: BFI Publishing, 1990), 87.

16 'Variety Entertainments', *Times*, 15 February 1910, 11.

17 *Living Pictures: Their History, Photo-Production, and Practical Working* (London: Optician and Photographic Trades Review, 1899), 208.

18 *Ulysses*, ed. Jeri Johnson (Oxford: Oxford University Press, 1993), 71.

19 *Letters*, vol. 1, 18.

20 *Inventions of the March Hare: Poems 1909–1917*, ed. Christopher Ricks (London: Faber and Faber, 1996), 16. References to Eliot's text will henceforth be included in the text as *IMH*.

21 *Inventions*, 139.

22 *Letters*, vol. 1, 45–6, 58.

23 *Inventions*, 256.

24 For useful accounts of Eliot's interest in philosophy at this period in his life, see Paul Douglass, *Bergson, Eliot, and American Literature* (Lexington: University of Kentucky Press, 1986); M. A. R. Habib, *The Early T. S. Eliot and Western Philosophy* (Cambridge: Cambridge University Press, 1999); and Donald J. Childs, *From Philosophy to Poetry: T. S. Eliot's Study of Knowledge and Experience* (London: Athlone Press, 2001).

25 *A Sermon Preached at Magdalene College Chapel* (Cambridge: Cambridge University Press, 1948), 5. See also the introduction to Josef Pieper, *Leisure:*

The Basis of Culture (New York: Pantheon, 1964), xi. Both remarks are cited by Douglass, *Bergson, Eliot*, 54.

26 The date proposed, after careful scrutiny of the available evidence, by Habib, *Early T. S. Eliot*, 61–2. For illuminating accounts of the essay, see Habib, ibid., ch. 2; and Douglass, *Bergson, Eliot*, 59–62.

27 Habib, *Early T.S. Eliot*, 42–7.

28 *An Introduction to Metaphysics*, authorised trans. T. E. Hulme (London: Macmillan, 1913), 4–5. Hulme was, of course, a close associate of Eliot and Pound. For his views on Bergson, see the essays and reviews reprinted in *Collected Writings*, ed. Karen Csengeri (Oxford: Clarendon Press, 1994).

29 *Time and Free Will: An Essay on the Immediate Data of Consciousness*, authorised trans. F. L. Pogson (London: George Allen/Macmillan, 1910), xxiii–xxiv.

30 *Introduction to Metaphysics*, 13, 18–19.

31 For an informative account of the poem's Bergsonian tendencies, see Childs, *From Philosophy to Poetry*, 52–62.

32 *Introduction to Metaphysics*, 42, 45.

33 *Creative Evolution*, trans. Arthur Mitchell (1911; New York, Dover Publications, 1998), 305–6, 336–7.

34 *Cinema 1: The Movement-Image*, trans. Hugh Tomlinson (London: Athlone Press, 1992), xiv, 24, 3. For a more general reflection on Bergson's uses for film theory, see Paul Douglass, 'Bergson and Cinema: Friends or Foes?', in John Mullarkey (ed.), *The New Bergson* (Manchester: Manchester University Press, 1999), 209–27.

35 As Ricks points out: *Inventions*, 134–7.

36 *Laughter: An Essay on the Meaning of the Comic*, trans. Cloudesley Brereton and Fred Rothwell (London: Macmillan, 1911), 29.

37 On Lewis and Bergson, see Paul Edwards, *Wyndham Lewis: Painter and Writer* (New Haven: Yale University Press, 2000), 71–6.

38 *Letters*, vol. 1, 70.

39 *T. S. Eliot and the Cultural Divide*, 38.

40 *Letters*, vol. 1, 62–4, 71–2, 76–7.

41 *Cinematic Modernism: Modernist Poetry and Film* (Cambridge: Cambridge University Press, 2005), 39.

42 Richard Abel, 'The "Imagined Community" of the Western, 1910–1913', in Charlie Keil and Shelley Stamp (eds), *American Cinema's Transitional Era: Audiences, Institutions, Practices* (Berkeley: University of California Press, 2004), 131–70, p. 143. See also, Robert Anderson, 'The Role of the Western Film Genre in Industry Competition, 1907–1911', *Journal of the University Film Association*, 31 (1979), 19–26; and Abel, *The Red Rooster Scare: Making Cinema American, 1900–1910* (Berkeley: University of California Press, 1999), ch. 6; and, more generally, Scott Simmon, *The Invention of the Western Film: A Cultural History of the Genre's First Half-Century* (Cambridge: Cambridge University Press, 2003).

43 'War in the Picture Drama', *Times*, 28 January 1915, 11.

44 *Letters*, vol. 1, 76–7.

45 Ibid., vol. 1, 63.

46 Barry Salt, *Film Style and Technology: History and Analysis*, 2nd edn (London: Starword, 1992), 94–5.

47 *Art of the Cinema*, in *Kuleshov on Film*, trans. and ed. Ronald Levaco (Berkeley: University of California Press, 1974), 41–123, p. 52.

48 '"Imagined Community"', 147–8.

49 *Letters*, vol. 1, 71–2.

50 Salt, *Film Style and Technology*, 139–40.

51 Tom Gunning, *D. W. Griffith and the Origins of American Narrative Film: The Early Years at Biograph* (Urbana: University of Illinois Press, 1994), ch. 4, esp. pp. 110–14.

52 See Hanns Zischler, *Kafka Goes to the Movies*, trans. Susan H. Gillespie (Chicago: University of Chicago Press, 2003).

53 *Letters*, vol. 1, 82–3 (27 January 1915), and vol. 1, 92 (21 March 1915).

54 'Readers and Writers', *New Age*, 21 (1917), 488–9.

55 These essays have been reprinted in *The Annotated Waste Land*, ed. Lawrence Rainey (New Haven: Yale University Press, 2005). References to them will henceforth be included in the text as *AWL*. See the 'London Letters' for May 1921 and July 1921.

56 'Religious Drama: Mediaeval and Modern', *University of Edinburgh Journal*, 9 (1937), 8–17. For an astute consideration of these issues, see Chinitz, *Cultural Divide*, 80–84.

57 Eliot offers an immediate qualification. We ought not to be affected by myth, he argues, 'as the newspapers say little boys are by cinema desperados. The myth is degraded by the child who points a loaded revolver at another, or ties his sister to a post, or rifles a sweet-shop' (*AWL* 143). The previous autumn, the British Board of Film Censors had voiced concern about the susceptibility of the public imagination to 'crime' films. 'Stories dealing with "costume" crime, however, such as cowboy films and Mexican robberies, are placed in a different category and regarded simply as dramatic and thrilling adventures with no connexion whatever with the lives or possible experiences of young people': 'Love and Crime on the Film', *Times*, 18 October 1920, 9. Some commentators could not see the difference. 'Why murder in Mexico should be shown on the film, while murder in Mile-end is anathema, it is difficult to see': 'Film Censorship', *Times*, 27 October 1920, 15.

58 'Dramatis Personae', *Criterion*, 1 (1922–3), 303–6, p. 306.

59 'The Beating of a Drum', *Nation and Athenaeum*, 6 October 1933, 11–12, p. 12.

60 'Art Notes', *New Age*, 26 September 1918, reprinted in *Ezra Pound and the Visual Arts*, ed. Harriet Zinnes (New York: New Directions, 1980), 78–81.

61 'Marie Lloyd', *Selected Prose*, ed. Frank Kermode (London: Faber and Faber, 1975), 172–4. Kermode prints the *Criterion* version of the essay.

62 'The Need for Poetic Drama', *Listener*, 25 November 1936, 994–5. Walter Benjamin, 'The Work of Art in the Age of Mechanical Reproduction', in *Illuminations*, 219–53.

63 'The Metaphysical Poets', *Selected Prose*, 59–67, p. 65.

64 *Letters*, vol. 1, 468–9.

65 *La Poésie d'aujourd'hui* (Paris: Éditions de la sirène, 1921), 57–8.

66 Ibid., 170–75. My translation.

67 *The World Viewed: Reflections on the Ontology of Film*, enlarged edition (Cambridge, MA: Harvard University Press, 1979), 23, 25–6, 107.

68 *The Waste Land: A Facsimile and Transcription*, ed. Valerie Eliot (London: Faber and Faber, 1971), 23–7.

69 *Facsimile*, 29.

70 'From the Captured Moment to the Cinematic Image: A Transformation in Pictorial Order', in Dudley Andrew (ed.), *The Image in Dispute: Art and Cinema in*

the Age of Photography (Austin: University of Texas Press, 1997), 263–91, pp. 268–9.

71 It was Thompson, Robert Crawford has argued, who 'let Eliot see Dante as a poet of modern London': The Savage and the City in the Works of T. S. Eliot (Oxford: Clarendon Press, 1987), 45–7.

72 T. S. Eliot and Prejudice (London: Faber and Faber, 1988), 136–41.

73 'The Lumière Cinematograph', in The Film Factory: Russian and Soviet Cinema, 1896–1939, trans. Richard Taylor, ed. Taylor and Ian Christie (London: Routledge & Kegan Paul, 1988), 25–6, p. 25.

74 The Waste Land (London: George Allen & Unwin, 1983), 97–8.

75 Times, 15 March 1921, 9.

76 Annotated Waste Land, 108–9.

77 'Pictures', Selected Stories, ed. Angela Smith (Oxford: Oxford University Press, 2002), 193–200. Eliot saw Mansfield occasionally at this time: Letters, vol. 1, 382, 389.

78 'Tiresias', Selected Poems, ed. L. M. Findlay (Manchester: Carcanet, 1982), 118–28, p. 119.

79 La Poésie d'aujourd'hui, 58–9.

80 For a more detailed version of this argument, see my The Making of the Reader: Language and Subjectivity in Modern American, English and Irish Poetry (Basingstoke: Macmillan, 1984), ch. 3. See also Mary Ann Doane's illuminating discussion of C. S. Peirce's interest in determiners as a form of indexicality: The Emergence of Cinematic Time: Modernity, Contingency, the Archive (Cambridge, MA: Harvard University Press, 2002), 91–103.

81 Her actions might be added to the examples of non-human or 'dehumanised' movement Grover Smith notes in 'Rhapsody on a Windy Night'. Smith adds that to depict someone in this way, as an automaton, captures for the art of poetry 'a flatness of conception discovered not by philosophers but by film-makers': The Waste Land, 7.

82 McCabe argues, on the contrary, that Tiresias's 'close observation' of the typist's intimate personal life 'hinges not upon desire for her but upon identification with her': Cinematic Modernism, 43–5.

83 Poetics of Impersonality, 97.

84 The Russian theorist Mikhail Iampolski has even understood Tiresias as a figure for cinema itself, as a cultural form which requires that the spectator assemble fragments and make sense of them retrospectively: The Memory of Tiresias: Intertextuality and Film, trans. Harsha Ram (Berkeley: University of California Press, 1998).

85 'Data', The Exile (London: Johnson Reprint Company, 1967), 104–17, p. 114; 'Paris Letter', reprinted in Ezra Pound and the Visual Arts, 175–7, p. 175.

86 'Data', 115.

87 For the most authoritative account of Pound's role as a go-between, which draws on unpublished correspondence, see Judi Freeman, 'Bridging Purism and Surrealism: The Origins and Production of Fernand Léger's Ballet mécanique', in Rudolf E. Kuenzli (ed.), Dada and Surrealist Film (New York: Willis Locker & Owens, 1987), 28–45, pp. 31–3.

88 Standish D. Lawder, The Cubist Cinema (New York: New York University Press, 1975), 137.

89   Richard Humphreys, 'Demon Pantechnicon Driver: Pound in the London
     Vortext, 1908–1920', in *Pound's Artists: Ezra Pound and the Visual Arts in London,
     Paris, and Italy* (London: Tate Gallery, 1985), 33–80, pp. 69–72.
90   *Camera Works*, 27.
91   'Cavalcanti', in *Literary Essays*, ed. T. S. Eliot (London: Faber and Faber, 1954),
     149–200, p. 154. John Alexander comes close to making a claim for a
     correspondence, at least, between Léger's ideas and the arrangement of
     Pound's cantos across as well as down the page. He points out that Pound, like
     Eliot, thought Cendrars worthy of attention ('Parenthetical Paris, 1920–1925:
     Pound, Picabia, Brancusi and Léger', in *Pound's Artists*, 81–120, p. 107).
92   'Data', 114.
93   *Ulysses*, 351–2. See Katherine Mullin, *James Joyce, Sexuality and Social Purity*
     (Cambridge: Cambridge University Press, 2003), ch. 5.
94   *Adolphe 1920*, in *Poems & Adolphe 1920*, ed. Andrew Crozier (Manchester:
     Carcanet, 1996), 133–74, p. 137.
95   *Poems & Adolphe 1920*, 86–7.
96   *Letters*, vol. 1, 540.

6

Virginia Woolf

Virginia Woolf's interest in the cinema has been a longstanding, if at best intermittent, preoccupation among her critics. The first book-length study of her work, by Winifred Holtby, published in 1932, devotes a full chapter to the topic.[1] There have been several recent investigations, some fruitful, some not.[2] And the idea that we should think of the movies when we read her experiments in fiction has been disseminated widely. Elaine Showalter, introducing the Penguin edition of *Mrs Dalloway* (1925), maintains that the novel's narrative technique is 'very cinematic'.

> Woolf makes use of such devices as montage, close-ups, flashbacks, tracking shots, and rapid cuts in constructing a three-dimensional story. Such transitional devices would have been familiar to her readers, who were flocking to the new cinema houses and seeing the latest American silent films.[3]

By this account, cinema has added a third dimension to the stories told in novels. Showalter's thesis is that the influx of 'American silent films' in the early 1920s helped to create an audience for literary experiment.

The argument Showalter advances is of a kind quite often advanced in relation to modernist writing, as I have already shown on more than one occasion in this book. It is an argument by analogy. Its basic proposition is that some works of literature are structured like a film. Thus Holtby claims that Woolf 'chose' for *Jacob's Room* (1922) the 'cinematograph technique' she had already tried out in *Kew Gardens*.

> There is no preliminary announcement, as on a film, 'Produced by - - - - - - Scenario by - - - - - - From the story of - - - - - - ' But the first chapter betrays her method. Its scenario might be summarised, 'Jacob as a small boy at the seaside in Cornwall,' and Mrs Woolf begins, as any producer might, by photographing a letter, word by word welling out slowly from the gold nib of Betty Flanders' pen. 'So of course there was nothing for it but to leave'. She shows us next the complete figure of the woman pressing her heels deeper in the sand to give her matronly body a firmer seat; then there is a close-up of her face, maternal, tearful, because Scarborough, where Captain Barfoot is, seems so far from Cornwall where she sits writing.[4]

Up to a point. Holtby has quite plausibly rewritten the opening of *Jacob's Room* as a fragment of scenario (most film-makers of the time would have started with an establishing long shot, and then cut in to a close-up of the letter, but there were other patterns available). To do so, however, she has had to overlook the order in which the words appear on the page. Here is the opening of *Jacob's Room*.

> 'So of course,' wrote Betty Flanders, pressing her heels rather deeper in the sand, 'there was nothing for it but to leave.'
> Slowly welling from the point of her gold nib, pale blue ink dissolved the full stop; for there her pen stuck; her eyes fixed, and tears slowly filled them.[5]

The first thing to go, in Holtby's rewriting of this passage in scenario-form, is a literary technique perfected by Charles Dickens: suspended quotation.[6] '"So of course," wrote Betty Flanders, pressing her heels rather deeper in the sand, "there was nothing for it but to leave."' In Woolf's version, we do not get the image of some words on a piece of paper, and then the image of a woman settling herself. Instead, the force of a feeling strongly felt but not yet articulated informs a physical thrust, of heels into sand, which itself then informs the feeling's articulation. The opening sentence of *Jacob's Room* is structured like a sentence in a Victorian novel rather than a sequence of shots in a film (though no Victorian novel would have opened with such a sentence).

Holtby and the critics who have followed her example are right to wonder about the relation between Woolf's writing and the cinema. They may be wrong to pursue analogies between literary and cinematic form, and to identify one as cause and the other as effect. It is more likely to be the case that there was, for a period during the mid-1920s, a fund of shared preoccupation; and that Woolf drew on this fund in developing a particular emphasis in her novels. The emphasis would no doubt have been developed anyway. But it gained in definition and force because she was in the intermittent habit of going to the movies.

The emphasis I have in mind, reiterated at the conclusion of *A Room of One's Own* (1929), is an emphasis on the 'common life' as the 'real' life.[7] Gillian Beer dwells on it in the introduction to her book about Woolf, arguing that the work 'declares' a kinship which might be regarded as more fundamental even than family romance: 'living in the same time, sometimes in the same place – whether or not you ever meet'.[8] This formulation is helpful in two respects. First, it insists that the principle upon which Woolf based her revisions of narrative form was not encounter, but coexistence, or co-observation. Secondly, it reminds us that in order to be properly encounterless, coexistence and co-observation must occur in a particular place at a particular time.

Existence as such, and the ways in which it might be conceived in the medium of literature was as fundamental a preoccupation for Woolf, during the 1920s, as it was for any other living writer. She also shared with some film-makers of the period a narrower interest in the ways in which movement (and in particular casual movement) defines space. The interest is clear in *Mrs Dalloway* (1925), and again in 'The Cinema' (1926), which was written at the same time as the 'Time Passes' section of *To the Lighthouse* (1927). My hypothesis is that the understanding of cinema Woolf evolved in very specific circumstances during the early months of 1926 made it possible for her to say things about the common life, and thus about existence as such, which she had not quite been able to say in *Mrs Dalloway.*

American movies

There is certainly cinema-going, if no particular grasp of or indebtedness to cinema, in *Mrs Dalloway*. Peter Walsh, lingering on the steps of his hotel, watches the office-workers, faces flushed with 'joy of a kind, cheap, tinselly, if you like, but all the same rapture', head off after work for their two hours at the pictures (p. 177). Peter himself will soon head off for Clarissa Dalloway's party, where Lord Gayton and Nancy Blow engage in an animated discussion of 'cricket, cousins, the movies' (p. 194).

The chances are that these would have been *American* movies, as Showalter suggests. By 1925, American movies were the norm. Hollywood dominated the international market. Cinema was a narrative art. It had had to become a narrative art in order to become a profitable mass-medium. The stories it told were tinsel not only for cinema's original working-class audience, patrons of the music hall, the fairground, and the nickelodeon, but for new audiences drawn in by the comfort and respectability of the proliferating picture palaces: Peter Walsh's office-workers, and on carefully chosen occasion Lord Gayton and Nancy Blow.[9] Cinema's spectacular character-driven narratives had displaced (by wholesale incorporation) melodrama and slapstick, on one hand, and the well-made play or novel, on the other.

Hollywood gained control of the international market by mass-production of narrative films made within the 'classical continuity system'.[10] The continuity system enforced some crucial distinctions; none more crucial, and from a certain perspective more damaging, perhaps, than that between movement and action. In his book on *Technique of the Photoplay* (1924), Frederick Palmer illustrated the differences between movement and action by devising a hypothetical scene. 'For instance, one might write: "The whirring blades of the electric fan caused the window curtains to flutter. The man seated at the massive desk finished his momentous letter, sealed it, and hastened out to post it."' According to Palmer, the fan and the fluttering curtain give movement only, while the writing of the letter constitutes an action. 'It is of action that photoplays are wrought.'[11] The spectator, grasping the significance of the letter, is absorbed into the narrative process.

the continuity system

Also at issue in the distinction between movement and action is a certain attitude to space. The aim of early films such as the 'actualities' produced by the Lumière brothers was to show rather than to tell. The movement the actualities frame is of interest in itself, primarily, and on account of the space it defines: a space in which the 'common life' could come into its own, perhaps for the first time, as the 'real' life. Cinema's increasing commitment to narrative, from around 1903 onwards, did not put an end to the pleasures of sheer visibility. The early chase films, for example, which are usually regarded as the first step towards a narrative cinema, still linger to some degree on movement as the demarcation of space (the space of the common life). What *did* in effect put an end to such pleasures, it could be argued, was the continuity system. The cut-on-action, for example, eliminated the 'white space' surrounding entrances and exits in the chase films. It was not so much of action as of cuts-on-action that the Hollywood photoplay was to be wrought. Hollywood method militated against any profound or consistent enquiry into space, because attention devoted to space for its own sake, like attention devoted to movement for its own sake, is attention withheld from narrative or symbolic meaning. The 'sheerly graphic space of the film image' became, David Bordwell observes, a 'vehicle for narrative'.[12]

Outside Hollywood, the pleasures of sheer visibility can be said to have survived, just about. While the continuity system was establishing itself, in the years between 1908 and 1917, a rival narrative cinema continued to flourish in Europe. This other tradition relied for its effects not on editorial process, but on long takes, staging in depth, and elaborate choreography.[13] In Britain, the development of film theory in the late 1920s coincided with the arrival of sound, and a certain nostalgia for early cinema's exposition of space through movement. Dorothy Richardson, a contributor to *Close Up*, the leading British journal of film theory, regarded such expositions of space as the great achievement of film practice in the silent era. 'In life,' Richardson observed, 'we contemplate a landscape from one point, or walking through it, break it into bits'; whereas a film, by 'setting the landscape in motion and keeping us still, allows it to walk through us'.[14]

This emphasis on film's ability both to 'record' and to 'reveal' the common life later found an echo in Siegfried Kracauer's *Theory of Film* (1960), a theory formulated in the light not only of developments such as Italian neorealism, but of Erich Auerbach's discussion, in *Mimesis* (1953), of the novels of Proust, Joyce, and Woolf. Kracauer relied heavily on Auerbach's argument that in *To the Lighthouse* Woolf had dwelt on 'random occurrence' as an event in itself, rather than as background to a 'planned continuity of action'. For him, cinema's 'redemption of physical reality' depended on just such a grasp of random occurrence. At the very end of his book, he returned once more to Auerbach's argument in *Mimesis* that 'the random moments of life represented by the modern novel concern "the elementary things which men in general have in common"'.[15] Kracauer's ready agreement with Auerbach suggests that it is worth pursuing the possibility that Woolf's engagement with cinema, in the early months of 1926, enabled her to say things about the common life which she had not been able to say in *Mrs Dalloway*. But we need first to establish what she *did* say, in that novel, about the common life.

Life and death in *Mrs Dalloway*

Mrs Dalloway, like the hypothetical scene outlined by Frederick Palmer, contains both the completion of a momentous letter and the fluttering of curtains. The letter is Lady Bruton's letter to the editor of *The Times* concerning emigration, completed, after a leisurely lunch, with the assistance of Richard Dalloway and Hugh Whitbread (120–21). It exemplifies, for Woolf, a certain claim to social and political momentousness: a narrowly ritualistic claim, but not altogether implausible. The curtain is one which blows out into the room at the start of Clarissa Dalloway's party, defining space. 'And Clarissa saw – she saw Ralph Lyon beat it back, and go on talking. So it wasn't a failure after all! It was going to be all right now – her party' (p. 186). The novel attends both to action and to movement. Its design is such as to ensure that the former does not eclipse the latter, as it would have done uniformly in the kind of novel (and the kind of movie) that Woolf disliked.

Woolf's reflections on the ordinary life in *Mrs Dalloway* are attentive above all to movement which defines space.

> Big Ben struck the half-hour.
> How extraordinary it was, strange, yes touching to see the old lady (they had been neighbours ever so many years) move away from the window, as if she were attached to that sound, that string. Gigantic as it was, it had something to do with her. Down, down, into the midst of ordinary things the finger fell making the moment solemn. She was forced, so Clarissa imagined, by that sound, to move, to go – but where? Clarissa tried to follow her as she turned and disappeared, and could still just see her white cap moving at the back of the bedroom. She was still there moving about at the other end of the room. (p. 139)

The sentence which introduces solemnity into the midst of ordinary things is itself excessively solemn in its reaching, through syntactic inversion, through metaphor, for poetic effect. But the ordinary, stimulated by the momentous, perhaps, nonetheless continues to move about to a rhythm of its own. It does matter, of course, that the person Clarissa Dalloway sees in the room in the house opposite is an old lady: an image of what she herself may well come to, and to that extent meaningful, even momentous. But the primary focus is on the movement, not the person moving. Clarissa discovers in the old lady's passage from chest of drawers to dressing-table what we might call, to revert to the terms I employed in discussing the films of D. W. Griffith, in chapter 3, a sense rather than a meaning. The sense the rhythm of 'movement about' makes is not one to which moral or narrative convention have contributed. 'Did religion solve that, or love?' (p. 140). The episode demonstrates the validity of Gillian Beer's point that in Woolf's fiction the apprehensions of kinship which establish the ordinary life as the real life are almost always encounterless. It is crucial that Clarissa and the old lady should have been neighbours for 'ever so many years' without, as far as we can tell, having met.

Later, Clarissa's response to the news of Septimus Smith's death is framed by another look across the square, at the old lady going to bed. 'It was fascinating to watch her, moving about, that old lady, crossing the room, coming to the window' (p. 204). The fascination, once again, is with space revealed by movement: the medium or dimension in which the common life stands out as the real life. It is a fascination in no way diminished by the presence of death. 'Suppose the idea of the book is the contrast between life & death,' Woolf had wondered in a note written on 9 November 1922.[16] The book does indeed bring life, in the shape of Clarissa Dalloway, into stark contrast with death, in the shape of Septimus Smith. The contrast depends, however, as has often been observed, upon an underlying affinity.

As the manuscript reveals, Woolf found it hard to formulate that sense of being-in-the-world which constitutes Clarissa Dalloway's claim to know the common life as the real life. 'But everyone [did that]; remembered; what she [did] <loved> was [to exist now. Lovelier than ever] this; in front of her; <now> [the very moment].'[17] The published version keeps the demonstratives, but adds a detail. 'But everyone remembered; what she loved was this, here, now, in front of her; the fat lady in the cab' (p. 9). The fat lady is a movement, or lack of movement, occupying space. But being-in-the-world, it seems, cannot be grasped on its own terms. We can never quite know what 'this, here, now' amounts to just by absorbing it. Clarissa's subsequent meditation on presence is from the point of view of absence. 'Did it matter, then, she asked herself, walking towards Bond Street, did it matter that she must inevitably cease completely; all this must go on without her . . .' (p. 9). It may be that in order to know what is happening in front of your very eyes, you have to imagine it as it would be if you were not there to see it. Clarissa, however, cannot quite hold on to the thought of her own necessary and constitutive absence: 'did she resent it; or did it not become consoling to believe that death ended absolutely? but that somehow in the streets of London, on the ebb and flow of things, here, there, she survived . . .' (p. 9). The sentence, vaulting its own question mark, hurrying forward regardless, is a willed consolation. It may have been Woolf, as much as Clarissa Dalloway, who could not yet quite hold on to the thought of a constitutive absence.

'The Cinema'

In a letter of 13 April 1926, Woolf told Vita Sackville-West that her mind was 'awash with various thoughts': pre-eminently of Vita herself, but also 'my novel' (she was hard at work on the conclusion to the first part of *To the Lighthouse*), and 'the cinema'.[18] The product of those thoughts about the cinema was an essay on 'The Cinema' which appeared in the New York journal *Arts* in June, and in the *Nation and Athenaeum* in July. The essay describes her response to three different kinds of film: documentary, mainstream narrative, and avant-garde.

Woolf begins with newsreel.

> Yet, at first sight, the art of the cinema seems simple, even stupid. There is the King shaking hands with a football team; there is Sir Thomas Lipton's yacht; there is Jack Horner winning the Grand National.[19]

These images are, it now needs saying, freshly minted. Jack Horner, ridden by Billy Watkinson, trained by Jack Leader, won the Grand National in 1926. A Pathé Gazette newsreel released on 29 March includes shots of the race, and of horse and jockey enjoying their triumph. George V had been the first reigning monarch to attend an FA Cup Final, in 1914, but the only football matches at which he put in an appearance in March 1926 were of the rugby variety (England beat France 11–0, but lost to Scotland). Topical Budget's 29 April release featured the launch of the yacht *Shamrock* at Southampton, in the presence of the proud owner, Sir Thomas Lipton, and a certain Captain Sycamore.

The point of the newsreel image is vivid topicality. All the more puzzling, then, that after a wonderfully incisive account of the metaphysical implications of such images, Woolf should suddenly start to speak of them in the past tense.

> Further, all this happened ten years ago, we are told. We are beholding a world which has gone beneath the waves. Brides are emerging from the abbey – they are now mothers; ushers are ardent – they are now silent; mothers are tearful, guests are joyful; this has been won and that has been lost, and it is over and done with. (p. 55)

Who are 'we'? And when were we told that 'all this' happened ten years ago? It sounds as though the new direction in Woolf's thinking was prompted by a specific event. There is certainly a change (it may just be an intensification) of emphasis. A further set of newsreel images, apparently of a sumptuous wedding, has supervened on Jack Horner, and the king shaking hands, and Sir Thomas Lipton. These images differ in that they are generic. They show brides emerging from the abbey, rather than Jack Horner, and the king, and Sir Thomas. And the events they record and reveal are over and done with in an absolute sense, Woolf notes, because the events they portray took place before the war 'sprung its chasm' (p. 55). Her oddly dislocated approach to newsreel seeks to elicit its rendering both of constitutive presence (Jack Horner passes the post as we watch) and of constitutive absence (a world gone beneath the waves).

'But the picture-makers', Woolf continues, 'seem dissatisfied with such obvious sources of interest as the passage of time and the suggestiveness of

reality' (p. 55). The picture-makers have gone over to narrative. They have
cannibalised literature.

> Then 'Anna falls in love with Vronsky' – that is to say, the lady in black velvet
> falls into the arms of a gentleman in uniform, and they kiss with enormous
> succulence, great deliberation, and infinite gesticulation on a sofa in an
> extremely well-appointed library, while a gardener incidentally mows the
> lawn. (p. 56)

Anna Karenina had been filmed seven times in all between 1910 and 1919
(twice each in Germany and Russia, once each in America, France, and
Hungary). I don't know which version Woolf saw (if any: she might have
inferred the scene from her experience of movies in general). The result, at
any rate, was a telling critique of the classical continuity system's insistence
on action rather than movement. 'A kiss is love. A broken cup is jealousy.
A grin is happiness. Death is a hearse' (p. 56). What Woolf didn't like about
films of this kind was what she didn't like about novels of a certain kind:
their determinism, their reduction of sense to meaning, of suggestiveness to
intelligibility.

The third and final part of the essay concerns what the cinema might
achieve if 'left to its own devices'. 'For instance, at a performance of Dr
Caligari the other day, a shadow shaped like a tadpole suddenly appeared
at one corner of the screen' (p 56). This time Woolf's emphasis is quite
explicitly on the occasion itself rather than on the film shown: Robert
Wiene's Expressionist masterpiece *The Cabinet of Dr Caligari*, first released in
1920, which does not receive any further mention. On the occasion when
Woolf saw *Caligari*, a flaw in the print cast a gigantic shadow on the screen:
a shadow she proceeds to imagine as the beginning of a new cinematic
language. 'For a moment it seemed as though thought could be conveyed
by shape more effectively than by words' (p. 56). This is cinema as it might
yet be; not cinema as it then was, even in Expressionist Germany.

What connects the otherwise puzzlingly discrepant accounts of newsreel
and avant-garde experiment is a sense of occasion. Somewhere, at some
time, 'we' were told that all this happened ten years ago; somewhere, at
some time, a shadow in the shape of a tadpole crept across the screen. I
want to suggest that there was indeed an occasion. My claim is that Woolf
attended a meeting of the Film Society in London on 14 March 1926.

The Film Society had been founded in 1925 at the instigation of Ivor
Montagu, a journalist on *The Times* and an enthusiast for German cinema.
Founding members included the director Adrian Brunel, the actor Hugh
Miller, and Iris Barry, film critic for *The Spectator*. Its purpose was to show
foreign films otherwise unavailable in Britain. The first screening, at the
New Gallery Kinema in Regent Street, on 25 October 1925, was attended by
1,400 people. During the fourteen years of its existence, the Film Society
screened approximately 500 films from eighteen different countries. The

emphasis tended to be on the continental avant-gardes: German Expressionism, to begin with, then Soviet 'montage' films. By 1929, the Sunday afternoon shows had become so popular that they had to be transferred from the New Gallery Kinema to the Tivoli Palace in the Strand. Audiences began to drop off in the mid-1930s, and the Society was dissolved in 1939.[20]

The Film Society was in effect the first step taken towards the establishment of an independent cinema circuit in Britain. It also created a forum for discussions of film as an art. Pudovkin and Eisenstein both gave lectures there in 1929. Furthermore, the programme notes Ivor Montagu provided throughout the 1920s were often fairly technical in nature. Equally significant, to my mind, is the fact that the Society also undertook an archaeology of cinema in its so-called 'Resurrection Series': early Griffith and Chaplin shorts were a particular favourite. Already, in 1925, it was possible to return to an origin at once remote and full of as yet unrealised potential.

Leonard Woolf's memorandum books reveal that on 20 December 1925, Vita Sackville-West drove him and Virginia to London, and that Leonard at least went on to a Film Society showing. On 17 January 1926, Clive Bell was involved in a near-riot at a Film Society showing of René Clair's wildly experimental *Entr'acte*; Virginia and Vita dined with him on the following evening.[21] On 14 March 1926, the Society showed *The Cabinet of Dr Caligari*. Montagu's programme note was sternly appreciative. 'Though its technique is in some respects old-fashioned (example, the continual use of iris in and iris out of scenes) in many respects it breaks new ground ...'[22]

'For instance,' Woolf was shortly to write, 'at a performance of Dr Caligari *the other day* ...' Could the other day have been 14 March? There could not have been many occasions on which *Caligari* was performed in the early months of 1926. Woolf was certainly in residence at 52 Tavistock Square over the weekend of the 14th. There is no proof that she went anywhere near the New Gallery Kinema. The reason for thinking that she may have done lies in the Society's 14 March programme, which included, among other items, a resurrection of documentary shorts from *Williamson's Animated Gazette* of 1910–12.

The first British newsreel, *Pathé's Animated Gazette*, was released in June 1910, as a response to the new pattern of regular viewing created by the construction of purpose-built cinemas. Competitors soon emerged: *Bioscope Chronicle, Gaumont Graphic, Topical Budget*. James Williamson was a chemist and photographer who began to produce actualities in 1897, but made his name at the turn of the century with some of the earliest and most adventurous multi-shot fiction films. The Williamson Kinematograph Company flourished for a while, but, like many other British companies, made little impact on the international market. By September 1910 the company's Brighton studio was up for sale. The only form of production to which Williamson clung was the topical and 'interest' films which made up his *Animated Gazette*.[23] Could it have been a viewing of items from the

Gazette at the Film Society which encouraged Woolf to associate documentary film not only with the topical and the immediate, but also with a world 'gone beneath the waves'? Was it there that the bride had emerged from the abbey who was now a mother? The ephemeral nature of newsreel as a medium means that we will probably never know.

What might matter, in the present context, is that the early newsreels had as much to do with the art of showing as they did with the art of telling. Each reel circulated for several weeks; the more out of date it was, the less cinema proprietors paid for it. Topics were chosen for their newsworthiness, to be sure, but also for the extent to which they permitted film to do what no other medium could. Parades, ceremonies, manoeuvres, launches, contests, arrivals and departures: in each case, movement defined a space. The early newsreels were not primarily a narrative medium. It was Williamson himself, speaking in 1926, who most vividly identified early cinema with the pleasures of sheer visibility. 'To see waves dashing over rocks in a most natural way, to see a train arriving and people walking about as if alive was admitted to be very wonderful.'[24]

Woolf altered the emphasis slightly, but to profound effect. In documentary film, she wrote, in a passage which links her experience of newsreels produced in 1926 to her experience of newsreels produced in 1910, events are not more beautiful, but more real, or, rather, 'real with a different reality'.

> We behold them as they are when we are not there. We see life as it is when we have no part in it. As we gaze we seem to be removed from the pettiness of actual existence. The horse will not knock us down. The King will not grasp our hands. The wave will not wet our feet. From this point of vantage, as we watch the antics of our kind, we have time to feel pity and amusement, to generalize, to endow one man with the attributes of the race. Watching the boat sail and the wave break, we have time to open our minds wide to beauty and register on top of it the queer sensation – this beauty will continue, and this beauty will flourish whether we behold it or not. (p. 55)

This seems to me to develop Clarissa Dalloway's meditation on being-in-the-world, and at the same time to take a risk she did not take. It celebrates the common life as the real life, but it does so by imagining what that life looks like when we are not there to see it. 'The horse will not knock us down. The King will not grasp our hands. The wave will not wet our feet.' Woolf can now take the risk because she has understood a fundamental fact about cinema. To reiterate: in cinema, unlike the theatre, actors and audience never coincide; for one party to be present, the other must be absent. Encounterlessness within the mutually acknowledged relationship of viewer and viewed was the medium's founding principle. The continuity system in full operation by the time Woolf wrote her essay could be thought of as an attempt to overcome this difficulty by staging a feature-length surrogate hermeneutic encounter in narrative form.

My hypothesis is that Woolf's viewing, within the same period, of newsreels from 1926 and newsreels from 1910 led her to realise that documentary film is inherently archaic, because the encounter it postulates will always in some sense be missed. The 'queer sensation' induced by late arrival, by knowledge that the event began without us, that it does not need us, opens our minds wider to beauty than any sense of command, of being throughout fully present and correct, ever could. What Woolf saw in the newsreel images, what Clarissa Dalloway had not seen in the fat lady in the cab, is that this beauty will continue, and will flourish, whether we behold it or not. Cinema had taught her a crucial lesson about constitutive absence. It gave a productive shape to her enduring preoccupation with 'the thing that exists when we aren't there'.[25] 'The Cinema' represents literary modernism's most profound acknowledgement of film's neutrality as a medium.

Life and death in *To the Lighthouse*   ~Bergson? Father knows Best~

Woolf's brief but intense engagement with cinema in the early months of 1926 altered her thinking about the common life. It encouraged her to suppose that one might grasp the commonness of the common life by means of a principle (or theory) of constitutive absence. According to this principle, encounters between people living in the same place at the same time were there to be missed; though, with a view to the survival of the species, some had better not be. A community would thrive only if it succeeded in maintaining the appropriate level of non-relationship among its members. It perhaps seemed to Woolf that cinema, and the newsreel in particular, might contribute to a better understanding of the principle of constitutive absence.

The novel Woolf was working on when she told Vita Sackville-West that her mind was 'awash' with various thoughts, including thoughts about the cinema, was *To the Lighthouse*.[26] In a diary entry of 18 April 1926, Woolf noted that she had just finished the novel's first part, and made a start on the second, 'Time Passes', which chronicles the abandonment of the Ramsay family's holiday home in the Hebrides during the period of the First World War, after Mrs Ramsay's death. The chronicle required, in her view, a radical departure from the established methods of this (or any other) novel. 'I cannot make it out – here is the most difficult abstract piece of writing – I have to give an empty house, no people's characters, the passage of time, all eyeless & featureless with nothing to cling to: well, I rush at it, & at once scatter out two pages.'[27] In the novel's first part, the choreography of points of view offers a great deal to cling to: an array of distinct but overlapping centres of consciousness. Its second part, by contrast, is 'eyeless': not rendered from any identifiable point of view. Constitutive absence, indeed; as subject matter *and* method.

Woolf knew from the start that the theme of *To the Lighthouse* was to be absence in the form given it by death, and by mourning. A diary entry of 27

~'constitutive absence'   Evan Dara~

June 1925 states the theme, blankly. 'I have an idea I will invent a new name for my books to supplant "novel". A new - - - - by Virginia Woolf. But what? Elegy?'[28] The book in which Woolf mourned her father and mother, her brother Thoby, and her half-sister Stella Duckworth, is not quite a novel. But it is not quite an elegy, either. For the abstract writing of the second part removes from the scene not only the objects of mourning (Mrs Ramsay, Prue, Andrew), but its subjects, as well. Those who will eventually come to terms with their grief (Mr Ramsay, his surviving children, and his house-guests, notably the painter Lily Briscoe) are reassembled for the purpose in the book's third and last section, 'The Lighthouse'.

If there is no mourner in 'Time Passes', there is at least someone who remembers. Laura Marcus argues that Woolf's engagement with cinema enabled her to conceive memory as projection. In 'Time Passes', the walls of the rooms in the abandoned house in the Hebrides become a picture-palace screen on to which the 'long stroke' of the lighthouse beam projects images of the past, and in particular of the dead Mrs Ramsay (pp. 180–81).[29] Seated in the picture-palace is the ancient caretaker, Mrs McNab, to whom, or for whose benefit, Mrs Ramsay appears.

> She could see her now, stooping over her flowers; (and faint and flickering, like a yellow beam or the circle at the end of a telescope, a lady in a grey cloak, stooping over her flowers, went wandering over the bedroom wall, up the dressing-table, across the washstand, as Mrs McNab hobbled and ambled, dusting, straightening). (p. 186)

It may be that Woolf substituted the telescope for the rather more cinematic yellow beam in order to indicate that Mrs McNab's memory of Mrs Ramsay is, after all, her own. But an examination of the terms in which that telescopic vision was framed in the original manuscript tends to strengthen Marcus's argument. 'It was [more] like an image seen through a rather feeble telescope; [it] was cut out like that – [a lady in a grey cloak] ...' The emphasis, here, is on a projected 'image' whose resemblance to what one might see through a telescope is fairly remote. This 'little picture', we are told, goes 'flickering about the bedroom for a moment', then vanishes.[30] There is more cinema in the draft, in the emphasis on the flicker of a cut-out image, than in the final version. It is worth recalling that a view through a telescope often provided the motivation, in early films, for a close-up. These films show a person looking through a telescope, and then, centred within a circular matte, what he or she saw. A *Variety* review of D. W. Griffith's *The Redman and the Child* (1908) described the 'clever bit of trick work' by which, when the 'Redman' looks through a telescope, 'immediately the field of the picture contracts to a circle', and the scene is 'brought before the audience' as though we are seeing what he sees.[31] A close-up is indeed an image 'cut out like that'. In the published text of *To the Lighthouse*, though not as it happens in the manuscript, a 'ring of light' encircles Mrs McNab's subsequent vision of Mr Ramsay, 'lean as a rake, wagging his head, as she came up with the washing, talking to himself, she supposed, on the lawn' (p. 190). It is quite possible that the experience of movie-going informed, even if it did not in the end shape, the conception of memory put forward in 'Time Passes'.

Did it inform Woolf's method, in *To the Lighthouse*, as well as her conception of memory? 'In the absence of "plot" in "Time Passes",' Marcus argues, 'Woolf produces a form of experimental cineplay, using visual images to express emotions and animating objects into non-human life.'[32] For reasons put forward in my critique of Winifred Holtby's analysis of *Jacob's Room*, I would not myself feel so confident in describing 'Time Passes' as a 'cineplay'. For the inspiration behind the pages scattered out in Woolf's first rush at this new kind of writing seems to be literary rather than cinematic. Consider, for example, the cadence needed to bring to a conclusion the prose poem about the 'little airs' permeating the empty house which makes up the second section of 'Time Passes'.

> At length, desisting, all ceased together; all together gave off an aimless gust of lamentation to which some door in the kitchen replied; swung wide; admitted nothing; and slammed to. (p. 173)

The cadence, if not the thought, derives from James Joyce's description of Leopold Bloom in church, in the 'Lotus Eaters' episode of *Ulysses*. 'All crossed themselves and stood up. Mr Bloom glanced about him and then stood up, looking over the risen hats. Stand up at the gospel of course. Then all settled down on their knees again and he sat back quietly in his bench.' Indeed, Woolf's familiarity with another episode in *Ulysses* may have helped to shape the structure of 'Time Passes'. In 'Proteus', Stephen Dedalus crosses Sandymount strand, encountering on the way two women who climb down some steps on to the beach. 'Number one swung lourdily her midwife's bag, the other's gamp poked in the beach.' Number one is 'Mrs Florence MacCabe, relict of the late Patk MacCabe, deeply lamented, of Bride Street'.[33] Woolf's Mrs McNab recalls Joyce's Mrs MacCabe; and she, too, has a companion, Mrs Bast. The section of 'Time Passes' which introduces Mrs McNab concludes with a description of a 'visionary' who, Dedalus-like, walks the beach asking 'What am I?' and 'What is this?' (pp. 177–9). Woolf took the plunge into abstract writing goaded by literature, not cinema.

However, it is important not to draw the distinction between literature and cinema in too absolute a manner. As Laura Marcus points out, Woolf's belief that cinema allows us to behold things 'as they are when we are not there' finds a direct echo in *To the Lighthouse* in the account Andrew Ramsay gives Lily Briscoe of his father's philosophical work on 'subject and object and the nature of reality': '"Think of a kitchen table then," he told her, "when you're not there"' (p. 33). Marcus shrewdly connects this concern for the way things are when we are not there with the anxiety Woolf felt about the 'Time Passes' section of the novel, which attempts to describe what the world might look like in the absence of a 'perceiving consciousness'.[34]

Film, I would argue, did not teach Woolf how to write eyelessly; but it did teach her how to imagine eyelessness as an element of the human condition. We must sometimes look without seeing, or see others not seeing us, if we are to miss our due proportion of encounters. The king will not grasp our hands, because, although he looks straight at us, he has not seen us. Woolf wants to say that his failure to see us, whenever we look at him looking, is in some sense necessary (part of being a monarch, a national figure). It is also frightening. It reminds that too often in life we look without seeing, or are looked at without being seen. 'But the stillness and brightness of the day were as strange as the chaos and tumult of night, with the trees standing there, and the flowers standing there, looking before them, looking up, yet beholding nothing, eyeless, and thus terrible' (p. 183). The eyeless flowers are immediately associated with Mrs McNab, who, 'thinking no harm, for the family would not come, never again, some said', picks a bunch to take home with her (p. 184). The manuscript, which inserts Mrs McNab's act of pillage parenthetically into the sentence about the flowers, denounces nature itself as 'eyeless, brainless, empty'.[35] Unlike Mrs Bast, who looks for and happily sees her son at work in the garden (p. 191), Mrs McNab takes nothing in: 'and again with her sidelong leer which slipped and turned aside even from her own face, and her own sorrows, stood and gaped in the glass, aimlessly smiling' (p. 178). The leer is an empty look. Mrs McNab's is the perceiving consciousness to whom the absent Mr and Mrs Ramsay appear. In order to remove the mourner from the mourning, Woolf had to define even that minimal consciousness as an absence. Class-prejudice did part of the job, reducing the caretaker to the status of dumb animal. Cinema may have done the rest. It may have helped Woolf to imagine the eyeless leer.

By Tom Gunning's account, a distinguishing feature of the earliest films is that the participants happily engage with the camera. They know that they themselves are, by the fact of their visibility, the main attraction. They stare at the camera, or tip their hats to it, or wave, or even on occasion shed their clothes.[36] But what exactly are they looking *at*? At an absence, at someone who will not be present when their visibility is put to its proper use (when they become worth seeing). They see no more than themselves being seen, on some other occasion. Yuri Tsivian quotes a remark by the poet Konstantin Ldov to the effect that characters in films are not just mute, but blind as well.[37]

Tsivian briefly explores this 'phenomenological aspect' of early cinema with reference to Woolf's essay, and to an episode in Thomas Mann's *The Magic Mountain*, published in 1924, but set in the years immediately before the First World War. In this episode, entitled 'The Dance of Death', Hans Castorp, inmate of an Alpine sanatorium, makes the rounds of the terminally ill, before repairing with some other patients to the local 'bioscope', where the show includes a scenic short shot in Morocco.

> A young Moroccan woman, in a costume of striped silk, with trappings in the shape of chains, bracelets, and rings, her swelling breasts half bared, was suddenly brought so close to the camera as to be life-sized; one could see the dilated nostrils, the eyes full of animal life, the features in play as she showed her white teeth in a laugh, and held one of her hands, with its blanched nails, for a shade to her eyes, while with the other she waved to the audience, who stared, taken aback, into the face of the charming apparition. It seemed to see and saw not, it was not moved by the glances bent upon it, its smile and nod were not of the present but of the past, so that the impulse to respond was baffled, and lost in a feeling of impotence. Then the phantom world vanished. The screen glared white and empty, with the one word *Finis* written across it.[38]

The scene's exoticism clearly includes the possibility, the promise, even, of sexual encounter. The young woman, her eyes full of 'animal life', engages with the camera. But she does so blindly. The spectators know, immediately, that the look and the wave are not for them. They feel bafflement, not arousal. Indeed, this missed encounter with a charming apparition prefigures, through its enactment of the power and the melancholy of constitutive absence, the blank screen (whitest of all white spaces) which brings each performance, whether at the bioscope or in the sanatorium, to an end.

The literature of early cinema has been an occasional topic, in this book. In its concentration on eyelessness, that literature might be said to have provided a context for Mrs McNab's leer. In Rudyard Kipling's 'Mrs Bathurst' (1904), for example, four men – the unnamed narrator; Hooper, a railway inspector; Pyecroft, a petty officer in the Royal Navy; and Pritchard, a Sergeant of Marines – drink beer on a sultry afternoon shortly after the end of the Boer War, in a railway-siding near Simon's Bay, in Cape Province. The conversation turns to Mrs Bathurst, proprietor of a hotel in Auckland, whose integrity and 'blindish' way of looking at a person have made a deep impression on the susceptible Pritchard. There is some connection between Mrs Bathurst and a warrant officer named Vickery, who has recently gone missing. Pyecroft describes how for five nights running he accompanied Vickery to Phyllis's Circus, in Cape Town, where there was a cinematograph. The show included an actuality featuring Mrs Bathurst. 'Then the Western Mail came in to Paddin'ton on the big magic-lantern sheet,' Pyecroft recalls:

> First we saw the platform empty an' the porters standin' by. Then the engine come in, head on, an' the women in the front row jumped: she headed so straight. Then the doors opened and the passengers came out and the porters got the luggage – just like life. Only – only when any one came down too far towards us that was watchin', they walked right out o' the picture, so to speak. I was 'ighly interested, I can tell you. So were all of us. I watched an old man

with a rug 'oo'd dropped a book an' was tryin' to pick it up, when quite slowly, from be'ind two porters – carryin' a little reticule an' lookin' from side to side – comes our Mrs Bathurst. There was no mistakin' the walk in a hundred thousand. She come forward – right forward – she looked out straight at us with that blindish look which Pritch alluded to. She walked on and on till she melted out of the picture – like – like a shadow jumpin' over a candle, an' as she went I 'eard Dawson in the tickey seats be'ind sing out: 'Christ, there's Mrs B!'[39]

Kipling has chosen to describe cinema's archetypal recognition scene, the arrival of a train at a station. Vickery, whose identification of the woman on the screen as Mrs Bathurst has been confirmed by Pyecroft, claims that her look at the camera was a look meant for him. He has put himself in the frame: at the place where he would have to be in order to be found by that look, where the look could be understood as for him and him only.

The frame, however, cuts both ways. The scene's automatism – the frontal assault, the looming, the abrupt disappearance – strongly suggests that while there is a good deal in it to recognise, at a distance, there may well be nobody in it to be recognised by. Mrs Bathurst's walk is unmistakable. But it is a machine she looks at, or looks *for*, as both target and beneficiary, rather than a person. Mrs Bathurst's 'blindish' look is the look of someone who sees herself being seen, in the future, rather than that of someone who expects to be met; or, perhaps, who wants to be met. Vickery's mistake about cinema (he has been taken in by its performance of mutual recognition) reproduces and is reproduced by a mistake about Mrs Bathurst: she is not there, and possibly never was there, *for him*. After Phyllis's Circus has left town, Vickery deserts. He has been driven mad, in Pyecroft's view, by exposure to Mrs Bathurst's image, by the missed encounter which is cinema.[40]

I make no claim for these examples drawn from Mann and Kipling other than that they demonstrate that the writers of the period thought *with* as well as *about* cinema. Woolf did the same. In *To the Lighthouse*, she imagined constitutive absence effectively. A diary entry of 27 March 1926 records an attempt to finish the 'rather long drawn out dinner scene' which now forms section 17 of the novel's first part.[41] At its conclusion, Mrs Ramsay rises and leaves the room. The moment, we realise, is a turning point, and as she is leaving the room Mrs Ramsay turns to look back at a scene which continues, and will continue, and yet is already over (because it no longer contains her). The look back is a look forward to this same scene without her, as it will take place again and again, in her absence, after her death. Woolf had already made the connection between leaving a room and leaving a life. A diary entry for 8 April 1925 explains that the recent death of the painter Jacques Raverat had lessened her respect for mortality. 'I like to go out of the room talking, with an unfinished casual sentence on my lips. That is the effect it had on me – no leavetakings, no submission – but someone stepping out into the darkness.'[42] Mrs Ramsay may not have an unfinished casual sentence on her lips as she leaves the room. But she does what Mrs Dalloway could not do. Stepping out into the darkness, with a look at once backward and forward, she enacts her own constitutive absence from the scene.

Mrs Ramsay then goes upstairs to look in on the children, comforted by the sure conviction that Paul Rayley and Minta Doyle will marry, and that the specificities of place and time which ensure 'community of feeling' – 'and this, and this, and this, she thought, going upstairs, laughing, but affectionately, at the sofa on the landing (her mother's) at the rocking-chair (her father's)' – will reliably outlast her (p. 153). She assumes too much, however. She has not gone all that far beyond Mrs Dalloway, because the future she imagines herself absent from is one she has done everything she possibly can to shape. Her hope is that the marriage she has brought about will be her monument.

It is the novel itself which removes Mrs Ramsay: which puts into effect a community of feeling predicated on her absence. In 'Time Passes', she continues to exist in the mind of a single human being only, Mrs McNab. The image projected of her during the years which elapse immediately after her death is almost no image at all. A brutal reduction to (almost) zero is the basis for her subsequent reconstitution, through ritual enactment, through loving memory, in the novel's final part. The absence that reconstitution is built upon, or around, now includes the knowledge that the Rayleys' marriage has been a disaster (p. 235). What Lily Briscoe calls Mrs Ramsay's 'mania' for marriage (p. 237) was one of the ways in which she had attempted to remain present: always there to behold things as they are. 'Time Passes' puts Mrs Ramsay's mania to the acid test of Mrs McNab's eyeless leer, embodiment of the principle of constitutive absence. That leer is an invention of cinema, or of the literature about cinema. 'Time Passes' is not in itself cinematic; but cinema made it possible.

Dead Mabelles

I want to conclude this chapter, as I concluded the last, with a very brief discussion of a couple of texts which, if not exactly in orbit around the texts I have been discussing, then at least bear some thought in relation to them. The female modernists whose interest in cinema has most often been considered in relation to Woolf's are, understandably, those who wrote for *Close Up*: H.D., Bryher, Dorothy Richardson.[43] It would be worth adding Mary Butts and Elizabeth Bowen to that list.

Butts's 'In Bloomsbury' (1932) makes elegant fun of the Curtins, a wealthy family whose intellectualism and taste for modish 'dissipations' suggests a milieu not a hundred miles from that inhabited by the Woolfs, Stracheys, and Bells. The story turns on the disturbance caused by the arrival in London of a pair of previously unknown American cousins, whose 'tanned faces and great bones' hold out the prospect, at once enticing

and repellent, of a regression to barbarism. The narrator, whose intervention has brought the two parties together, conceives of the encounter in
terms of primitivist fantasy: 'Ghenghis Khan's men' come to 'gentlefolk in
an eighteenth-century house'. To her, the newcomers are like 'powerful
animals' in their predatoriness. But they are modern as well as primitive.
When she first meets them, in a café in Paris, the words they speak
communicate little: 'the picture of them completed itself, image by image, as
we sat'. In order to understand their otherness, the narrator must first recall,
not some novel by Jack London, but film's original neutrality as a medium.
'Picture, it was a cinema, an *actualité*, infinitely prosaic; and not until I had
listened for some time with the minimum of polite interrogation and
response, did I notice that it was creepy.'[44] Whatever the size of their bones,
or the depth of their tans, these American cousins have the creepiness of the
people who come and go in the first films. To see them at all is to see them
as they are when we are not there to see them. If the narrator's initial
encounter with the cousins has already been missed, even as it happens, in
the infinitely prosaic succession of images, then the prospects for family
reunion appear slim.

Like Woolf, Elizabeth Bowen associated cinema with death rather than
life, or with death-in-life. 'Dead Mabelle', published in *Joining Charles and
Other Stories* (1929), finds something creepy not in ancient actualities or
newsreels, but in the very latest Hollywood feature film: the sort that
colours Peter Walsh's office-workers with tinselly rapture, in *Mrs Dalloway*.
The story concerns the compelling effect exercised on 'cinema-shy' bank-
clerk William Stickford by Mabelle Pacey, a rising star in the Clara Bow or
Louise Brooks mould. Lured into the Bijou Picturedrome at Pamsleigh on
the misunderstanding that cinema is an 'art-form', Stickford discovers in
the images on the screen at once too much presence and too much absence.
Mabelle on screen seems to him an abstraction among abstractions: every
movement she makes is an outrage to his understanding of the physical
world. And yet her relation to him, as viewer, could scarcely be more
immediate. 'When she looked up again that dark, dancing, direct look came
out as it were from hiding, taking one unawares. It was as though she
leaned forward and touched one.'[45] Bowen has invented a rube, a viewer
unready for cinema, in order to prise cinema's constitutive creepiness out
from within the narrative identifications made possible – made natural – by
the continuity system.

Stickford, however, soon readies himself for Mabelle. He becomes a fan,
buying into her manufactured 'real-life' star persona. A colleague discovers
a copy of the *Picturegoer* hidden among the books on his shelves. 'On the
cover Mabelle, full length, stood looking sideways, surprised and ironical,
elegantly chocked by a hunting-stock, hair ruffled up as though she had just
pulled a hat off, hand holding bunched-up gauntlets propped on a hip'
(p. 279). The star, like Eliot's Fresca, can be known, or recognised, by
mediation alone, in and through the parts she plays; the function of stardom

is to create a general immediacy which incorporates and transcends those specific mediations. The *Picturegoer* has at once raised Mabelle Pacey above the parts she is known to play by appearing to put her in the company of the English landed gentry; and lowered her beneath them by appearing to catch her unawares, hair ruffled, hand propped on a hip. Hyper-mediation, in the form of a photograph which derives from and comments upon the effect of the moving image, creates a new immediacy.

Bowen, however, obviously felt that Stickford's performance as a rube was not in itself enough to prise cinema's constitutive creepiness out from beneath the continuity system's assiduous suturing. Mabelle Pacey comes to a sticky end; and her death, or 'absolute dissolution', far from dissolving in its turn the immediacy she has for her admirers, reinforces it. 'He faced round to the empty doorway. Mightn't she as well be *there* who wasn't anywhere? Who was not' (p. 281). To cash in on Mabelle's death, the Picturedrome shows one of her first hits, *The White Rider*. Stickford, watching her wheel her horse round and hurl herself at the camera, recoils, rube-like, from the visual assault. The rube, however, is now a fan. He has *chosen* to be disabled, and re-enabled, by immediacy. 'He looked up with a wrench at his being; advancing enormously, grinning a little at the moment's intensity, Mabelle looked down. They encountered' (p. 282). This is one encounter Stickford is determined not to miss, whatever the wrench.

Not missing the encounter results in dementia. Leaving the Picturedrome, Stickford takes Mabelle with him. 'Here, by him, burning into him with her actuality all the time. Burdening him with her realness' (p. 284). Woolf had suggested, with documentary film in mind, that the burden realness imposes is a knowledge of death (of constitutive absence). Bowen, with the very latest product of the Hollywood continuity system in mind, seems to agree.

Notes

1 *Virginia Woolf* (London: Wishart, 1932).
2 Laura Marcus amply demonstrates the significance of Woolf's interest in cinema, in a brief but perceptive discussion to which I shall return: *Virginia Woolf* (Plymouth: Northcote House, 1997), 99–102. See also Maggie Humm, *Modernist Women and Visual Cultures: Virginia Woolf, Vanessa Bell, Photography, and Cinema* (New Brunswick: Rutgers University Press, 2003).
3 *Mrs Dalloway*, ed. Elaine Showalter (Harmondsworth: Penguin Books, 1992), xxi. References will henceforth be included in the text.
4 *Virginia Woolf*, 117–18.
5 *Jacob's Room*, ed. Kate Flint (Oxford: Oxford University Press, 1992), 3.
6 Mark Lambert, *Dickens and the Suspended Quotation* (New Haven: Yale University Press, 1981).
7 *A Room of One's Own* (London: Triad, 1977), 108.
8 *Virginia Woolf: The Common Ground* (Edinburgh: Edinburgh University Press, 1996), 2.

9   Nicholas Hiley, '"At the Picture Palace": the British Cinema Audience, 1895–1920', in John Fullerton (ed.), *Celebrating 1895: The Centenary of Cinema* (London: John Libbey, 1998), 96–103; and '"Let's Go to the Pictures": The British Cinema Audience in the 1920s and 1930s', *Journal of Popular British Film*, 2 (1999), 39–53; Robert Murphy, 'Under the Shadow of Hollywood', in Charles Barr (ed.), *All Our Yesterdays: 90 Years of British Cinema* (London: BFI Publishing, 1986), 47–71.

10   David Bordwell, Janet Staiger, and Kristin Thompson, *The Classical Hollywood Cinema: Film Style and Mode of Production to 1960* (London: Routledge, 1985).

11   Quoted by Bordwell, 'The Classical Hollywood Style, 1917–60', in *Classical Hollywood Cinema*, 1–84, p. 15.

12   'Classical Hollywood Style', 50.

13   Tom Gunning, 'Notes and Queries about the Year 1913 and Film Style: National Styles and Deep Staging', in Thierry Lefebvre and Laurent Mannoni (eds), *L'Année 1913 en France* (Paris: Centre National de la Cinématographie, 1993), 195–204; David Bordwell, *On the History of Film Style* (Cambridge, MA: Harvard University Press, 1997), ch. 6.

14   'Narcissus', first published in *Close Up*, in September 1931; in James Donald, Anne Friedberg, and Laura Marcus (eds), *Close Up 1927–1933: Cinema and Modernism* (London: Cassell, 1998), 201–3, p. 203.

15   *Theory of Film: The Redemption of Physical Reality* (Princeton: Princeton University Press, 1997), 219, 298, 304, 310.

16   *'The Hours': The British Museum Manuscript of 'Mrs Dalloway'*, ed. Helen M. Wussow (New York: Pace University Press, 1996), 414.

17   Ibid., 264. Square brackets indicate words under deletion; angle brackets indicate words added above or below a line.

18   *Letters*, ed. Nigel Nicolson, 6 vols (London: Hogarth Press, 1975–84), vol. 3, 254.

19   'The Cinema', in *The Crowded Dance of Modern Life*, ed. Rachel Bowlby (Harmondsworth: Penguin Books, 1993), 54–8, p. 54. References will henceforth be included in the text. Leslie Kathleen Hankins has very usefully placed the essay in relation to a range of comment on film: '"Across the Screen of My Brain": Virginia Woolf's "The Cinema" and Film Forums of the Twenties', in Diane F. Gillespie (ed.), *The Multiple Muses of Virginia Woolf* (Columbia: University of Missouri Press, 1993), 148–79.

20   Jen Sansom, 'The Film Society, 1925–1939', in *All Our Yesterdays*, 306–13.

21   An episode described by Hankins, '"Across the Screen of My Brain"', 154–5.

22   *The Film Society Programmes 1925–1939*, ed. George Amberg (New York: Arno Press, 1972), 23.

23   Martin Sopocy, *James Williamson: Studies and Documents of a Pioneer* (Madison: Fairleigh Dickinson University Press, 1998).

24   Quoted by Sopocy, *James Williamson*, 30.

25   *Diary*, ed. Anne Olivier Bell and Andrew McNeillie, 5 vols (Harmondsworth: Penguin Books, 1977–84), vol. 3, 114.

26   *Letters*, vol. 3, 254.

27   *Diary*, vol. 3, 75–6.

28   Ibid., vol. 3, 34.

29   *Virginia Woolf*, 102.

30   *To the Lighthouse: The Original Holograph Draft*, ed. Susan Dick (London: Hogarth Press, 1983), 226–7. Square brackets indicate words under deletion.

31 Quoted by Tom Gunning, *D. W. Griffith and the Origins of American Narrative Cinema* (Urbana: University of Illinois Press, 1994), 72.

32 *Virginia Woolf*, 101.

33 *Ulysses*, ed. Jeri Johnson (Oxford: Oxford University Press, 1993), 79, 38.

34 *Virginia Woolf*, 106. A passage in the original draft envisages Mrs Ramsay as closest to an understanding of life and death when she thinks mechanically (as though, one could perhaps add, she was at the cinema): 'as if a shade had fallen, & robbed of colour, she saw things truly; & then, not of her own willing, but independently like the pulse of a machine, which, inexplicably stopped, inexplicably begins again, the old familiar life began' (*To the Lighthouse: The Original Holograph Draft*, 134). I am grateful to Beci Carver for drawing my attention to this passage.

35 *Holograph*, 223.

36 'The Cinema of Attractions: Early Film, Its Spectator, and the Avant-Garde', in Thomas Elsaesser (ed.), *Early Cinema: Space, Frame, Narrative* (London: BFI Publishing, 1990), 56–67.

37 *Early Cinema in Russia and Its Cultural Reception*, trans. Alan Bodger (London: Routledge, 1994), 159.

38 *The Magic Mountain*, trans. H. T. Lowe-Porter (Harmondsworth: Penguin Books, 1965), 318.

39 'Mrs Bathurst', first published in *Traffics and Discoveries* (1904), reprinted in *Short Stories*, 2 vols, ed. Andrew Rutherford (Harmondsworth: Penguin Books, 1971), vol. 2, 73–92, pp. 82–3, 85. Nicholas Daly has recently proposed the Boer War as a context for Kipling's cinematographic reflections on loss: 'The Boerograph', in *Literature, Technology, and Modernity, 1860–2000* (Cambridge: Cambridge University Press, 2004), 56–75.

40 There is also a sociological point, I think, to Kipling's story, which may be of interest in relation to the audience for early cinema. Pyecroft's habits of speech mark him as lower-class, and his description of the scene at Paddington Station puts him (almost) in the state of unreadiness for the moving image of the rustic protagonist of *The Countryman and the Cinematograph* (1901), who responds with voyeuristic delight to shots of a woman dancing and a rural courtship, and with terror to a shot of a train entering a station. The middle-class Hooper, by contrast, takes it all for granted: ' "Seen 'em all. Seen 'em all," said Hooper impatiently' (p. 84). According to Pyecroft, Vickery is 'what you call a superior man' (p. 83); he can afford to treat Pyecroft and himself to expensive (shilling) seats for five nights in a row (p. 84). And yet, like Pyecroft, he is not ready for cinema.

41 *Diary*, vol. 3, 72.

42 Ibid., vol. 3, 7. Beci Carver, once again, drew my attention to this passage.

43 For example, Humm, *Modernist Women*, ch. 5. See also Rebecca Egger, 'Deaf Ears and Dark Continents: Dorothy Richardson's Cinematic Epistemology', *Camera Obscura*, 30 (1992), 5–33.

44 'In Bloomsbury', in *From Altar to Chimney-Piece: Selected Stories* (New York: McPherson, 1992), 39–57, pp. 41, 45. Rochelle Rives has made good use of this story in 'Problem Space: Mary Butts, Modernism, and the Etiquette of Placement', *Modernism/Modernity*, 12:4 (2005), 607–27.

45 'Dead Mabelle', in *Collected Stories* (Harmondsworth: Penguin Books, 1980), 276–85, pp. 277–8. References will henceforth be included in the text.

7

Charlie Chaplin

I want to conclude my account of the relation between early cinema and literary modernism with a case-study which will enable me further to explore and to substantiate its basic hypothesis: that some early film-makers shared with some writers of the period a conviction both that the instrumentality of the new recording media had made it possible for the first time to represent (as well as to record) *existence as such*; and that the superabundant generative power of this instrumentality (the ever-imminent autonomy of the forms and techniques it gave rise to) put in doubt the very idea of existence as such.

I began with stereoscopy's presence-effects: that visualisation of tangibility which fascinated film-makers (the Lumières, Hepworth, Pastrone, Gance, Eisenstein) and writers (Kafka, Joyce, Proust) alike. I went on to discuss Griffith as a film-maker whose films make sense of the world, as well as, by means of montage, a significance for it. Griffith found in the poetry of Tennyson and Kingsley, and in Naturalist fiction, not just the elements of character-driven or polemical narrative, but a powerful way to describe the lived world: a model for the productive excess, in representation, of mimesis over meaning.

Therein lay the problem. For imitation to excess creates the effect not just of presence, of what is palpably *here, now*, in front of us, but of absence: of what had to appear and then disappear so that its palpable trace remains vividly for us. Examining a stereoview of Ann Hathaway's cottage, Oliver Wendell Holmes noted the marks and stains left by passage through the doorway.[1] Griffith almost certainly read on in *Leaves of Grass* past 'Out of the Cradle Endlessly Rocking', to 'As I Ebb'd with the Ocean of Life', which meditates not on the World-making emblem, in Heidegger's terms, but Earth itself: the waste-matter of windrow, sea-gluten, and salt-lettuce. An absence-effect – the trace of what has passed through the scene, of what has gone missing – configures each presence-effect. These absence-effects speak to the constitutive absence of the human observer whose authority and compassion might have mediated the scene: might have made a meaning for it, rather than sense of it.

My topic has not been waste-matter, as such, but rather the new automatisms of vision which brought waste-matter back into view, in the mechanically reproduced image. 'We cannot hope to embrace reality', Kracauer announced, 'unless we penetrate its lowest layers.' Film has a duty not only to record, but to reveal – to expose, to lay bare – the visible world. The camera sees what the human eye cannot, or through habit, scruple, or stubbornness will not see. The direction of its gaze is not upwards, Kracauer thought, towards moral intention, but downwards into material existence, into contingency. It looks '*under* the table', refusing to conceal its interest 'in the refuse, in what is just there – both inside and outside the human being'.[2]

The automatism of the mechanically reproduced image became increasingly both a preoccupation and a method, for film-makers and writers alike, in the period during and immediately after the First World War. Looking for life, in documentary film, Virginia Woolf saw only death. Joyce and Eliot, the main exponents of a poetics of impersonality, wanted urgently to find out what automatism looked like from the inside. As, I think, did those film-makers (Tucker, Griffith, Gance, Vidor, Dreyer) who made a point of – and instituted a counter-narrative through – their use of lateral tracking shots.

Anti-mimesis, or the polemical overthrow of then predominant modes of representation, has usually been regarded as modernism's calling-card. In this book, however, I have drawn attention instead to scenes which, rather than abandoning such methods altogether, stretch them to the very limit by converting them into a topic: the mock-ceremony of mutual acknowledgement which catches up performer and (in some cases involuntary) audience in 'Wandering Rocks'; the mechanical seduction mechanically shown by Tiresias, that mutoscope equipped with consciousness, in *The Waste Land*; Mrs Ramsay's backward look, in *To the Lighthouse*, at an event which her departure has brought to an end, but which continues after she has gone, automatically, its continuation a foretaste of her death. These scenes, like the scenes from *Napoléon*, *The Crowd*, and *Vampyr* in which a lateral track distends the tableau, pulling it sideways to reveal it as a mask, constitute at once an enactment and a critique of mimesis. They lay bare the automatism within mimicry, not to dispel it, but rather to explore its (often fatal) attraction. The departure they negotiate from 'natural' lines of sight and movement is a *willed* departure. The modernist will-to-automatism should be understood as at once a concession of human self-presence to the machine, and a refusal to recognise the machine as the principle or mythology of absence, of the non-human.

All this may seem a long way from Charlie Chaplin. Chaplin, however, was by any account not just the supreme exponent of imitation, but its epitome. The Tramp is all imitation. There are scenes in Chaplin's films, I hope to demonstrate, which make imitation their topic as well as their method. 'Charlie Chaplin is not English, or American,' T. S. Eliot observed, 'but a universal figure, feeding the idealism of hungry millions in Czecho-Slovakia and Peru.'[3] Chaplin ministered to the fantasies of the many and the few alike (in Eliot's case, disdain for the merely cosmopolitan). To conclude this book with a discussion of some of his films is to confirm an emphasis upheld throughout it: that the study of literary modernism's indebtedness to cinema should not be restricted to a handful of avant-garde *jeux d'esprit*. Mainstream cinema mattered, to Joyce, Eliot, and Woolf; Chaplin's films help us to understand why.

Hypermimesis

My proposition is that Chaplin should be thought of as modern, and even modernist, by virtue not of anti-mimesis (supposedly modernism's calling-card), but of what I shall call hypermimesis.[4] Several of Chaplin's most remarkable short films demonstrate an interest in mimicry for mimicry's sake. Charlie imitates to excess. Why?

Anglo-American modernist writers went so far, on occasion, as to define their hostility to mimesis by reference to Chaplin. Modernism has long been regarded, from a wide variety of critical perspectives, as constitutionally anti-mimetic. Modernism is that, or it is nothing. One of the most fruitful recent developments in the study of Anglo-American modernism has been to attribute to its constitutional anti-mimesis a politics and a sociology. Anglo-American modernism's anti-mimetic initiatives have been understood as a critique of the principle of *social* mimesis informing modern bourgeois democracy. Wyndham Lewis, the czar of Anglo-American anti-mimesis, wrote abstract novels and campaigned against the various cults which he thought had made social mimesis more or less compulsory: the time-cult, the child-cult, the cult of 'inversion', and so on. As Peter Nicholls puts it, the 'polemical thrust' Lewis and his contemporaries gave to an 'anti-mimetic art' was directed against the 'imitative tendencies associated with the mass politics of a democratic age'.[5] One can, I think, trace this anxiety back in Anglo-American political thought at least as far as John Stuart Mill, who worried that the all-inclusive democratic social order in prospect from the 1850s onwards would extinguish 'variety of situations'.[6] In the 1920s, Lewis was to speak, in very much the same spirit, of mass democracy's fundamental drive towards the 'suppressing of *differences*'.[7] The politics and the sociology of Anglo-American modernism's anti-mimesis amounted to an anxiety about the wholesale suppression of differences.

In *Time and Western Man* (1927), Lewis described Charlie Chaplin as the very epitome of the cult of childishness which in his view was systematically undermining the ability of grown men and women to take responsibility for their own actions. His argument echoes that put forward as early as 1915, in a review of *The Tramp* in the American avant-garde magazine the *Little Review*, which was later to serialise James Joyce's *Ulysses*. The reviewer describes Chaplin as a 'Mob-God' whose gyrations draw purgative laughter from a previously supine audience, a 'sodden mass inclined toward protoplasmic atavism'. 'He is the Mob-God. He is a child and a clown. He is a gutter snipe and an artist. He is the incarnation of the latent, imperfect, and childlike genius that lies under the fiberless flesh of the worshippers. They have created Him in their image.'[8] Chaplin, Lewis declared in *Time and Western Man*, 'is *a child-man*, rather than merely *a small man*'. Since the child-man triumphs over authority by maintaining his childishness intact, by resolutely not growing up, he exemplifies, in Lewis's view, a politics and a sociology. The tramp's 'irresponsible epileptic shuffle', which combines playfulness with 'scurrilous cunning', was a licence to his millions of admirers not to grow up, not to undertake the responsibilities of difference.[9] Imitating a child, Chaplin is himself imitated: he becomes the very medium of the social reproduction of mimesis, and thus capitalism's most valuable asset.

Lewis's strategy, in *Time and Western Man*, is to Chaplinise his literary rivals, to make Charlies out of writers such as Gertrude Stein and Marcel Proust. The 'I' of Proust's novels, Lewis maintains, 'is that small, naïf, Charlie Chaplin-like, luxuriously-indulged, sharp-witted, passionately snob-bish, figure, a model for many variations bred thickly everywhere'.[10] The politics of this thesis is evident enough in the genetic or epidemiological metaphor it so readily deploys (recall the piece in the *Little Review*, and its preoccupation with protoplasm).[11] In a delirious passage, Lewis speculates gleefully about the sudden proliferation of pocket-size *avant-gardistes*. Nature, he observes, has evidently decided to turn out geniuses who are 'eternal sucklings' in both spirit and flesh. 'Picasso . . . is very small as well; with, however, a slightly napoleonic austerity lacking in Chaplin; though he has the same bright, darting, knowing eyes, the same appearance of microscopic competence. He is built on strictly infantile lines.'[12] And so on.

This, then, is how modernism at its most mimeticidal viewed Chaplin: Chaplin embodies that social reproduction of mimesis which if unchecked will extinguish for ever difference of situation. There were some writers, it is true, like T. S. Eliot, whose desire to reintroduce elements of myth and ritual into modern society, and into modern literature, rendered them rather more susceptible to Chaplin's creation of a universally recognisable comic figure. Chaplin's 'egregious' merit, Eliot thought, was to have 'escaped in his own way from the realism of the cinema', and thereby 'invented a *rhythm*'.[13] But what seems to me informative in the more forthright modernist critiques of Chaplin is his identification as the creature and exponent of likeness. Eliot and Lewis, one with reluctant admiration, the other with a contempt stopping just short of complete disavowal, might both have understood Charlie's compulsive mimicry as a way to be modern without being anti-mimetic.

The moments I want now to draw attention to, in Chaplin's films, are the moments when he chose to dwell on, and to make a performance of, imitation itself. The films which interest me most from this point of view are the films Chaplin made during and immediately after the First World War, at Essanay, Mutual, and First National, in which the figure of the tramp became something more than a costume and a set of mannerisms, something less than a 'character'. Various useful accounts have been offered of the tramp's emergence as an icon or universal figure. John Kimber, for example, has distinguished between three successive but overlapping 'incarnations' or 'selves' in the films of this period: over-bearing, creatively high-spirited, and 'fully human'.[14] Rather than identify a 'self' in the tramp's antics, I have sought to define a specific preoccupation which, because it provoked Chaplin to feats of film-making, can be said to constitute an attitude, a view of the world, a critique of modernity.

As the figure of the tramp took shape, in the Essanay films, so imitation became in the most pressing sense an issue for Chaplin. His rapidly escalating popularity encouraged a wide variety of imitators, from Stan Laurel, whose Chaplin imitation was overt, and thus flattering, to Billy West, a smalltime vaudevillian who copied Chaplin's costume and make-up in more than fifty one- and two-reel comedies. In 1916, Charles Amador, a Mexican actor, changed his name to Charlie Aplin, and copied Chaplin's most successful routines. Chaplin sued, and won, though not without difficulty.[15]

I want to concentrate on two scenes of imitation, in particular, which occur with some frequency in the films of this period. The first involves Charlie's imitation of and by another person, who thereby becomes a stooge or accomplice; following Chaplin himself, I shall refer to it as 'The Biter Bit'. The second involves Charlie's imitation of a mechanical apparatus of some kind (including persons in an unconscious state). It amounts to an exercise in camouflage.

The first scene, apparent in the earliest Essanay films, and no doubt deriving from vaudeville, is the product of a casual encounter, in a public or semi-public space, between Charlie and another man. The other man has intentions upon Charlie, more often than not involving robbery. Charlie realises immediately what is going on, but decides not to resist. There is a happy recognition, first on the part of the victim, then on the part of the assailant, of the full extent of the indignities in progress. Both are willing to allow these indignities to continue after the original motive for the encounter has been exhausted. The two participants imitate each other madly, in complicitous resistance, or resistant complicity, in a *pas de deux* charged with an astonishing intensity of feeling on both sides: an intensity not at all incompatible, as we shall see, with a certain nonchalance.

We might compare the performance with that put on by literary modernism's pseudo-couples: the pairs of mismatched and yet inseparable male protagonists, in Wyndham Lewis, in Lawrence, in Beckett. The term is Beckett's.[16] Fredric Jameson has argued that the pseudo-couple became in modernist writing from Flaubert to Beckett a 'structural device for preserving narrative as such'. In his view, the modern plotless novel, with its anti-hero and its compensatory weight of 'abstract stylization', was a result of the extinction of the 'older' passions and interests by *ennui* and *anorexia*. The pseudo-couple is the 'unstable, acrobatic resolution' of the need to keep narrative going.[17] That the resolution is unstable and yet acrobatic would, of course, suit Chaplin perfectly. What I would take from Jameson's account is the sense of the pseudo-couple as a stimulus to new and in essence contrary formal energies. The *pas de deux* does not constitute an obstacle to narrative as such. It constitutes, rather, a counter-narrative, a story told about something else altogether. Writers from Flaubert to Beckett found that they needed to tell that story. So, I think, did Chaplin.

Perhaps the most carefully conceived of Lewis's pseudo-couples, worth brief consideration before I turn to Chaplin's films, is to be found in *The Childermass* (1928), the first part of *The Human Age*, a trilogy completed by the publication of *Monstre Gai* and *Malign Fiesta* in 1955. Pullman, a writer bearing a resemblance to James Joyce, and Satterthwaite, who had been his fag at Rugby, and appears to have met his end during the First World War, bump into each other in the afterworld, in a huge encampment on the banks of the River Styx where those awaiting admission to Heaven morosely congregate. Pullman, musing beside the river, 'a lost automaton rather than a lost soul', is suddenly confronted by Satterthwaite's 'pink young mask'. 'Eye in eye they dart and scent each other's minds, like nozzling dogs.' The companionship which develops between them is a compound of the most urgent darting and nozzling and utter incuriosity, or 'respectful strangeness'. Mechanical adjustments of attitude and feeling to each enforced change of shape or status will preserve intact the sheer arbitrariness of this first encounter in the afterworld. And yet they cannot bear to be apart. 'Their minds continue to work in silent rhythm, according to the system of habit set in motion by their meeting.'[18]

Promenading in a landscape defined as much by time as by space, they eventually reach an amphitheatre where a bureaucrat-demagogue known as the Bailiff considers applications to enter the city across the river, while the followers of his arch-enemy Hyperides hotly contest his right to do so. Alectryon, the Hyperideans' chief spokesman, carries cheerfully on where *Time and Western Man* had left off. He claims that the 'class-conscious orthodoxy' of modern societies has reduced those possessing 'conspicuous undemocratic abilities' to pariah-status (p. 302). As Alectryon prepares to state his case, the Bailiff looks over at Pullman: 'his trusty and well-beloved Anglo-Saxon admirer gazes back at him through his glasses in steadfast silence while the sucker-like fore-paw of Satters wakes into activity and massages the muscles of his patron's arm in secret' (p. 300). There is no danger that either of them will give a moment's thought to what Electryon has to say. Pullman exists by ideological mimicry alone, Satterthwaite by physical mimicry alone.

In *Time and Western Man*, Lewis had characterised Joyce, Pullman's model, as a craftsman pure and simple, and thus endlessly susceptible both to social and political doctrine and to literary influences. Joyce, Lewis concluded, had neither the will nor the ability to conceive of literature as anything other than imitation. Little hope for Pullman, then. Satterthwaite, by contrast, is the child-man produced by consumer capitalism. His talk is baby-talk, or Stein-talk, his actions pure reflex. These men exemplify the everything Lewis had campaigned against for so long. In imagining them, he abandoned Vorticism, the pursuit of abstraction, and became instead, for whole paragraphs at a time, James Joyce, or Gertrude Stein. When not dedicated to studious literary pastiche, the narrative goes binge-shopping in the 'warehouse of cultural and mass cultural cliché'.[19] And yet Pullman and Satterthwaite cannot be dismissed as creatures of social mimesis: an example to us all, held comfortably up for inspection by satire or jeremiad. There is something other than creaturely in the 'normal posthumous relationship' (p. 27) constituted by their pseudo-coupling: an intent whose ferocity exceeds any discernable purpose. Pullman may want simply to 'rattle along these beaten tracks', as Lewis himself does, in this instance, by settling for cliché; but sometimes to rattle along is to shake loose, or be shaken loose – to agitate the beaten track, without dislodging it, or departing from it (p. 17). The story the pseudo-couple's adventure tells is a story about imitation for imitation's sake: about hypermimesis, and the will-to-automatism of which it is at once enactment and critique. Pullman and Satterthwaite want so badly to become automata that they thereby remain (posthumously) human.

Lewis's rendering of the will-in-automatism in the first 130 pages or so of *The Childermass* – by critical enactment, rather than by satire, pastiche, citation, or other anti-mimetic manoeuvre – is a tour de force and utter vindication of modernist literary technique. Cinema evidently played a part in its conception. It is not at all remarkable, perhaps, that an afterworld conceived in the late 1920s should resemble Hollywood product. 'The whole city like a film-scene slides away perceptibly several inches to the rear, as their eyes are fixed upon it' (p. 29). But the sliding film-scene is not simply a metaphor for synthetic space and time, for the manufacture of illusion. What interested Lewis about such film-scenes was that they could not be conceived of as wholly immaterial.

Early on in their adventure, Pullman and Satterthwaite encounter a party of 'peons' equipped with picks, shovels, wheelbarrows, and other implements. Satterthwaite stares in awe at these 'halted human shells'.

> Here and there their surfaces collapse altogether as his eye falls upon them, the whole appearance vanishes, the man is gone. But as the pressure withdraws of the full-blown human glance the shadow reassembles, in the same stark posture, every way as before, at the same spot – obliquely he is able to observe it coming back jerkily into position. One figure is fainter than any of the rest, he is a thin and shabby mustard yellow, in colouring a flat daguerreotype or one of the personnel of a pre-war film, split tarnished and transparent from travel and barter. He comes and goes; sometimes he is there, then he flickers out. He is a tall man of no occupation, in the foreground. He falls like a yellow smear upon one much firmer than himself behind, or invades him like a rusty putrefaction, but never blots out the stronger person. (p. 22)

The tall thin man exerts much the same fascination on Satterthwaite as the spectral passer-by in *Intolerance* was to exert on Sergei Eisenstein. He, too, has no occupation; but rather comes between or in front of purposeful activity, obtruding his gaunt hollowness, which then begins to look like the stuff of existence. Like a figure from a pre-war actuality, he is not held in focus for the viewer by the part he plays in the action, or by the discovery in him of psychological depth. 'He comes and goes; sometimes he is there, then he flickers out.' However, this flickering in and out, as the product of automatic vision, does not reduce the man entirely to a spectre. He has, it turns out, a kind of materiality. He is transparent, but also tarnished: a smear or rusty putrefaction which seems more vivid, in its way, than mere non-transparent existence. To exist by means of automatic vision, for a viewer external to the scene viewed, as an absence-effect, is, it would seem, to establish a certain distinctive presence. Small surprise, then, that this figure should suddenly 'come to life'. 'His neck sticks out there is a black flash and a stream of sputum stained with betel-nut strikes Satters upon the cheek' (p. 25). The figure comes to life, as the passer-by in *Intolerance* had come to life, by random violence. There is nothing immaterial about sputum.

If the afterworld on show in *The Childermass* is a product of the continuity system, Pullman and Satterthwaite, like the peons from whom they are notionally to be distinguished, belong instead to the cinema of attractions. Lewis, like Joyce, Eliot, and Woolf before him, found in what was by the 1920s a superseded mode of representation, in its awkwardness, its flickering in and out, a way to expose that which more recent modes, literary or cinematic, had sought to conceal: an excess, in human as well as post-human existence, of mimesis over meaning. Pullman and Satterthwaite have an astonishing density, as literary creations, because Lewis conceived them as lost automata rather than lost souls, as the product of cinema's automatic vision.

The concept of the pseudo-couple enabled Lewis to withdraw his protagonists from a narrative driven by sexual desire or ambition. It created a descriptive laboratory in which mimesis could be tested to destruction (but not, I think, beyond). The pseudo-couple's density is not in itself cinematic. It is an effect of literary language. Paul Edwards has usefully revised Jameson's account of the style of *The Childermass* by demonstrating that the book is 'replete with specialised discourses beyond the cultural horizon of most readers'.[20]

Even more striking, to my mind, is a descriptive vocabulary which, although well within the cultural horizon of most readers, causes a certain disquiet by the fanaticism of its determination to specify. This vocabulary comes into play at moments when Pullman and Satterthwaite, lost in pseudo-coupling, are furthest removed from sexual desire, ambition, or any other motivating force. It finds in the very mechanism of mechanical behaviour a life not apparent in non-mechanical behaviour. We have already seen them approach each other 'like *nozzling* dogs'. 'Nozzling' is an unusual term, but perfectly comprehensible in its context. It does not call forth specialised knowledge, or the dictionary. Instead, it insists (fanatically) on pseudo-coupling's specificity: on the combination it provokes of phallic prod or probe (nozzle) with a demand for nurture (nuzzle). Locomotion seems particularly susceptible to literary hypermimesis: far from rattling along beaten tracks, the two men 'stog and plod, leg and leg' (p. 18). At one point during the promenade, Satterthwaite, feeling himself an impostor from head to foot, removes all his clothes. 'A formidable elongated bladder of meat, Satters cloppers up his arms flapping fin-like as he runs, useless paddles of dough beating the air up into invisible suds' (p. 111). There are familiar words in the vicinity of the neologism 'clopper' or 'clopper up'. Satters, always liable to clobber someone, is presumably engaged in 'running like the clappers' towards the inscrutable Pullman. Lewis wants us to think with familiar language, but also beyond it, to what the specificity of the life in the very mechanism of mechanical behaviour might actually be. By and large it is the things the pseudo-couple does together, leg and leg, or the 'engines of unmeaning melting expressiveness' (p. 29) the two men turn on each other, which provoke Lewis to feats of literary hypermimesis. There is a critique, in these descriptions, of the will-to-automatism, but a critique hard to distinguish from enactment.

The promenade undertaken by Pullman and Satterthwaite terminates at the amphitheatre where the Bailiff holds court, assessing the arguments put forward by various petitioners for salvation. The two men become spectators at a tournament of dialectic which provides little or no scope for the exercise of the will-to-automatism on their part. At this point in *The Childermass*, Lewis gave up on hypermimesis. The account I have offered of the experiments undertaken in his descriptive laboratory does not apply to the remainder of the book (the bulk of it).[21] I hope, however, that it will throw some light on the films made by a film-maker who also discovered in the very mechanism of mechanical behaviour a life not apparent in non-mechanical behaviour.

Chaplin: from Essanay to First National

My first example of a Chaplinesque pseudo-couple is from *In the Park* (1915), an Essanay quickie made in a week, and generally dismissed as a 'park' comedy in the Keystone mould. 'All I need to make a comedy', Chaplin once told Mack Sennett, 'is a park, a policeman, and a pretty girl.'[22] On this occasion, he began with the pretty girl. A nursemaid (Edna Purviance) sits on a bench reading a book entitled *Why They Married*. She glances with open admiration at a genteel (or faux-genteel) couple seated on another bench, who fondle each other enthusiastically. The pattern of cuts leaves us in no doubt that she would like (and indeed expects to get) some of what her middle-class counterpart is having. However, this burgeoning heterosexual idyll is about to be rudely disturbed. An intertitle announces: 'The biter bit'. Elsewhere in the park, Charlie, at a loose end (Jameson's *ennui*, perhaps), stands twirling his cane, gazing down at the ground. A thief approaches him from behind, and staring ostentatiously in the opposite direction (or perhaps in no direction, since he would appear to be blind), reaches out a hand towards his jacket pocket. Charlie sees what is going on, but at first chooses not to react. The thief removes a handkerchief from Charlie's pocket, which Charlie, observing the manoeuvre with interest, seizes, and uses to blow his nose, thanking his collaborator. Unabashed, the thief tries again, this time prospecting in Charlie's trouser-pocket. One thinks of Satterthwaite's sucker-like fore-paw, in *The Childermass*, a 'reluctant muscle-taking-root' which perpetually massages Pullman's arm in secret (p. 16). Charlie reciprocates by fishing a cigarette out of the thief's jacket pocket, and putting it to his lips. The look he now gives his assailant-turned-collaborator is a mixture of coyness and reproach. The pair swop places, feigning indifference, and Charlie strikes a match on the back of his partner's neck, before tipping his hat to him and waving goodbye. There is intimacy, in this encounter, and profound mutual understanding; but never for an instant the mutual regard which might become the basis of relationship, as opposed to durable co-presence. The biter bit is Chaplin's version of a pseudo-coupling. What holds the *ennui*-struck pair together is imitation. The biter gets bitten, that is, imitated; he bites again, imitating his imitator. Each knows what the other is up to. Neither wishes to bring the performance to a premature end.

This counter-narrative to heterosexual romance (*Why They Did Not Marry*) immediately produces another scene which, although comparably awkward, does not constitute a pseudo-coupling. Elsewhere in the park, a policeman stands, looking off to his right (our left), twirling his baton. Charlie backs cautiously into view from the right, until he comes to rest against the policeman's solid form, when without looking round he reaches out a hand to fondle first the policeman's hand, then his badge, then the buttons on his tunic, then, lightly, the baton. He is still locked in imitation of his original blindly fondling assailant. But, in another place at another time, the imitation misfires. Coming to, abruptly, Charlie twirls his cane in embarrassment, and then, oddly unabashed, resumes. This time he fondles the tip of the baton, which the policeman holds at an angle of 45 degrees across his groin, rather more deliberately. As the policeman looks down, Charlie wanders off, twirling his cane. The scene is set off from its predecessor by the striking disparity, in terms both of physical size and of power, between the two participants.

Between such a pair, there is not the equivalence which permits imitation (as there is, for example, between Pullman and Satterthwaite, whose shared class history has already taken the edge off disparities in size and authority). For we have, here, in Charlie's pleasuring of phallic authority, a Rabelaisian Chaplin whose wild invention requires a different kind of analysis from the one I shall develop.[23]

The most nearly Rabelaisian of Charlie's pseudo-couplings occurs, to brilliant effect, in *Police* (1916), officially the last film Chaplin made for Essanay. The film's celebrated flophouse scene pales by comparison with the muscle-taking-root episode which follows it. Charlie has been thrown out of the flophouse because he has no money, and is mugged in a dark alley in a manner verging on the orgiastic. He and the mugger ransack each other's persons in what appears to be full mutual knowledge and consent. The mugger rummages through Charlie's rear trouser-pockets a second time, even after he has discovered that they are empty, a manoeuvre which Charlie interprets as sexual. In this case, the mutual rummaging has reunited a pseudo-couple: the pair were cell-mates in prison; they go on to rob a house together.

Desire, however, is not the point of pseudo-coupling (it has no point). Chaplin wove a certain nonchalance into Charlie's participation in these bouts. Nowhere more so than in *The Floorwalker* (1916), his first film for Mutual, which redescribes the encounter between biter and bitten as a mirror-imaging. The encounter takes place in an outer office on the upper level of the shop. The manager and his assistant have conspired to empty the safe. The assistant, having disposed of his accomplice, emerges into the outer office, loot in hand, to be confronted by Charlie, who is coming the other way, with a store detective in hot pursuit, and who looks an awful lot like him. Both think that they have seen their own image in a mirror. Each imitates the other's actions, uncertain whether he is looking at himself, or at someone else. Each reaches out a hand to touch the surface of a nonexistent mirror. Looking down simultaneously, they realise that Charlie has a cane in his hand, rather than a briefcase full of money. After a futile attempt to escape from each other's presence, they engage in close mutual inspection. The assistant manager knocks Chaplin's hat off, pinches his cheek, and gets a kiss in return. They swop clothes. Although thoroughly expedient, from both points of view, imitation is in this scene also an end in itself: a reason to come together, a profound pleasure. It is Charlie's nonchalance, an awareness preceding and not dependent upon full knowledge, although further extended by it, which reconfigures the episode as an investigation of the wish to conform to another's wishes.

So much for the biter bit. In the other characteristic scene I have in mind, Charlie engrossedly imitates an object, or mechanism, at first in order to elude pursuit, then for reasons harder to fathom. The piece of the world into which he sinks himself in these episodes takes the form of a contrivance, or contraption (a term evolved from 'contrive', with a strong implication of the makeshift, and just a hint of entrapment). In acting like a machine, Charlie does not cease to be himself. Indeed, he becomes rather more himself. He fulfils himself. The wish fulfilled, the wish to act like a machine, is a new and defining solitude. There may well be other persons present. But they will never know what he knows. They will never see the world as he sees it from within his contraption.

Chaplin's last and most popular film for Mutual, *The Adventurer* (1917), has two parts. The first part, in effect a reversion to Keystone methods, has convict Charlie chased up and down the Santa Monica hills by a posse of trigger-happy warders. In the second part, Charlie masquerades as a wealthy yachtsman at a party given in his honour by the heroine, whose mother he has saved from drowning. Suspicions are soon aroused, and the warders arrive. Placing a lampshade on his head, Charlie stands stock still as the hot pursuit swirls around him, and away, at the motionless centre of motion. He removes the lampshade, in order to assault the villain, but then replaces it on his own head, as though he now cannot do without it, and walks out onto the veranda. He would like above all to extend the enchanted interval. But other perils await, and he cannot expect the trick to work again, in another place at another time. He tosses the lampshade aside. Now no one will ever know what he knew (not even Edna Purviance, stood right next to Charlie-the-lampstand while the pursuit swirled by).

In Chaplin's first film for First National, *A Dog's Life* (1916), Charlie discovers the automaton he needs in another human being. He returns to the Green Lantern dance-hall to retrieve from a pair of pickpockets the contents of a wallet they had stolen and buried, which his dog had dug up, thus making it his. The pickpockets sit in an alcove curtained at each end. Charlie knocks one of them out through the curtain, and inserts his own arms on either side of the man's body, engaging in a vividly mimed conversation with the other pickpocket, in order to elicit the money due to him. His eyes visible through a slit in the curtain, Charlie converts his victim into an automaton. The mime utterly mesmerises its interlocutor, who appears not to have noticed that his previously loquacious colleague has been struck dumb. His fascination is our fascination.

Both kinds of scene enact imitation, as Charlie's body conforms itself to a machine, or to someone else's expectations; and both kinds of scene comment upon imitation, through sheer excess, and the pleasure taken in excess. Both kinds tell a story. Slapstick comedy reproduces in fantasy the insult the body suffers in the world. By contrast, Chaplin's tramp comedy insists, as Mark Winokur has pointed out, on the intelligence of the body in *avoiding* insult (or at least terminal insult) through self-transformation.[24] It seems to me, however, that the intelligence at work in tramp comedy amounts to something more than avoidance, something less than self-transformation. By defining this intelligence as hypermimesis, we acknowledge it as a counter-narrative, as at once enactment and critique of imitation. Why did Chaplin take up hypermimesis? What was it about the nature and circumstances of imitation that provoked him to feats of film-making?

Aura and mechanism

The place to begin might be the contradiction at the heart of the role Chaplin devised for himself in the Essanay and Mutual films. On the one hand, the Tramp has generally been regarded as the very embodiment of the illusion of presence cinema alone can generate, of an immediacy given rather than made. Chaplin, as Michael North puts it, had 'succeeded more completely than any other screen actor in turning himself into a purely visual object'.[25] He had become universally recognisable. His arrival in Europe in 1921 without the moustache, the large shoes, the derby, and the cane was the cause of considerable disgruntlement. 'There are grave doubts', he reported, 'as to whether I am Charlie Chaplin or not.'[26]

The moustache, large shoes, derby, and cane had meanwhile ensconced themselves in European film-theory as the very epitome of screen beauty, of *photogénie*. In becoming Charlot, Louis Delluc claimed in 1917, Chaplin had gone beyond the actor's art. 'Not for him the art of traditions, disguises, tricks, acrobatics, eccentricities, and clownings, but a prodigious truth, at bottom, the truth of what he does for himself rather than for the spectator.'[27] Yet what did the prodigious truth consist of if not of disguises, tricks, acrobatics, and the rest? The stylisation that went into the Tramp created a mechanism rather than a persona: a mechanism, what's more, consistently exposed as mechanism by acts of hypermimesis. Essential to Charlot's 'vision of the world', Louis Aragon remarked, was the 'discovery of the mechanical and its laws', so that by an 'inversion of values' objects become people and people pieces of machinery whose starting-handle must be found.[28]

The concept of *photogénie* could be said to have prepared the way, by its emphasis on description rather than on narrative, on mise-en-scène rather than on montage, for André Bazin's account of the ontology of the photographic image. Bazin, as is well known, thought that the photographic image had at last fulfilled the profound human need to 'give significant expression to the world both concretely and in its essence'. It could be at once concrete and essential because its relation to the object was primarily indexical. 'The photograph as such and the object in itself share a common being, after the fashion of a fingerprint.'[29] For Bazin (and Eliot may have thought the same), there were performers whose performances were myth's fingerprint: whose concrete person disclosed an essence, a meaning universally understood. 'The greatness of *Limelight*', he declared in 1953, 'is one with the greatness of the cinema itself – it is the most dazzling display of its very essence, abstraction *by way of* incarnation'. The meaning and value of Chaplin–Calvero's death lay in the public exhibition made of it, a narrative effect 'daringly based on the flesh and blood ambiguity of the cinematographic image: see and understand!'[30]

The incarnations Bazin had in mind were, however, always and everywhere *abstract*. Their credibility depended upon the intervention between observer and scene of a 'non-living agent', a machine. 'For the first time an image of the world is formed automatically, without the creative intervention of man.'[31] In a remarkable essay on Chaplin's myth as the creation specifically of cinema, first published in 1948, Bazin found himself pondering not the flesh and blood ambiguity of the gags 'peculiar' to Charlie, and therefore the stuff of myth, but rather their persistent 'use of the mechanical'.

One of Bazin's most instructive examples is the moment in *Shoulder Arms* (1918), Chaplin's war-movie, in which Charlie, on a mission behind enemy lines, conceals himself in or as a wood and canvas contraption painted to look like a tree. Caught out in the open when some German soldiers begin gathering wood for a fire, Charlie has no choice but to hide behind appearances. He completes the deception organised through camouflage by standing stock still, arms held out at approximately branch-like angles, his eyes just visible through a slit in the tree-machine, as they had been visible through a slit in the curtain in *A Dog's Life*. He has removed himself from the scene, while remaining throughout at its centre. From within this radical solitude he is able, as he was in *The Adventurer*, to counter-attack. He clobbers a succession of hapless German soldiers as they wander beneath the branches of his tree-machine. Camouflage subsequently becomes a technique of mise-en-scène when Charlie, pursued into a wood, once again holds himself immobile, as effectively hidden from the audience as he is from his pursuer. 'One is reminded', Bazin observes, 'of those little stick-like insects that are indiscernible in a clump of twigs or those little Indian insects that can take on the appearance of leaves, even leaves that caterpillars have nibbled. The sudden vegetable-like immobility of Charlie-the-tree is like an insect playing dead.'[32]

It isn't quite true to say that Charlie disguises himself as a tree. He disguises himself as a machine disguised as a tree. As in *The Adventurer*, there is good reason for these efforts at concealment. But one might once again want to say that the mechanism in the machine has brought out the mechanism in Charlie. Bazin almost says as much, by comparing the man-myth to an insect. Where does the comparison come from? It comes, I believe, though I cannot prove as much, from the work of the philosopher and naturalist Roger Caillois, Bataille's collaborator at the Collège de Sociologie in Paris during the late 1930s. In *Méduse et compagnie* (1960), which assembles arguments developed during the previous twenty-five years, Caillois had put forward the hypothesis that mimicry is, for animals, insects, and human beings alike, a compulsion rather than a survival strategy. Among the examples he gives are insects which mimic twigs and leaves nibbled by caterpillars. Camouflage, Caillois says, is 'a feigned loss of individuality, which dissolves itself and can no longer be found out'. That is, it begins as a feint, but outlasts its original purpose. The term Caillois uses for this 'aimless delirium of perfection in mimicry' is *hyperthely*, or the excessive development of an organ. Human beings, he adds, like animals and insects, get caught up in hyperthely, or mimicry for its own sake. 'The success of man, or his misfortune perhaps, is to have introduced an element of play into the rigid machinery.'[33] Caillois, then, leaves it open to doubt as to whether or not in human behaviour the element of play overrides the element of compulsion. Is Charlie playing dead? Or would he like to be dead (an insect, a machine)?

Or has he gone mad? In an uncollected essay which Bazin may or may not have known, Caillois compares the mimicry undertaken by animals and insects to that undertaken by schizophrenics. He speaks, in a wonderful phrase, of a 'temptation by space' in schizophrenia. Tempted by space, the imitator dissolves into the world.[34] There might then be a psychopathology of imitation. Bazin emphasises Charlie's rapid recovery from mad mimesis. He has contracted a kind of 'mechanical cramp', which soon eases. Or we might regard 'mechanization of movement' as his 'original sin', a 'ceaseless temptation'; a temptation he is, however, capable of overcoming. What distinguishes Charlie from an insect or a schizophrenic, Bazin concludes, is the speed with which he returns from his 'spatial dissolution into the cosmos' to a state of readiness.[35]

Bazin, however, cannot altogether approve of the conclusion it seems reasonable to draw from Caillois's understanding of mimicry: that Charlie has developed a liking for automatism, that he has got the habit. So he insists on the rapidity of Charlie's recovery from the habit, on the rapidity with which he resumes a state of readiness. But is the recovery in fact all that rapid? For Charlie continues to imitate a lampstand or a tree long after these imitations have fulfilled their immediate purpose. He has been possessed by the idea of mimicry, and continues to try it on even when there is no need to do so. 'Aimless delirium of perfection in mimicry', Caillois's phrase for hyperthely, a phrase which finds no echo in Bazin's argument, would seem rather more appropriate to Charlie-the-lampstand or Charlie-the-tree than invocations of original sin.

In Chaplin's films, the tableau still possesses the sense of spatial and temporal volume it had possessed in the first Lumière actualities. These films exemplify Stanley Cavell's claim, in *The World Viewed*, that the limits of the screen are 'not so much the edges of a given shape as they are the limitations, or capacity, of a container'. 'The screen *is* a frame,' Cavell goes on; 'the frame is the whole field of the screen – as a frame of film is the whole field of a photograph, like the frame of a loom or a house. In this sense, the screen-frame is a mold, or form.'[36] What the container contains, in Chaplin's films, contains in such a way as to shape, is Charlie: the Charlie-effect.

The World Viewed was first published in 1971, in the aftermath of an explosion of 'technique' in cinema worldwide, a development which might well have appeared to offend Cavell's Bazinian belief that cinema should 'communicate only by way of what is real'.[37] Still, Bazin's declaration that cinema should communicate only by way of what is real occurs during an enquiry into that 'dialectic of concrete and abstract' which informs it throughout.[38] Cavell's attention to the abstract in cinema takes the form of an attention to its constitutive automatism. 'Photography', he observes, 'maintains the presentness of the world by accepting our absence from it.' A film is a 'succession of automatic world projections'.[39]

For Cavell, one suspects, as for Bazin, Chaplin and the other great silent comedians exemplify that combination of the 'intensity of mystery' with the 'intensity of mechanism' which he considers unique to cinema. As ever, though, his method is to approach the 'particular mode of presence' of these figures on the screen by way of the 'particular mode of absence' from them of their audience. Movie performers 'cannot project, but are projected'. It is the fact of projection, Cavell argues, which 'permits the sublime comprehensibility of Chaplin's natural choreography'.[40]

The choreography (the rhythm, Eliot might have said) is 'natural'. But it signifies, is made comprehensible, by the shape it takes within the (loom-like, house-like) screen-frame, within the shot understood as tableau: by a centring, for all eyes at once, which could not be achieved in the theatre. Chaplin's habit of retaking a shot over and over again until it felt right bears witness to his reliance on the comprehensibility delivered by the automatism of the photographic image. It is not surprising that Cavell should wish to describe his achievement in this respect as 'sublime'. The sublime, however, is precisely that which cannot be comprehended. This is perhaps the point at which Cavell's thesis about the ways in which cinema has maintained the world's presentness exceeds, for a moment, its own otherwise illuminating terms. The comprehensibility of Chaplin's tableau is sublime because it centres on that which cannot be comprehended: on that in it which 'represents' absence rather than presence.

In becoming a contraption, Charlie becomes, in his solitude, the vacuum at the centre of a vortex, a whirlwind of activity. The biter and the bit swop roles across a fold in narrative space which presents each to the other as mirror-image. It is this fold in space which Charlie and his double simultaneously reach out to touch in *The Floorwalker*. Such effects could only have been achieved by and as an 'automatic world projection': take after take, until it felt right, until it felt like (an image of) second nature. A constitutive absence from or within the mise-en-scène (a hollow centre, an object which does not exist) ensures that hypermimesis will function both as enactment and as critique.

Chaplin's career could be understood as the supersession first of slapstick comedy by tramp comedy, and then of tramp comedy by a socially and psychologically acute comic drama. Hypermimesis could be taken to define an aspect of tramp comedy. Indeed, its productiveness in those films, as enactment and critique, should be enough to thwart any inclination to view Chaplin's career as a development from an emphasis on body to an emphasis on spirit.[41] Even so, I have to acknowledge that hypermimesis was from the outset shadowed by a contrary preoccupation with the mimesis proper to serio-comic drama. As Chaplin's films conformed more and more closely to the model of a 'cinema of narrative integration', in David Bordwell's phrase, a cinema which 'absorbs cinematic techniques and engaging moments into a self-sufficient world unified across time and space',[42] so he found less use for hypermimesis.

The divergence is apparent as early as *His New Job* (1915), which was in fact Chaplin's first job at Essanay. The film turns on the construction of an idea of the pro-performative, on a space outside, or supplementary to, the arena within which the performer performs. Charlie is an aspiring actor hired as a stage hand who ends up, briefly, as a film-star. The space of the pro-performative is defined in large part by comic business in the inner and outer offices at Lodestone Studios, including a biter-bit episode between Charlie and another aspiring actor. The two aspirants are seated side by side in the outer office. Turpin sneezes violently in Charlie's face, and hooks his leg over Charlie's knee. Charlie doesn't like the smell. They turn to face each other. Turpin has a cigarette between his lips, which Charlie impudently fellates, before striking a match on the plaster covering Turpin's cheek. He gets confused as to which end of the cigarette should be in his mouth. This is a pseudo-coupling undertaken in full mutual knowledge. Turpin stalks Charlie for the rest of the film.

The space of the performative is defined by the presence in it of actors and actresses in period costume, and by an event which has always struck me as strangely moving, in more senses than one. The director issues instructions to the leading man and lady, while his assistant fiddles with the lens of a camera fully visible in the foreground of the shot. As they retire behind the on-stage camera, the off-stage camera tracks forward past them and in on the leading man and lady. Such movement is a rarity, of course, in Chaplin's early films. Here, it indicates 'cinema'. So great was the reputation at this time of Giovanni Pastrone's *Cabiria* (1914) that the tracking shot on a static or partly static scene rapidly became known as a 'Cabiria movement'. In *His New Job*, the track forward glides effortlessly around and past the whole awkward business of film-making itself. It expresses a desire for cinema, for film-art rather than film-making, which cannot be extinguished even by the tawdriness of the costume-drama it absorbs us momentarily into.

Chaplin may even have prepared for his new job by studying *Cabiria*, the last word in high-toned European costume drama. I have already discussed the scene in *Cabiria* in which the camera tracks to the right around a wooden post in the centre of the room, to move in on the strongman Maciste, who holds Cabiria, while Fulvius Axilla peers out of the window behind them; and then, after the inn-keeper's appearance, back and to the left, around the post, to resume its original position (above, p. 102). In *His New Job*, Charlie's big scene in the costume-drama requires him to act the raffish cavalryman for the benefit of the statuesque heroine. As the extravagance of his gestures increases, the camera moves diagonally to the left, to disclose a pillar. Charlie, at the height of tragic intensity, leans against the pillar, which, being a prop, topples over.

Later, there is a lengthier track-in on Charlie as he once again courts the heroine, and a track-out, after she has disappeared up the stairs in the background. What these Cabiria movements cannot gloss over is Charlie's physicality: a physicality which either erupts, as yet untamed by performance, from beyond the set; or stands out within the performance as an obtrusive remnant. They cannot seal the performative off from the pro-performative. In the cinema of narrative integration, in Chaplin's later films, that is exactly what they would do.

Chaplin's preoccupation with hypermimesis, then, could not be said to have defined a phase in his career; or, indeed, any of the films he made during that phase. But it did prove astonishingly productive. And it does allow us to consider some of his films as the work of a modernist of a particular stripe. In *The Childermass*, Lewis envisaged a tracking shot which would slide a whole city away; but it was the memory of pre-war cinema's ferociously material apparitions which gave him Pullman and Satterthwaite, and their 'engines of unmeaning melting expressiveness'. Something similar might be said, perhaps, about Chaplin's taste for contraptions and shameless mutual rummaging.

In his autobiography, Chaplin recalled a meeting with Gertrude Stein, during which Stein held forth on the feebleness of film plots. 'She would like to see me in a movie just walking up the street and turning a corner, then another corner, and another.'[43] Modernist Charlie, turning invisible corners at right-angles, so that his planted leg acts as a mechanical pivot, has introduced geometry into 'natural' narrative space. Stein would have liked to convert an occasional event or gesture into an abstract rhythm, into modernist anti-mimesis. But that was not the only way to be modernist. Karl Rossman, in Kafka's *The Man Who Disappeared*, escaping from the police, skids on one leg round a corner in a way that seems thoroughly Chaplinesque, without thereby inaugurating an abstract rhythm.[44]

As it exists, in the films, the skid aims at hypermimesis: at imitation, for imitation's sake, of the geometric in movement, of that mechanism in mechanical behaviour which has more life to it than non-mechanical behaviour. Hypermimesis puts a wrinkle, a twist of sublimity, into homogeneous narrative space. The laughter it induces is at the spectacle not of a person inadvertently behaving like a machine, as Bergson might have supposed, but of a person who wants to behave like a machine. What is laid bare in and through hypermimesis is the structure, not of the imitated, but of the imitator. Charlie has chosen at the very least to tolerate the contraption or pseudo-coupling thrust on him; when he might have chosen to reject it, after it had served its purpose, or to protest against it. His behaviour need not be construed as an allegory of the damage done to the human body by a machine age. Charlie could perfectly well find another way to turn a corner; the joke is that he does not want to.

Notes

1   'The Stereoscope and the Stereograph', in Alan Trachtenberg (ed.), *Classic Essays on Photography* (New Haven, CT: Leete's Island Books, 1980), 72–82, p. 80.

2 *Theory of Film: The Redemption of Physical Reality,* ed. Miriam Bratu Hansen (Princeton: Princeton University Press, 1997), 298; and comments from the Marseille notebooks, quoted by Hansen in her Introduction, xvii, vii.

3 'The Romantic Englishman, the Comic Spirit, and the Function of Criticism', in *The Annotated Waste Land,* ed. Lawrence Rainey (New Haven: Yale University Press, 2005), 141–3, p. 142.

4 My understanding of hypermimesis is close to, and has been coloured by, Theodor Adorno's theory of modern mimesis as 'identification with' rather than 'identification of'. I decided not to try to extend this line of enquiry, or the distinctions which follow from it (for example, between imitation and mimesis), because it derives from a particular conception of modernism, and of the 'crisis of critique' of which modernism was allegedly a consequence. For a helpful exposition, see Michael Cahn, 'Subversive Mimesis: Theodor W. Adorno and the Modern Impasse of Critique', in Mihai Spariosu (ed.), *Mimesis in Contemporary Theory: An Interdisciplinary Approach,* 2 vols (Philadelphia: John Benjamins Publishing Company), vol. 1, 27–64.

5 *Modernisms: A Literary Guide* (Basingstoke: Macmillan, 1995), 251.

6 *On Liberty and Other Essays,* ed. John Gray (Oxford: Oxford University Press, 1991), 81. This anxiety is the topic of my *Paranoid Modernism: Literary Experiment, Psychosis, and the Professionalization of English Society* (Oxford: Oxford University Press, 2001).

7 *The Art of Being Ruled,* ed. Reed Way Dasenbrock (Santa Rosa, CA: Black Sparrow Press, 1989), 29. Lewis's emphasis. The book was first published in 1926.

8 'The Mob-God', reprinted in George C. Pratt, *Spellbound in Darkness: A History of the Silent Film,* rev. edn (Greenwich, CT: New York Graphic Society, 1973), 198–9.

9 *Time and Western Man,* ed. Paul Edwards (Santa Rosa: Black Sparrow Press, 1993), 64–5.

10 Ibid., 52.

11 Or, indeed, T. S. Eliot's remarks about the 'encroachment' of the 'cheap and rapid-breeding cinema' on the music hall: 'Marie Lloyd', in *Selected Prose,* ed. Frank Kermode (London: Faber and Faber, 1975), 172–4. p. 174.

12 *Time and Western Man,* 66.

13 'Dramatis Personae', *Criterion,* 1 (1922–3), 303–6, p. 306.

14 *The Art of Charlie Chaplin* (Sheffield: Sheffield Academic Press, 2000), 66–72. See also Charles J. Maland's concise account of the 'further "refining"' of Charlie during the Mutual period: *Chaplin and American Culture* (Princeton: Princeton University Press, 1989), 29–35.

15 John McCabe, *Charlie Chaplin* (London: Robson Books, 1992), 88–90.

16 'Two shapes then, oblong like man, entered into collision before me', reports the narrator of *The Unnamable.* 'They fell and I saw them no more. I naturally thought of the pseudocouple Mercier-Camier': *The Unnamable,* translated by the author, in *Three Novels* (London: Picador, 1979), 272. See *Mercier and Camier,* translated by the author (London: John Calder, 1974).

17 *Fables of Aggression: Wyndham Lewis, the Modernist as Fascist* (Berkeley: University of California Press, 1979), 59.

18 *The Childermass* (London: John Calder, 1965), 11, 13, 14. References will henceforth be included in the text.

19 Jameson, *Fables,* 73.

20 *Wyndham Lewis: Painter and Writer* (New Haven: Yale University Press, 2000), 325.

21 For an informative account of *The Childermass* as a whole, and of the (minimal) changes Lewis subsequently made to it in the 1950s, in order to convert it into the first volume of *The Human Age*, see Edwards, *Wyndham Lewis*, 322–39, 528–9.

22 *My Autobiography* (Harmondsworth: Penguin Books, 1966), 159.

23 The kind of analysis developed to illuminating effect by William Paul in 'Charles Chaplin and the Annals of Anality', in Andrew Horton (ed.), *Comedy/ Cinema/Theory* (Berkeley: University of California Press, 1991), 109–29. Paul draws upon Freud and Bakhtin to describe Charlie's 'coquettish' behaviour towards his bigger and stronger antagonists, with reference primarily to *City Lights* (1931). I am grateful to Lindiwe Dovey for conversations which forced me to clarify the rather different kind of analysis I propose in what follows.

24 *American Laughter: Immigrants, Ethnicity, and 1930s Hollywood Film Comedy* (Basingstoke: Macmillan, 1996), 104.

25 *Reading 1922: A Return to the Scene of the Modern* (Oxford: Oxford University Press, 1999), 166. North provides an informative account of the nature and breadth of Chaplin's appeal in the early 1920s.

26 *My Trip Abroad* (New York: Harper and Brothers, 1922), 29.

27 'Beauty in the Cinema', *Le Film*, 6 August 1917, reprinted in *French Film Theory and Criticism: A History/Anthology*, ed. Richard Abel, vol. 1 (Princeton: Princeton University Press, 1988), 137–9, p. 139. In his 1928 essay on 'Sex Versus Loveliness', D. H. Lawrence proposed Chaplin over Valentino as the epitome of screen-beauty. See Linda Ruth Williams, *Sex in the Head: Visions of Femininity and Film in D. H. Lawrence* (Hemel Hempstead: Harvester Wheatsheaf, 1993), 72–3.

28 'On Decor', *Le Film*, 16 September 1918, in *French Film Theory*, 165–8, p. 167.

29 'The Ontology of the Photographic Image', in *What Is Cinema?*, ed. and trans. Hugh Gray, 2 vols (Berkeley: University of California Press, 1967), vol. 1, 9–16, pp. 12, 15.

30 'The Grandeur of *Limelight*', in *What Is Cinema?*, vol. 2, 128–39, p. 138. For Stanley Cavell, the point about the great movie comedians is that they 'realized the myth of singularity': *The World Viewed: Reflections on the Ontology of Film*, enlarged edition (Cambridge, MA: Harvard University Press, 1979), 35–6.

31 'Ontology', 13.

32 'Charlie Chaplin', in *What Is Cinema?*, vol. 1, 144–53, pp. 149–50.

33 *Méduse et compagnie* (Paris: Gallimard, 1960)/*The Mask of Medusa*, trans. George Ordish (London: Victor Gollancz, 1964), 81/63 (my translation), 113–15/86–7, 166/127.

34 'Mimicry and Legendary Psychasthenia', trans. John Shepley, *October*, 31 (1984), 17–32.

35 'Charlie Chaplin', 149–51.

36 *World Viewed*, 25.

37 'Theatre and Cinema: Part Two', in *What Is Cinema?*, vol. 1, 95–124, p. 110. Quoted in *World Viewed*, 16. Cavell's subsequent claim that the 'presented magic' of Stanley Kubrick's *2001: A Space Odyssey* (1968) is no more than 'another way of confirming the physicality of our world' (p. 40) recalls not only Bazin, but Kracauer asserting in the *Theory of Film* that the 'very staginess' of *The Kid* (1921) demonstrates a 'primary concern for physical reality' (p. 86).

38 'Theatre and Cinema', 110.

39   *World Viewed*, 23, 72.

40   Ibid., 210, 37.

41   As it is, for example, by Winokur, *American Laughter*, 104.

42   *On the History of Film Style* (Cambridge, MA: Harvard University Press, 1997), 127.

43   *My Autobiography*, 302–3.

44   *The Man Who Disappeared*, trans. Michael Hofmann (Harmondsworth: Penguin Books, 1996), 147. Posthumously published, as *Amerika*, in 1927. Kafka had six chapters of the novel in draft by December 1912, and resumed work on it in the autumn of 1914; Chaplin's tramp took shape in *Kid Auto Races at Venice*, a Keystone comedy released in America on 7 February 1914.

Index

Adorno, Theodor 142, 199n
Arvidson, Linda 52, 67

Barry, Iris 52, 166
Baudelaire, Charles 39, 129–30, 147
Bazin, André 3, 60–62, 73, 79, 82n, 193–6, 200n
Beckett, Samuel 185–6
   The Unnamable 199n
Belasco, David 78
Benjamin, Walter 4, 24, 31, 46n, 129–30, 143
Bennett, Arnold 7, 25–6, 128
Bergson, Henri 133–7, 198
Blanchot, Maurice 28, 31
Bolter, Jay David 10–12
Bordwell, David 74, 80n, 106, 112, 162, 196
Bowen, Elizabeth 1, 11
   'Dead Mabelle' 22, 176–7
Bowser, Eileen 58, 66
Brewster, Ben 57, 67, 71, 75, 104
Brown, Karl 105
Bruno, Juliana 28–9
Burch, Noël 40, 91, 99–101, 112, 130
Butts, Mary
   'In Bloomsbury' 22, 175–6

Caillois, Roger 194–5
Cavell, Stanley 145–6, 195–6, 200n
Chaplin, Charlie 9, 12, 142, 146–7, 181–98
   The Adventurer 191–2, 194
   A Dog's Life 192, 194
   The Floorwalker 191, 196
   His New Job 197–8
   In the Park 189–90
   The Kid 200n
   Limelight 193
   Police 190–91
   Shoulder Arms 194
   Close Up 5, 162
Conrad, Joseph
   Heart of Darkness 6
   The Nigger of the 'Narcissus' 51
Cooper, James Fenimore
   The Last of the Mohicans 26

Crary, Jonathan 4, 30, 39, 81n

Deleuze, Gilles 135
Delluc, Louis 193
Dickens, Charles 51–2, 160
Dreyer, Carl-Theodor 9, 115, 182
   Leaves from Satan's Book 106
   Vampyr 105, 111–13

Edison, Thomas 18–19, 29, 53, 93
   The Gay Shoe Clerk 41
Eisenstein, Sergei 3, 40, 49, 51–2, 60, 72, 87–91, 140, 167, 181, 187
Eliot, T. S. 5, 10, 122n, 125–53, 156n, 184, 193, 196, 199n
   'The Dry Salvages' 130
   'Interlude in a Bar' 132
   'Interlude in London' 132
   'The Love Song of J. Alfred Prufrock' 12, 127–31, 137, 151
   'Mandarins' 132, 136, 145
   'Oh little voices of the throats of men' 132
   'Portrait of a Lady' 126, 137
   'Preludes' 131–2, 134
   'Rhapsody on a Windy Night' 125, 134
   The Waste Land 2–4, 12, 22, 111, 126, 132, 144–51, 153, 176, 182
Epstein, Jean 144–5, 150–51

Flaherty, Robert 61, 73
Ford, Ford Madox
   Mister Bosphorus 21–2
Forster, E. M.
   Howards End 5–8
   Freeman's Journal 93–4, 96
Freud, Sigmund 56–8, 62, 200n

Gance, Abel 9, 39–40, 47, 115, 151, 181–2
   Napoléon 40, 105–9, 111, 113
Gish, Lillian 64
Gorky, Maxim 19, 92, 97, 99, 118, 148
Griffith, D. W 9, 11, 15–16, 49–80, 82n, 87–91, 106, 141, 163, 181–2
   After Many Years 52–6, 60, 65, 71, 89

The Birth of a Nation 88
Broken Blossoms 88
Confidence 57
A Corner in Wheat 51, 71–7
The Country Doctor 53
The Drive for a Life 59
A Drunkard's Reformation 79
Enoch Arden 51, 65, 67–71
The Fatal Hour 54–6
Fisher Folks 65
For His Son 71
Gold Is Not All 71
The House of Darkness 57–9
Intolerance 40, 49, 60, 64, 88, 91–2,
　105–6, 187–8
Judith of Bethulia 88
Lines of White on a Sullen Sea 65–6, 68
The Lonedale Operator 52–4
The Lonely Villa 52–5, 89
The Note in the Shoe 57
The Prussian Spy 57
The Redman and the Child 170
The Restoration 57–9
The Sands of Dee 65
The Song of the Shirt 53, 71
The Unchanging Sea 51, 65–7, 69
The Usurer 51, 71, 76–9
Way Down East 88
Grusin, Richard 10–12
Gunning, Tom 8, 18, 51–2, 59, 62, 65,
　71–2, 74, 93, 104, 172

Hansen, Miriam 15n, 39, 46n, 64
Heath, Stephen 50, 60, 81n, 100
H.D. 13n, 175
Heidegger, Martin 63–5, 181
Hepworth, Cecil 39–40, 93, 95, 97, 143,
　181
Hildebrand, Adolf 29
Holmes, Oliver Wendell 30–31, 34, 39,
　70–71, 181
Holtby, Winifred 159–60, 171
Hopwood, V. W. 131

Jacobs, Lea, 71, 75
James, Henry 11, 44n
　The Ambassadors 20
　'Crapy Cornelia' 19–21, 115–16, 127–8
Jameson, Fredric 5–8, 63–4, 185, 188–9

Jolas, Eugene 3
Joyce, James 2, 5, 9–10, 87–118, 122n,
　162, 181–2, 186
　Finnegans Wake 6
　Ulysses 3, 11–12, 22, 27, 30, 41–2, 45, 48,
　　87–100, 111, 113–18, 131–2, 152–3,
　　171, 182–3

Kafka, Franz 26, 31–2, 34, 141, 181, 198
Kenner, Hugh 4, 95, 114, 117, 125, 127
Kenyon, James 94–5
Kingsley, Charles 51, 65–6, 181
　'The Three Fishers' 66
Kipling, Rudyard
　'Mrs Bathurst' 22, 173–4, 179n
Kracauer, Siegfried 40–41, 46n, 60–61,
　70, 82n, 162, 181–2, 200n
Krafft-Ebing, Richard von 56, 58
Kuleshov, Lev 139–40

Lawrence, D. H. 11, 128, 185, 200n
　The Lost Girl 22–7, 97
　Studies in Classic American Literature 26
　Women in Love 22, 25–6
Leavis, F. R. 142
Léger, Fernand 152
Lewis, Wyndham 5, 10, 137, 142, 183–9
　The Childermass 12, 186–90, 198
　Time and Western Man 183–4, 186
Lindsay, Vachel 40, 64
London, Jack 176
　Before Adam 19
　Martin Eden 19
Lumière, Auguste and Louis 5, 8, 18–19,
　39, 47n, 49, 92, 94, 96, 99–101, 148,
　162, 181

MacNeice, Louis 2
Mallarmé, Stéphane 14n
Mann, Thomas 9
　The Magic Mountain 172–4
Mansfield, Katherine
　'Pictures' 22, 149
Marey, Etienne-Jules 62
Marinetti, F. T. 12–13
Marks, Laura 28–9, 62
Méliès, Georges 8
Metz, Christian 8, 24–5, 96

Milestone, Lewis
  All Quiet on the Western Front
  110–11
Mitchell, Sagar 94–5
Montagu, Ivor 166–7
Moore, Marianne 4–5, 13
Münsterberg, Hugo 29, 81
Murnau, F. W. 61, 106
  Nosferatu 111, 113
Musser, Charles 14

Nabokov, Vladimir 50, 80n
Norris, Frank 11, 23
  'A Deal in Wheat' 72, 75–6
  McTeague 17–22, 75, 79
  The Octopus 19, 75

Orage, A. R. 141

Palmer, Frederick 161, 163
Pastrone, Giovanni
  Cabiria 39–40, 102–3, 108, 181,
  197
Paul, R. W. 18
Peirce, C. S. 61, 83n
Pope, Alexander 146–7
Porter, Edwin S. 104
Pound, Ezra, 5, 7 143, 146–7, 151–3
Promio, Alexandre 94
Proust, Marcel 9, 11, 43, 162, 175,
  181, 183

Reade, Charles
  Drink 78
Richardson, Dorothy 5, 162
Riegl, Aloïs 28–9
Rodker, John 151–3
  Adolphe 1920 22, 152–3
  'Wild West Remittance Man' 153
Ruskin, John 32, 43
Ruttmann, Walter
  Berlin: City Symphony 151–2

Sackville-West, Vita 164, 167, 169
Salt, Barry 102, 106
Sennett, Mack 189
Shaw, George Bernard 44n
Smith, G. A. 40
  As Seen through a Telescope 43, 128–9,
  132
Stein, Gertrude 13, 184, 186, 198
Stewart, Garrett 4–8, 99, 126
Stroheim, Erich von 61, 79

Tennyson, Alfred, Lord 51–2, 181
  Enoch Arden 52, 65, 67–8
Thackeray, W. M.
  Vanity Fair 77–8
Thompson, Kristin 50, 57–8
Tucker, George Loane 9, 182
  Traffic in Souls 103–5

Valentino, Rudolph 26, 200n
Vidor, King 9, 182
  The Big Parade 109
  The Crowd 105–6, 109–10, 113

Weber, Lois 66, 122n
Wells, H. G. 44n
Wharton, Edith
  Lily Bart 120n
Whitman, Walt 64–6, 69, 181
Wiene, Robert
  The Cabinet of Dr Caligari 151, 166–7
Williams, William Carlos 13
Williamson, James 167–8
Winter, O. 96–7
Woolf, Leonard 167
Woolf, Virginia 5, 10, 159–77, 188
  'The Cinema' 12, 161, 165–9
  Jacob's Room 159–60
  Mrs Dalloway 12, 22, 159–64, 168–9
  To the Lighthouse 12, 22, 162, 164,
  169–75, 179n, 182

Zola, Emile 75, 84n
  L'Assommoir 78

Made in the USA
Lexington, KY
04 October 2012